SHORELINE

A Memoir of Wandering, Friendship, and Finding Home

GUERNICA WORLD EDITIONS 82

SHORELINE

A Memoir of Wandering,
Friendship, and Finding Home

SHIRA NAYMAN

GUERNICA
World
EDITIONS

TORONTO–CHICAGO–BUFFALO–LANCASTER (U.K.)
2024

Guernica Editions Founder: Antonio D'Alfonso

Michael Mirolla, general editor
Margo LaPierre, editor
Cover design: Allen Jomoc, Jr.
Interior design: Jill Ronsley, suneditwrite.com

Guernica Editions Inc.
1241 Marble Rock Rd., Gananoque (ON), Canada K7G 2V4
2250 Military Road, Tonawanda, N.Y. 14150-6000 U.S.A.
www.guernicaeditions.com

Distributors:
Independent Publishers Group (IPG)
600 North Pulaski Road, Chicago IL 60624
University of Toronto Press Distribution (UTP)
5201 Dufferin Street, Toronto (ON), Canada M3H 5T8

First edition.
Printed in Canada.

Legal Deposit—Third Quarter
Library of Congress Catalog Card Number: 2024930076
Library and Archives Canada Cataloguing in Publication
Title: Shoreline : a memoir of wandering, friendship, and finding home /
Shira Nayman.
Names: Nayman, Shira, 1960- author.
Series: Guernica world editions (Series) ; 82.
Description: Series statement: Guernica world editions ; 82
Identifiers: Canadiana (print) 2023062393X | Canadiana (ebook)
20230623964 | ISBN 9781771839167 (softcover) | ISBN 9781771839174 (EPUB)
Subjects: LCSH: Nayman, Shira, 1960- | LCSH: Authors, American—21st
century—Biography. | LCGFT: Autobiographies. | LCGFT: Creative nonfiction.
Classification: LCC PS3614.A96 Z46 2024 | DDC 813/.6—dc23

*For the beloveds in my life,
past and present, alive and gone,
whom words will never come close
to evoking, honoring, or equaling—*

Contents

This Acre   1

Author's Note   2

Prologue   5

1   Moon Landing   23

2   Imaginary Life Buoy   55

3   The Jazz Band   76

4   Dark Night of the Moon   100

5   I'm Dying, Egypt, I'm Dying   118

6   There for the Taking   138

7   What Do You Do Once You Have Seen God?   147

8   I Wish I'd Had You as a Mother   177

9   A Mahogany Door, Leading Down   206

10   The Moving Forward   220

Epilogue   239

Texts   250

Film and Television   251

Acknowledgements   252

About the Author   254

[T]hese shores, so different in their nature and in the inhabitants they support, are made one by the unifying touch of the sea ... these coastal forms merge and blend in a shifting, kaleidoscopic pattern in which there is no finality, no ultimate and fixed reality—earth becoming fluid as the sea itself.

—Rachel Carson, *The Edge of the Sea*

This Acre

Of all the broken fields
Scattered like cracked dolls face up
In the mud of the earth

This acre, torn and fresh
Where the plow's wound aches
In the violet afternoon

Lies flat and breathes into the air
Its faint aroma
Of trees once felled

Of shadows wed to
Floating summer clouds
Of sheaves of hay awaiting harvest

The river dried one sultry eve
As cowhands tossed their beers

—SN, 1987

Author's Note

MEMOIR IS a tricky and somewhat elastic term. In casting a backward eye on my life, I was aware of how often my own deep habits as a fiction writer came to the fore. As I explored recollections and ideas, conversations appeared on the page. These incarnations of the past are not, of course, transcriptions, but rather attempts at peering back, at capturing or evoking moods or events. Names have been changed throughout, and events collapsed or crafted in service of narrative flow. In some obvious examples, such as an imagined conversation with a writer who died before I was born, entire scenes have been imaginatively conjured.

I trust the reader will pass judgment only on the author of this book, and not on any of the people with whose realities I have taken liberties. This is the anguishing pitfall of writing memoir. I'd have avoided these incursions into other people's lives had I been able to. However, in attempting to write my own story, I had no choice but to involve others, since I am only me through and involving them. I ask those living and those gone to forgive any indiscretions and to know that my overarching feelings toward them are gratitude, respect, admiration, and love.

Prologue

I'm at the end of a very long birthing labor, in a crisis of pain as I'm being ripped in two. I am stifling my screams. The earth is being wrenched open. The universe is gaping with agony. I am hanging on to that strange thing I'd called dignity before knowing the ineffable, unbearable cosmology of childbirth. And then, the pain evaporates, and I open my eyes to see the smiling face of my young doctor. *It's a girl*, she says, handing my baby to me. I reach out across the ages, a woman reaching for her child, and then, the first touch. Flesh on flesh. My flesh on my flesh, her flesh on her flesh, the two of us one, reunited after that timeless tearing apart. Together again, at last.

I look down. Her eyes, seeing for the first time, blink through a white coating, glimpsing the world that is Mother, the world that is me. *My baby*, I say again and again, naming her, naming me anew— now, I am Mother—from the deepest part of both the universe and me. *My baby* is all I feel, all I can say.

The oneness of me became a twoness that day. The splitting was at the same time a strange unifying, a finding of oneself in something more complete. It is what the old-fashioned expression attempts to make sense of: *She had a baby, she's so fulfilled.* Something my mother used to say about women who'd had babies. Full-filled, no longer empty. Oneness. The whole.

It struck me at my daughter's high school graduation that she really was going to leave. The next day, I was walking down Court Street, one of the commercial drags in our Brooklyn neighborhood, when I felt overcome by a hurricane of emotion that brought me, doubled over, to a halt, gripped by a silent sob. Winded. People moved around me—an eye strayed my way, then another—as I struggled to draw in breath.

All through that last summer before she left for college, the awful soul-siege would fell me in the middle of whatever I was doing. The *two* slammed back to a diminished *one* that was more like *a half*. An ax brought down in an empty forest. The thing that was *me* teetered and then crashed to the ground.

My daughter couldn't bring herself to pack up her room. I understood I would not see much of her that summer—senior prom, high school graduation, work. And of course, her friends, each of them an indispensable piece in their kaleidoscopic becoming as they reached for a new sense of identity. My husband and thirteen-year-old son were in Bogotá, Colombia, beginning another year away, our third, that we'd planned so our son could do his eighth-grade year immersed in Spanish. I would be joining them at the end of the summer, after dropping our daughter at college. We'd sublet our Brooklyn apartment for the year, so I needed to pack everything up. Every now and then, I'd ask my daughter when she planned to take on her room—she'd kept everything from her growing-up years: books, notebooks, keepsakes, clothing. *Soon, Mama, I'll get to it soon.*

I slogged through each room, dismantling our lives, making piles—giveaway, throwaway, storage—swallowing the panicked feeling that my life would forever be this Sisyphean purgatory of sorting through the leavings of my precious child-rearing years.

And then, there it was, staring me in the face. My daughter's room.

This time the pile-making took place as if in a swimming pool, everything seen through tears. The "to college" pile was the hardest—the place away, where there'd be nothing of me.

I found myself zombie-like, at one in the morning, wandering the empty house. Our lives sorted, packed into boxes and vacuum-sealed bags, the rest discarded. My daughter out with her friends, making brief text appearances—*Getting in a cab ... Gonna sleep at Juliet's.* Me keeping tabs, as I had through her four years of high school, knowing that even this texting-update kind of connection would soon be over once she was at *college*, that mythical place we'd talked about for such a long time, which always had a thrilling sound but was never actually real.

The drop-off on her first day of college was awful, at least for me. None of the special moments I'd planned ended up happening. It was all a frenzied rush. At the last minute, we dashed off to Bed Bath & Beyond. We sat in choked traffic, then a miserable half hour negotiating the horde of other college students and parents in the crowded store, emerging with a shower caddy and wardrobe contraption for hanging shoes. We got back to campus five minutes before the freshman orientation meeting: no time for the relaxed afternoon tea I'd imagined, no time for anything but the most hurried goodbye. She sat in the passenger seat for a moment, the shower caddy in her lap, and gave me a sweet smile.

"Don't cry, Mama, okay?" she said.

Her little face. She looked like she was nine years old.

I nodded. "Bye, darling," I said, reaching for her hand.

She got out of the car, stood for a moment looking at me through the open window. I jumped out of the driver's seat and ran around the car to give her a hug. She hugged me back, a tight little-girl hug, gentle and fierce at the same time. We pulled apart. Her lip quivered, our eyes filled at the same time, and the tears trickled down. Hers, mine, ours.

While leaving the college campus, the heavens opened in a deluge. As the torrential rains continued unabated, I inched along the highway, able to see only a few yards ahead. I berated myself for not having checked the weather. The five-hour drive took eight. I battled a migraine the whole way, at times barely able to keep my eyes open. It's an undoing kind of pain, something I've lived with as long as I can remember, an acid searing that dissolves who you are. I'd learned from early on that the world was not safe—racing panic was my heart's natural rhythm. In my childhood home, I understood it was best to be cheery and bright and never complain, to keep any troubles to myself. It never occurred to me to say anything when my head ballooned with pain and I had to squint against the lacerating light. It wasn't until I was in my forties, during a routine physical, that a kind doctor asked a few more than the usual questions and suggested I see a neurologist, who named the condition.

When a migraine takes hold, you know somewhere, in a distant place, that you must keep doing what a person does, though you're no longer a person, only an imploding skull, a body racked with nausea, all the world an onslaught. You are reduced to a single, primitive desire for all experience to end, perhaps akin to suicidal longing, and yet you also feel you've already died, death not a release but a brain-crushing purgatory.

I could see the windshield and the lashing rains, the windshield wipers frantic but almost useless, though I could not see the highway, only the waters bearing down. I wondered vaguely through the pain if there was even a remote chance I would make it safely back to Brooklyn. A thought fragment broke through—*have to pick Sparky up from the dog-sitter*—along with a shadowy recollection that, the next day, I was flying to Bogotá.

As I boarded the plane, the years flashed before me, cycling through all the ages of my daughter: the little baby, the toddler, the kindergartner, and on through her school years, scary little existential leapfrogs through time. Blurry images of me as well, the young mother. How different I must look now to her. I doubled over in my tight-squeezed airplane seat as Sparky plaintively yelped from the dog carrier under the seat in front of me. The awful, familiar silent shriek took hold—the sundering of *me*, the cleaving in two.

As the plane reached its altitude of ten thousand feet, I stood up and stumbled down the aisle to the bathroom where I washed my face, then stood for a moment looking into my own stricken eyes. I recalled the words of my boss's wife, speaking to my new reality: *I love the relationships I have with my adult children.* And from another couple we'd known for years: *You're going to love the freedoms.* I knew in my heart the other truth, that the impossibly beautiful thing I had built my world and self and life around was over. The young-children family, the all-of-us being and growing, the endless daily joys. Living in a shining bubble of visceral togetherness, our identities interwoven. I knew that life's natural order involves family connections that shift in nature and intensity and yet endure, but I couldn't put a good face on it. I didn't want to.

In the Atlanta terminal, I counted the hours since I'd stood holding Sparky outside our dog-sitter's house in Brooklyn and hailed a taxi to JFK Airport. With the vet-service check, then customs and the long wait to board, we'd already clocked six hours. With this layover, the four-hour leg to Bogotá ahead of us, then customs and the wait for the luggage—if he didn't go now, surely Sparky's Yorkshire-terrier-sized bladder would explode. I took him to the bathroom and held him over the bowl. He looked at me quizzically, his little legs dangling down. *For heaven's sake, woman, what are you doing?* He averted his gaze. Okay, I thought, try to recreate normal conditions. I laid paper towels down in the corner of the stall, then plopped him beside them. He gave me his judge-y eye as he did whenever I scraped a plateful of tantalizing scraps into the garbage. I leaned down and gingerly lifted his hind leg, hoping the muscle memory would kick in. His eyes deepened with disapproval: *Can we please just stop this awkward madness?* I could see it was not going to work and gave up.

I felt the pressure in my teeth the moment we touched down in Bogotá, as if someone had tightened a monkey wrench around my jaws. After a long delay in customs dealing with Sparky's travel papers, I walked out onto the street, holding the leash while trying to manage the trolley with the suitcases bearing everything I'd need for a year away. Sparky trotted nonchalantly through the door and cocked his head at the feel of the fresh air on his face. He chose a rusty length of pipe jutting up from the curb and lifted his hind leg.

My jaw bones were now pulsing with pain. I made my way to the taxi stand, then waited my turn. The driver had a kind manner and was patient with my halting Spanish. Speeding along the highway, I held on tightly to Sparky, who squirmed in my lap, furiously panting, craning to see out the window.

"It's okay," I said, and he looked up at me with his sweet, trusting face, though I saw panic in his eyes. "Really, Sparkles, everything's going to be fine."

For some miles, the buildings were modern and boxy and in various stages of dilapidation. Barbed wire in imaginative forms sprouted everywhere like an invasive species of blooming night-shade. People swarmed, though there was something orderly in the feel of it, something practiced about the choreography that I associated with life in the big cities I'd known. I felt like I was in a Colombian *Truman Show* movie, all of it a vast stage set where the actors had been instructed to make me feel invisible—to shut me out and refuse to engage.

The buildings became more upscale: anonymous-looking high-rises flanked by doormen in uniform, stretches of elegant storefronts. Still the orderly swarms of people, but many more now seeming well-heeled and giving off a groomed sense of privilege and ease.

What had happened to my delight in exploring new places? Why this feeling of bloodless panic, the sense that even the clouds in the sky were banks of anodyne refusal? Weary from the journey and feeling vulnerable from the pain ricocheting around my teeth and jaws, I was eager to reunite with my husband and son. Perhaps once we were back together, I'd feel enthusiastic about being here.

Sparky had settled down in my lap, his face resting on his paws. He'd given up on trying to take in the novel surrounds.

"We're almost there," the taxi driver announced. "This is the Plaza Usaquen."

We were skirting an elegant square bordered by towering trees where people milled about, sitting on benches, walking the path-ways, or talking in the mottled shade. I rolled down the window: the smell of roasted corn on the cob and barbequed meat wafted in. Vendors dotted the space, selling steaming foods, iridescent balloons, hand-painted wooden toys, and leather goods stitched with patches of brightly colored tapestry. We turned off the square onto a side street. The driver pulled up in front of a metal gate set into a high brick wall that was topped with metal spikes and giant barbed-wire coils.

I rang the bell. A uniformed doorman, middle-aged and trim with warm, intelligent eyes, opened the gate. Behind him, I could see a small courtyard dominated by a glorious chicalá tree, its yellow bell flowers in full bloom. The carefully tended flowerbeds held species of flowers I'd never seen before—orangey-red stars, purple wheels with tubular yellow stamens, miniature sunflowers hanging from velvety gray stalks. The courtyard was encircled by six tiny narrow townhouses, one of them my new home.

Sparky set up watch on a turquoise ottoman in front of the picture window looking out onto the courtyard, a front-row seat to the outside world he'd never had access to in the elsewheres he'd lived. He'd sit there for hours in a state of serene alertness, ears pert, tracking anything that moved—the gardener raking, residents coming and going, the Colombian variants of sparrow and thrush hopping about. Such a sweet doggie, patient with the life he'd fallen into when we'd found him nine years earlier in a small village in the south-central mountains of Mexico. I counted the countries he'd lived in on my fingers: Mexico, the US, France, Spain, and now Colombia. Three shy of the countries I have lived in, which includes South Africa, Israel, and Australia, where I'd grown up.

"We're nomads, hey," I said to him that first day. He swiveled his head to face me.

Not really, I read him saying. *We just like to live in different places.* He seemed to be shaking his head. *Nomads don't have homes.*

I recalled something my daughter said, the summer we spent in Oaxaca when she was fifteen. One morning, sitting in the courtyard of our run-down rental, under the cacaloxúchitl tree with its spindly branches and extravagant white blooms, she'd remarked, "Home is wherever we are." Her voice was matter of fact, but something lovely glistened in her eyes. "I mean, when we're together, our family, we're home."

I looked up at the courtyard aware of nothing but foreignness, then glanced around the narrow space of the kitchen/living room that made up the ground floor. The little house comprised three rooms stacked on top of each other, joined at one side by a tiny stairway that wound treacherously, the steps cramped and too steep.

An hour later, my son arrived back home on the school bus just as my husband was walking in the door from work, teaching at the university. They were excited to share stories of their adventures since we'd last been together. I was especially eager to hear how our son's new school was working out.

But the pain in my jaw had grown steadily worse. I waited until our son went upstairs to start his homework to say something to my husband, who called his colleague. *Baradontaglia*, she said. *It's from the altitude. It will likely settle down after a few days.*

It did not. That first week, while my son was at school and my husband was teaching, I was alone at home with Sparky. I went out for long walks, looking for coffee shops where I might sit and write, but every time I ventured out, I found myself slamming up against a sense of impenetrability. Our son's school was a forty-five-minute bus ride from where we lived. I visited for parent orientation and tried to connect with other parents but again, I faced a brick wall. I later learned that casual short-term social relations were generally not part of the fabric of life for people in Bogotá.

Several weeks passed and the tooth and jaw pain got worse, so I got the name of a dentist from my husband's colleague.

"It's the root," the dentist said once he'd had a chance to examine my mouth. "Let me take you to the endodontist down the hall."

The endodontist was disarmingly beautiful and dressed like a fashion model, high heels and all. I couldn't imagine how she stood all day over open mouths on those heels. When she was through getting into the tooth, she said: "My god, this is awful! The infection is raging!"

A pungent, rotting odor filled the air and then she pulled something out of my jaw and held it up. A skinny, blackened worm.

"Necrotic root. The infection has dissolved a piece of your jawbone—the size of a large olive."

I could not speak, since my mouth was being held open by a wooden chunk jimmied into place by the woman I had unwittingly come to think of as my beautician. I shut my eyes, allowed my consciousness to swim along the current of the strange, inviting/repelling term, "necrotic root." Perhaps she'd meant to say "necrotic nerve," but *root* seemed more apt.

Woozy from the anesthetic, I focused on an image in my mind's eye: a worn chair with faded blue upholstery before a narrow window, looking down at a congested street below. Seated in the chair was an elderly woman, dressed simply and wearing a bonnet. It was an image from a book I'd been reading about Mayer Amschel Rothschild, born in 1744 in a slum tenement in the Jewish ghetto of Frankfurt, patriarch of what would become the Rothschild dynasty. Established in 1462 outside the city wall, the ghetto was on a sliver of land originally intended to house the city's handful of Jewish families. As the population grew, they were denied permission for extra land. Houses were built behind and in front of the original ones, floors were added, jutting into the narrow Judengasse—Jews' Lane—until the upper stories almost touched. By Rothschild's time, the ghetto was crammed with three thousand souls—10 percent of Frankfurt's population, and the largest concentration of Jews in Europe. Property, therefore, was at an absurd premium.

For forty-two years, Rothschild lived in a tiny decrepit tenement. Then, having amassed a small fortune in his business, he moved his growing family to a house on the Judengasse. The exorbitant cost of Rothschild's modest new house would have bought a mansion across town, like the one Goethe lived in with his family. But Jews were not allowed to live, or buy property, outside the high ghetto walls.

I pictured Mayer Amschel Rothschild in his later years, hobbling down the Judengasse to the synagogue, nodding up at the window to his wife, Gutle Schnapper. As the endodontist labored over me, I held on to the image of the elderly Gutle, sitting in that faded blue chair well into her nineties, long after the laws were changed and her progeny were free to live outside the ghetto. She bore nineteen children, ten of whom survived to adulthood. She would outlive her husband by thirty-seven years. Gutle's children entreated her to leave the ghetto house. She refused.

What, I wondered, was she clinging to?

As I struggled to peer through time, something marvelous occurred. A decorative swirl, a vivid shade of Prussian blue, grew from Gutle's seat as if the faded chair had all these years harbored a tank filled with bright paint. A marigold yellow dotted the blue swirl as it thickened and grew—Van Gogh's stars plucked from the starry night to fall into the earth. The burrowing swirl straightened as it grew.

The voice of the endodontist broke through. I snapped open my eyes.

"The infection is deep in the jaw. I'm having trouble clearing it all out." She explained I'd have to return every few days for a while to have her clean and disinfect.

My eyelids sank back down. What had started out as a swirl beneath Gutle's chair had become an enormous root, thick as a tree trunk.

I met Arturo at the taxi stand outside the hotel around the corner from our house. Three times a week, for a month, he ferried me back and forth to the endodontist, a six-mile journey that would take an hour or more because of the clogged traffic that is a defining feature of Bogotá life. Arturo was patient with my inadequate Spanish. He was a kind man with a love of poetry ingrained in him by his father, a civil servant who was also a poet. In the course of that year, Arturo was the only Bogotano I came to know. He took me to and from the airport for work trips I made back to the US, when I would slip in a quick visit to my daughter at college, or for family trips, one to see my very ill mother in Australia, another to South Africa for my niece's wedding. That year, I took two of the longest nonstop flight legs on the planet: Dallas to Sydney, clocking in at seventeen hours, and Johannesburg to Atlanta, sixteen hours and twenty minutes. On those trips, the sense of thrill and adventure I'd always felt when traveling evaporated. Each flight became something to endure, carrying me from one location to another, neither of them home.

It hit me on one of those taxi rides back to the little Usaquen house, talking to Arturo and doing my best to make good on his ever-patient tutelage, that I had reached the end of the line. I couldn't understand what Arturo was saying. The world was a blur. I was coursing through streets I didn't know, that didn't know me, that cared nothing for my presence. For a moment, I had no idea where I was. What was I doing here? It was my own life after all, not imposed by the gods but orchestrated—by me. I closed my eyes. The motion of the car and the pain in my exploding skull felt like the tug of a violent ocean that intended to suck me down.

* * *

In Melbourne, growing up, we were a small island of six: my mother, father, and three siblings. On distant continents were three grandparents, countless aunts and uncles, and dozens of first cousins. I'd been told, from earliest memory, that the Jewish people, who had wandered homeless since biblical times, through more years and generations than my young mind could make sense of, were *my* people. Their saga converged with the record of my own extended family, who were mythical to me since I'd not met any of them.

My grandparents fled Eastern Europe in the first decade of the twentieth century, when their villages were being set on fire by Cossacks, their babies thrown from buildings, their men beaten to death, their women raped before they were murdered. These massacres were given a name—pogroms (Russian for "devastation" or, more specifically, "destroy by use of violence"). There is a rich terminology attached to the brutalities in the annals of this people I was told were mine. Exile, expulsion, ghettos. Crusades and inquisition. And more recently, concentration camps, gas chambers, death marches, and medical experiments, such as timing how long it took for a child immersed in ice water to die. The umbrella term for the latest terminology, *Holocaust*, is derived from the Greek translation (*holokauston*) of the Hebrew word *olah*, meaning "burnt sacrifice," chosen, it is thought, because the ovens the Nazis built in the extermination camps burned bodies whole. The Holocaust had sucked up numbers of my own family—my parents' aunts, uncles, and cousins, whose names surfaced rarely and in hushed, alarmed whispers. *My uncle Yosele was dragged into the street and shot*, my mother would say, *along with his wife and children*, or, *Cousins Miriam, Chaya, Rosa, they all perished in the camps*. The word *perished* caught in my throat, as if these people, my relatives, had died in some unfortunate natural calamity, an avalanche or mudslide, rather than being tortured and murdered. The Nazis certainly weren't shy about using the more accurate term. *Extermination*.

To escape the pogroms, my grandparents fled the villages their families had inhabited for generations. They ended up in South Africa, a place my own parents left as a young married couple for the distant shores of Australia, which I first left when I was seventeen, acting on the plan I'd hatched at the age of twelve. I wanted to *get away*. It's as if there was something in my blood, a kind of historical fever that sought relief in flight, a pattern laid down in the setting of epigenetic switches deep in my DNA—a propulsive response to just, well, being alive. As if somewhere below my consciousness, an ancient algorithm, developed in the name of survival, exerted its influence: *We were forced to leave ☒ You're going to have to leave ☒ You better make sure you leave.*

But the escape I yearned for was also rooted in my own personal present. I had never felt safe in my childhood home. I lived in a state of confusion about this. I loved school and was happy there, where I understood the rules and knew what it took to please—to get good marks, to have a shot at winning the weekly spelling bee. Where sports were fun, and friendships blossomed. Everything sparked my interest; I hung on my teachers' words, gobbled up books, relished handwriting exercises and math problems.

Home was different, surreal in its external perfection and veering unpredictably into gloomy fright. I lived in a home crafted with flair by my mother and made possible financially by my father's success as a surgeon. I was proud of my parents' worldly talents and charm, and the respect they seemed to command. I was also afraid of my mother, disconnected from my father, and at painful odds with my siblings. I never knew when the mood of the house would shift, when my heart would pound, and I'd have trouble breathing. Dread, spring-coiled with a readiness to react, followed me into my dreams. It didn't take much delving to know why I became a psychologist, though I was surprised to discover, in my training and work, that the standard psychodynamic explanations for my own experience never fully satisfied and did little to change the noisily ticking panic that was never far away.

When I was a child, I'd lie awake for hours staring into the night and feeling both the future and the past. I saw people and places from worlds I didn't know and yet felt I'd inhabited or would one day inhabit. Worlds that were foreign and yet, impossibly, mine. Lying there, I would strain my eyes and ears, waiting for something—a message or an image I could grab hold of and then worry into magical, uncertain life. That blackness filled me, shimmering like gold on the bottom of the ocean where light cannot reach it—shimmering within itself, knowing the possibility of light exists a thousand leagues above. I didn't then call this feeling *reincarnation*, or *epigenetics*, and I'm still not sure of the right word for it.

I see now that my parents' struggles and confusing ways were long in the making, across generations. Was my family's generational history coursing through my veins? Oxygen tainted with nitrogen dioxide, mother's milk laced with arsenic, bright light projected by a black sun. A people whose mantra was *survival*, defined by massacres and exile and fleeing, and a personal family history also replete with dislocation and flight. My bright, sparkling childhood home often came alive with music, learning, and spirited dinner conversation, but could also fill with agitation, discord, and misery, where the atmosphere readily shifted to lashing out, criticism, and blame.

The brightness gave me the confidence and courage to leave. But even as I told myself of the grand adventures I would have far away, catapulting from the one shore I'd known, I also intuited that the plan I'd hatched was one of escape. Each flight was an attempt to discard, to leave behind, so that I might claim myself anew.

When you fly for long hours—twenty or more at a time, with brief stops to refuel—you discover that time and space collapse. On those many journeys, static in that propulsive silver projectile, I glimpsed that history was like the impenetrable ocean beneath me, its strata of obscurity pulsing with life. I had only to squeeze my eyes shut to know it, to see it, to find little bits of it, like darkly glimmering shards from the seabed, jagged in my hand.

I married a man with his own peripatetic urges. On one of our first dates, he mentioned in passing that he was a rolling stone, that moss was not his thing. As life unfolded with our young family, it made sense that we would spend each summer abroad, and then plan yearlong immersions in other cultures, where our children could learn first one language, then another. We arranged jobs that made this possible—most of the travel was paid for, the rest made up by subletting our Brooklyn apartment whenever we were gone. We lived modestly when abroad and with the cost of living usually cheaper than life in New York, our travels typically allowed us to save. It was all part of our deliberate, overarching life plan. The years passed in a flurry of packing and unpacking, setting up one home and then another, planes and trains and cars. I have a friend who used to say that I was the only person she knew whose regular life included four continents.

Those child-raising years were a happily frenetic whirl—until my jaw infection in Bogotá. Six months into our time there, my husband had to return to New York for work, unable to finish out the year with us, though he visited briefly every few weeks. Something undid my seams. I was not a *me* I recognized, the image in the mirror staring back strangely. What frightened me was the fear and dullness in my eyes. The defeat.

Nine years later, we're four years into a global pandemic. Sparky lived to be fourteen. He died not long before the pandemic hit. I find myself looking back and trying to understand what that something was that undid the seams of me. Yes, I was struggling with my daughter's departure for college. I had landed in a culture I could not find my way into, and after my husband's departure, I felt alone. Also, the headache and migraine pain I battled on and off for much of my life ramped up to a daily challenge. But there was something else. Was it too many flights to too many elsewheres? Too many decades living oceans away from extended family? Too many generations settling too lightly on too many foreign shores? How could I not have noticed all the *too many* untetherings?

But there were also other clues as to the possible causes of my undoing. As a child, whenever I saw a mother being kind and loving to their child, a panicky sob would rise in my chest. Then, the vicious longing would grip me. I had nightmares of shadowy figures looming in doorways, a child being dangled, its face filled with terror, wet cobblestone streets, late at night, and me running, gasping for breath, the sound of jackboots on my heels. I thought about Melbourne not as home, but as the place I once grew up in, the one spot on earth that held for me a negative allure, calling and repelling in equal measure, impossible to escape. I would hanker to return, though each visit back felt fraught, the subsequent departure a renewed escape.

It may be misguided to look for causes of the states of undoing that can engulf us at some point in our lives—perhaps feeling undone is simply an inviolable part of the human condition. Perhaps to be alive is to be inconsolable. It is to be a lost infant, an abandoned lover, a daughter or husband or mother or son left stranded on the shoreline of life when the beloved is snatched away by death. Yes, there are adventures and passion and giving birth, more glories than can be counted, and the basis, perhaps, for notions of heaven. But are all these just puzzle pieces that at any moment might be snatched by a gust? In the end, after *everything*, do we end up being—well, only a pile of scraps?

I do not know if I was wrong to think, after the birth of my daughter those many years back, that I was complete. I do not say that the full-wattage happiness, strangely unruffled by all that I did know back then of reality and life, was deluded or false. I only know that from where I now view things, there can only be pieces. Lapses and gaps, seams that threaten to split open and often do. As this book has unfurled, I've come to see that the wish to reclaim some kind of whole, unfractured *me* was misguided—that people and life are, by definition, compromised, imperfect, incomplete. And to respond to this with a sense of crushing disappointment is to squander the gift of life.

But wait—. I read back over this prologue, aware of how many themes I raise here, of the way in which I toggle between dimensions and domains. The end of the glorious child-raising years, my dread-filled childhood home, the burden of history and yearning for a place to belong. Perhaps when it comes to living, the true nature of coordinates is that they ricochet wildly, pointing up the false sense of order implied by the neat lines of the cartographer's map.

The writing of this book has been a deeply personal undertaking, one that has felt soul baring, though the beam of attention is not always explicitly on the narrative *me*. Perhaps this has something to do with the kind of *me* that might be more common among storytellers, whose center of gravity is not necessarily separable from the stories of others. Most of the chapters that follow explore a single relationship that has shaped the course of my life, likely shining more light on the nature of my own being than on the other person. The book zigzags through time, and across continents, veering toward the end into the kinds of imaginative realms that are for some (many?) of us an integral part of the world we inhabit.

I look behind me and there they are: the countries I've left, the people I've left, and those who've launched forever away from me and from this life, their bodies plunged into graves while I stood weeping, the smell of the fresh dirt like the world on fire, incinerated, the ash pouring into me.

But then, as I wrote, I found myself experiencing anew the extraordinary power of words—to plunge me directly into the living-breathing past, to bring the dead back to life, to give meager form to inchoate longings and fears, to the invisible forces that guide us in powerful, mystical ways.

I have a beloved aunt, named Gloria, who died the week before I wrote this. I was twelve when we met, on my first trip abroad to meet my extended family. On that first meeting, I had only to look into Auntie Gloria's eyes to know we were kindred spirits. On our final Zoom call, she talked about the tragedy of her daughter's death, by suicide, in her thirties, leaving a young son whom my aunt then raised with her husband. "Aside from the tragedy of her death," my aunt said, "I've had an absolutely marvelous life." She then showed me the pictures on her wall of her children, grandchildren and seventeen great-grandchildren. Some weeks later, on her deathbed, slipping in and out of consciousness, Gloria opened her eyes and announced, "It's amazing." My cousin sat beside her, holding her hand. "Gloria, what's amazing?" Her reply: "Everything."

– 1 –

Moon Landing

The house was one of the unpretentious orange-brick boxes that sprang up around the edges of the older Melbourne suburbs in the 1950s and 1960s, the brick almost the sunburnt rust of the red desert at the heart of Australia, our new country. These houses had about them the echo of the same vast and mysterious openness, of glaring light and secrets hidden in plain sight. It was the house my father found when he arrived as an immigrant from South Africa, six weeks ahead of my mother and the three small children, me the youngest, aged eight months.

We played on the vacant lots that punctuated the streets. But North Balwyn, a newer outer suburb with good public schools, was being rapidly developed. One by one, those vacant lots disappeared. Ground would be broken, and then we'd have adventures within the square wooden frame that quickly rose. I got to see how the bones of sister houses to ours were laid and bricked over. We'd explore the emerging interior, breathing in sawdust, until the windows and doors were put in place, blocking our entry. Then we'd move on to the next vacant lot, until the chainsaws and backhoes were brought in, felling trees and yielding up the rich smell of broken soil.

Everything about our orange-brick house was unadorned. The square rooms, no door or ceiling moldings to catch the eye, antiseptic 1950s kitchen and bathroom. We owned little from before my parents' arrival from South Africa where they'd grown up, a different halfway across the world from where their own parents had been born and raised in the Jewish shtetls of Lithuania and Latvia.

One grandfather supposedly stowed away at age fourteen, though I was never able to lay hands on the facts. My other three grandparents were also refugees fleeing pogroms and poverty, branches snapped from massive ancient family trees.

Over the years, a few material fragments of family history made their way to our household, miraculously transported by my fleeing, impecunious forebears. A cuckoo clock brought to South Africa from Lithuania was, years later, waylaid en route to my mother in Australia, forgotten for more than a decade in my uncle's London attic. A brass samovar, which throughout my childhood had pride of place in our living room, evoked the kind of Imperial Russian drawing-room scenes I later read about in Turgenev and Lermontov. There was also my grandmother's wedding china, received by her as a young bride in the tiny rural town of Koppies in South Africa's Orange Free State, decorated in orange and gold and etched with the fine lines of age. These objects were ghosts that kept to their place in daylight but broke free at night, in my dreams, taking root in my imagination as if seeking there some sort of ground-steady, continuous home.

Three of my grandparents were still alive, though being so far away, in a country as foreign to me as the moon, they were more like fictional characters than real people. I'd memorized their names, the way that at school we memorized the names of centuries' worth of British monarchs. When I did finally meet them, on a few brief visits they made to Australia, those old people felt like strangers, with their heavy Eastern European accents and perplexing ways. They peered at me thickly, their faces sticky with emotion. Their history never felt even remotely like mine. The rare visits sit in my memory like tiny uninhabited islands, far from the small landmass of our actual family of six, my little brother the only Aussie-born, just us, with no connection to anything larger or historically rooted.

The only hiddenness in that new-world openness of the house was the crawl space beneath it, what we called, aptly, *underthehouse*. I delighted in flopping to my belly and wriggling into the space, which opened to allow a crouch. My mother would sometimes send me down to retrieve something she kept stored there—canned goods or cleaning supplies. I'd leap to that chore, more adventurous than other tasks, like sweeping the floor, ironing shirts and sheets, or the one I found particularly tedious, combing the fringes of the living room rugs.

My heart would pound at the feel of the imposing darkness as I wriggled my way into the crawl space and then slowly pulled myself up to a crouch. It was as if I'd always known there was another dimension beneath the brightness and visibility of daytime life, a hidden realm I had only to drop to my belly and wriggle into, where all kinds of mystery beckoned. I would quiver with fear, the dirt pressing up against my face, electric with certainty that, here, I would find out what was really going on. Here, all the pretense and excruciating boredom of normal life would fall away.

That last time I went down, my mother asked me to fetch a box of laundry detergent. The boxes she bought were enormous and heavy—an early reader, I could clearly make out the words "family size" plastered on the side.

"Anything else, Mum?" I asked. My mother was removing fat with a spoon from the pot of chicken soup on the stove, letting the clear globules slip into a jar, where they would congeal in the fridge to schmaltz that my father would spread on challah and eat with relish for breakfast.

"That's about enough for a little girl to manage, don't you think?" she said, a smile on her lips, her eyes filled with warmth. I froze, my heart swelling with joy. She would do that sometimes, send a sunbeam of love my way. I would pocket the moment with fastidious stealth, masking the shame I felt at the feeling of having to filch.

It was a warm day. I'd been playing outside all morning and my skin was clammy with the heat. I skipped around the back of the house and fell to my belly, anticipating the pleasant waft of coolness. The crawl space was even cooler than usual, in contrast with the hot sun. I felt like I was foraging in a cave. My eyes adjusted to the dimness. I rose to a half crouch then made my way to the shelves up against the side wall. I pulled a box of laundry detergent from the bottom shelf and dragged it across the floor. From out of the gloom, two bright eyes were suddenly looking directly into my own. A pale wash of light filtered in from behind me, revealing the contours of a furry face and needle-sharp whiskers, slightly trembling. An enormous rat! I dropped to my belly, leaving the detergent where it lay, my body slithering rapidly backward of its own accord. Within seconds I was outside in the bright sunlight, staring with horror at the band of darkness below the last line of orange brick.

From then on, I insisted on other chores, the rug-fringe combing suddenly a reprieve from having to venture back down *underthehouse.*

Until the night that Whisky gave birth to her puppies.

Whisky was a lively, scruffy sandy-haired terrier we'd found wandering the streets in a daze and had brought home. For months, her belly had been growing and now, in the wee hours of the morning, my mother awoke us to say it was time. I was five years old. I don't think I'd ever been up at this hour—what we called the *middle of the night.* I crept from my bed and followed my mother, who led us out into the back garden. Sleep lifted away like morning mist. I found myself softly alert, aware that something momentous was unfolding. I saw it in my mother's eyes, which shone with calm joy. No sign of the black cloud that would often overtake her, snuffing out the light. My father vibrated with his usual enthusiastic intensity, a kinetic energy that made him seem like a group of people, rather than just one. My mother stewarded us down the path, holding my sleepy baby brother in her arms. The sky was glowing with sunrise, pale pink and orange hanging about the craggy trees and shrubs. The deep olive of the eucalypti, with their dryly curling leaves and peeling gray trunks. The frothy yellow pom-poms of the golden wattle, shaggy and overgrown. The low-slung banksia, harboring its arsenal of red brush-like blooms. I was too enchanted with the unusual cool feel of the garden at this early hour to register fright as we approached the opening of the crawl space.

In an instant, we were all crouching, attempting to peer in. Dad slid the cold beam of the flashlight into the darkness, feeling around for his target, and then there she was, Whisky, looking startled in the stark halo of illumination.

Dad lowered the beam. "Let's give her a moment to get used to the light," he whispered.

He let the beam rest in the dirt, leaving only an insipid upwash of light that turned Whisky to shadows. She swiveled toward us. Her eyes glowed dully, showing confusion and pain. She wavered, her swollen frame teetering, then let out a slow moan, settling into a half crouch with her back legs lowered. The sound of her rapid panting filled the space, and then she seemed to hold her breath. We held our breath with her.

"There," Dad said, raising the eye of the flashlight to catch Whisky's body, leaving her head in shadow.

We watched as three puppies dropped to the ground, one by one, then waited to see if any more would emerge.

After a time, Dad shut off the flashlight. "I think that's it," he said. "Small litter. Better leave her now so she can clean them off."

We all went back to bed, though I was too excited to sleep.

The next morning, my mother found two smothered puppies in Whisky's sleeping basket. Whisky was distraught, my mother said, telling us she'd howled when my father removed the tiny unmoving bodies. I don't remember what happened to the one puppy who survived.

Some months later, I was walking home up the steep hill from school when I spied something lying in the gutter near our house. I got close enough to see it was a dog who seemed to have been hit by a car. The familiar sandy-colored fur. But it was not until I was staring down at the body, my gaze fixed on a fly that was walking in and out of the poor animal's open eye, that I realized it was Whisky.

* * *

Life in that orange-brick house was perfect yet off-kilter, like a trick house with optical illusions baked into its design, built to seem normal and yet set on an angle that makes it difficult to find one's footing. That house held a tense, topsy-turvy world, presided over by a dangerous, capricious woman who would slip, from time to time, into the skin of my often charming, sometimes loving, always beautiful mother.

It was a hazy night and there was the sound of beating rain. I was six years old, sitting in the car with my mother and three siblings. The car wasn't moving, and yet we were in the middle of the road. Through the windshield, I could see a man standing in front of the car waving his hands. Moments earlier, the man had appeared from nowhere right in front of the car as we were driving along the rainy road, and my mother had screeched to a halt. Rain slanted down, the windshield a dreamy lens onto the nighttime world. I could feel my mother's panic but also sensed she was excited. She swiveled to face us in the back seat, where we four huddled together.

"Stay in the car, children," she said, a high-drama look on her face. "This man might need my help. I'm going to see what he wants."

Then, she was outside in the rain. I could see the man talking to her. The rain dripped down the windows so that everything looked wobbly, the man's face, my mother, wobbling like Jell-O.

The front door opened, and she was back in the car. "I was right. He does need my help," she said. "Stay put. Do not move. I'll lock all the doors and I'll be back soon."

We were in the car; the doors were locked. *All the doors*, my mother had said. I wondered about that. Would there be any point locking only some of the doors? Or was it only safe if *all* the doors were locked? Time moved in droplets, like the rain, gathering in shallow pools. The occasional car moved slowly by; the road beyond the windows glistened slick and black in the heavy rain. I gripped my brother's hand; my sisters were singing a round. *Come follow follow … Wither shall I follow … To the greenwood tree*—I loved that round but could not join in. My throat was shut tight.

I wondered where my father was, then remembered he was probably *operating*. At that time, I didn't understand what that meant—only that it was something my surgeon father did.

My brother fell asleep, his head in my lap. We three girls pressed up tightly against each other in the back seat.

We were startled by a loud rapping on the window; it was the man, his face still trembly through the rain pouring down the window. He had thick features and was unshaven, there was something haunted about his eyes. Terror leapt to my throat. I heard a rapping on the other side of the car and turned to see my mother, her face urgent and oddly animated. She didn't look afraid, though, and this reassured me. She gestured to me to unlock the car door, which I did.

"We need your help," she said. She had her politeness-for-visitors face on, with the voice to match, though it was colored with a gravity brought on by crisis.

"Come, girls," she said, impatient now. "Get out of the car! Wake up your brother. Quickly!"

I didn't say: *But it's raining. It's the middle of the night. You left us alone in the car in the dark forever. I'm scared, and I want to go home!*

In a flash, we were out on the street and within minutes, soaked through. I held my little brother's hand tightly in mine. He stumbled beside me, half-asleep, shivering in the rain. We hurried after our mother, who was teetering in her high heels. We turned sharply off the main road onto an alleyway. There seemed to be no moon; away from the streetlamps, we were sunk in even gloomier obscurity. The tarmac beneath my feet glowered menacingly; I could feel its wetness through the thin soles of my sneakers. The terror in my throat choked all of me and all the world. The only thing I had to grip on to was the sight of my mother's heels up ahead, and my brother's little hand squeezed tightly between my fingers.

"Ow, it hurts," he called up in his thin toddler voice. I loosened my grip.

We turned into a darkened doorway. Smells I couldn't place, cooking that reminded me of the take-out hamburger place our father sometimes took us to. And a heavy, padded silence, not a peep from any of us, until my mother said again, "Come on, hurry up! This way!"

We found ourselves in a small room dominated by a window with a venetian blind that hung unevenly down, a streetlight beaming white light in through the open slats. That's when I saw the woman, lying face down on the bed up against the wall. She had long hair and it was tangled, like it hadn't been brushed for days. My mother's hair was always perfect; she slept on her stomach so as not to disturb the teasing and lacquer imposed by the hairdresser every Saturday morning. Friday was the only night my mother allowed herself to sleep comfortably on her side, since the next day she'd be getting her hair done. The woman on the bed clearly did not get her hair done. Her arms and legs were in a funny position, like a doll who'd been messed with by a naughty boy. Was she even alive? Was this man her husband? His face was all twisted up, a scowl that started at his brow and crunched its way all the way down to his chin. An awful, sour odor swelled in the room.

"Stay with your brother," my mother said to me. And then, to my older sisters: "Girls, come."

She led them to the bed. "Help the man," she said to my eldest sister, and then to my next older sister, "You help me."

They arranged themselves, the four of them, so that two were at each end of the woman, and then I saw that they meant to lift and carry her. Out of the room we went, then into the alleyway. We went in the opposite direction from the one we'd just come, the two grown-ups and two children swinging the body of the woman between them, my brother and I following behind. My legs propelled me forward and I gripped my brother's hand, feeling that the fate of the world depended on my keeping hold.

Rounding the corner as we turned onto another darkened street, my brother stumbled, and I pulled him up, back to his feet. The rain had slowed to a drizzle. My thin raincoat stuck to my wet shirt, my wet shirt stuck to my skin, my hair hung in dripping strings. We came to a halt beside a large car, what I know now to be a pickup truck. The man gestured to my mother and sister to let the woman down onto the pavement. My eldest sister looked stunned and scared. I dared not look at my other sister; I feared she might be crying. The man opened the door to the truck and the four of them picked up the woman again and heaved her into the cabin. She toppled down sideways, her head falling where the driver would need to sit. I stared at her chest and saw that it was moving, very slightly and erratically, up and down. Alive, at least. My child's mind was a scramble—had someone hurt her? Everything was frightening—the man, the broken-doll woman, the rainy night, but most of all my mother, changeable and dangerous, fragile, and in full command of our fates. Before I had a chance to see how the man was going to arrange the barely breathing woman so he'd be able to drive, we'd taken off down the street.

I panicked when I realized my brother's hand was no longer in mine. How had I let go? What would become of him? Had the scary man with the big truck taken him? Would I ever see him again? And then I saw that my mother had him in her arms as she ran down the street, the three of us girls racing behind her to keep up. Around this corner and that, then we seemed to backtrack again. My mother was crying; I could hear it, coming from somewhere far away. She was always getting lost. Always lost, always late. Now, I knew from the sound of her sobs that she had no idea where we were, that we were, all of us, lost. I turned to look behind me: a long, wet street, the haze illuminated at intervals by the glaring eyes of the streetlamps.

My mother stumbled, and then I saw her rip off her shoes, one of them broken, a stump where the heel had been. She flung them into the street. We ran and turned and ran some more and the terror lifted from me. Suddenly, I felt almost ecstatic—realizing I was no longer alone with my siblings locked up in the car. The unmoving woman had vanished, also the man with the gravelly voice. Reality suddenly, inexplicably rearranged itself, giving rise to my escape, leaving only freedom …

The rain stopped and now, we were all together, and the night erupted with vitality. How different it was from the daytime, how strange and heightened, the world not the same world—and me no longer the same me. Something hidden had cracked open, and in a rush of intense feeling, I recognized it, as if it had been within me, all along, just waiting—

I was no longer struggling as I ran along the street behind my mother; no, I was flying—actually flying! A foot or so above the ground, my legs free from effort and stretched out behind me, my arms reaching forward to steer in the glide. This was entirely new. A cushioned soaring, the air soft as it rushed by my ears. All of me suddenly a ripple of calm. The barbed agitation and hot alarm that often frazzled my world whisked away to reveal that the glistening tarmac beneath me was really the vast skin of an unruffled ocean, the streetlights the reflection of a hundred moons. Below the ocean's surface was a deep upon deep filled with secret gliding sea animals, their splendid colors masked by endless tons of water, the plant life exotic and wildly waving. Who knew there was so much more? The terror that had been a stabbing beak and grasping claws was now a freewheeling bird with a capacious wingspan, circling higher and higher, sharp eyed and farseeing, the landscape stretched out below.

Was this, for me, the first split?

How extraordinary, to be above everything, and free, away from the things that made my heart pound, from the mother I longed for and feared, and as fleet as the imagination, airborne, everything visible, sky and earth within my grasp, the wind a song I could sing myself. I never wondered if all children could take flight. I only knew that *I* could, and I held this secret tightly, breathless with a sense of my own power.

Later, I realized that this experience was replicated in my dreams, which were filled with heart-stopping threats—and had been there, all along. There, too, I would actively will my dragging feet to move, fueled by electric panic, my breath seized in my chest—but then, magically, I would soar. When I awoke, these forces stayed with me, pulsing invisibly through the daylight hours of "normal life," the life everyone else seemed to be effortlessly living, as if unaware of the unbalancing truths I glimpsed within and behind the dailiness.

I have, however, wondered if we are all propelled by the dangers we face, if feeling trapped, and finding ways to escape, is what defines us. I have wondered if all journeys involve fleeing, if ecstasy is always paired with a knowledge of dread, if the laws of the emotions run parallel to those of the physical world—equipoise a matter of opposite and competing charges. When I first heard the phrase "flights of the imagination," I knew exactly what it meant.

But I am getting ahead of myself. That rainy night, when I found my feet could lift off the ground, when I discovered I could escape, and also see things from a dizzying height, that was when I knew I could change—everything. I could go wherever my imagination might take me.

A week later, I heard the raised voices of my parents. The night often pinched me awake, leaving me charged with its hidden goings on. That night, hearing the upset tone of my parents' voices, I crept from my bed. My sister was asleep on her side of the room, I could hear the slow heavy pull of her breathing. I tiptoed down the short hallway, hugging the wall. The curtains had not been drawn. A fat moon sat high in the sky, scattering flinty beams. I stopped outside the closed door of the kitchen and pressed my ear to it.

"Where is your sense?" My father's voice was boiling with anger. He almost never sounded angry, not like my mother, with her frequent rages. "What were you thinking?"

My mother was petulant. "The man needed my help."

"He could have called an ambulance. Jesus Christ." My father sounded desperate.

I wasn't sure what Jesus had to do with all this. We were Jewish, so it was not a name that freely floated about in our household.

"Four children in the car. Our little boy, two years old. Do you realize the danger you put them in? Do you?"

My mother said something in her crying voice, but I couldn't make out what it was. My insides felt wobbly, the way everything had looked that rainy night. I tiptoed unsteadily back down the hallway and carefully climbed into bed.

Now, I try to peer into that kitchen of so long ago—to see my mother, her face crumpled with crying, and my father in that angry moment. What was between them? Did my father know how abandoned and alone my mother felt, wholly responsible for raising four kids, while his outsized career (surgeon, medical director, researcher, university lecturer) gobbled up his time and attention? The long hours also, I learned much later, an alibi for his infidelities. *I had no one, ever, to help me*—over and over, my mother would recount the trauma of being a new immigrant, with no family or established community, and a husband who was always gone. I see them there, at the kitchen table, the night eating away at itself, each of them lonely in their mismatched marriage, forlorn in that faraway spot they'd landed in—and yet also, in their way, devoted to each other and to their family, doing the best they could. They couldn't know their third child was shivering on the other side of the door, all of it pouring into her like hot gas, filling her with a frenzied desire to fix things, to somehow set things to rights.

* * *

When I was seven, we moved to Kew, a more established suburb closer to the city. The new house sat at the base of a cul-de-sac. An enormous monastery dominated one side, home to Redemptorist monks, who wore brown habits fastened with cord and had a lurking sense about them. The grounds of the monastery flared out to a beautiful campus of maroon-brick buildings and sweeping lawns. A circular driveway was governed by a statue of Saint Majella, protector of children and pregnant women, slender in white marble robes, his arms raised in welcome. We played British Bulldog in the wide, curving driveway, a full-tackle version of tag. The statue stood in a little circle of grass that had a brass faucet at its edge, a godsend in the blistering summer, when we'd crouch beneath it and let water pour into our mouths.

Our next-door neighbor and chief source of interest was an older boy named Bazza, whose mother would declare, "Tonight, we're having an easy tea," a word Australians also use for dinner. "Chops on the grill!" Lamb was plentiful and cheap, and the thick-slab chops were considered a solid and inexpensive meal. Everyone I knew had an indoor gas grill that sat high up above the stove. Walking into Bazza's house at dinnertime meant seeing the blue and yellow flames busily alive over chops.

It was Bazza's friend Neil—an older, almost unbearably handsome boy who lived around the corner and suffered from a mysterious illness no one ever talked about—who told us he'd seen one of the monks sneaking into the house two doors down from us. The house was inhabited by Miss Featherstone, a plump woman with sparkly eyes who was cheerful and easily embarrassed, and unusual, in our world, for being unmarried, the word *spinster* attached to her like a sticky tail. One day, Bazza let out his urgent whistle-code, *Cooo-wee*, and we ran outside, then snuck around the side of Miss Featherstone's house to where Neil was perched on top of the fence, peering through the branches of a tall tree into a high window. We scrambled up to join him.

The sight was a strange one—Miss Featherstone in bed with a man, locked in embrace. Draped over a chair was the monk's brown habit, looking like a discarded hide. I glanced at the boys. Their faces were serious and there was something sad and old about their eyes. I scrambled back down the fence and ran home. I knew I had no business peering into our neighbor's bedroom window and felt ashamed. It only heightened my sense that the monks were to be avoided.

The monastery was bordered in front by a low brick wall, maybe two feet high, fun to walk on or leap over, hurdle style. All that open space in the middle of the suburbs was a luxury; it felt special that our house was right across the street, like having our own private park grounds. The monks allowed us to run about those front areas. We did not venture behind the buildings, where we could see the vast grounds stretching back. Occasionally, we skirted the side of the main building, though that always felt scary, taking us beyond eyeshot of the street and the other houses. On one of those

occasions, when I was about nine, a portly monk appeared from
a side door. I see him still—of middling height and fat, the cord
around his waist slicing through his large, overhanging belly. He
was holding a tin of Vanity Fair chocolates, the only luxury chocolates I knew of, and there was something strange about the look
in his face, an expression I'd never seen before that frightened me.

"Would you like a chocolate?" he asked.

In my memory, his face trembles with excitement and his
watery eyes hold an aggressive pleading. I did want a chocolate, but
something told me it would be dangerous to take one.

"Yes," I said, "I would."

"Well then." His smile grew tight. "You'll have to come and get
it." He took a step backward.

I took a step forward, to close the gap.

"You can have more than one, if you like," he said, moving back
another step, closing the distance to the small side door in the
building behind him, which stood open. That doorway was a black
hole, leading to an evil cave, and I knew he was trying to lure me
there with the chocolates. There was little in my life at that age that
held greater allure than chocolate, especially those Vanity Fair ones,
their brightly colored metallic wrappers glistening with promise.
My mother limited sweets. I'd made a minor career of finding her
hiding places and pilfering the contraband—chocolate, of course,
but also cookies, marzipan, Turkish delight.

Another step closer to the black mouth of the doorway. My eyes
were locked on the open tin, on the bits of shiny foil gleaming in
the afternoon sun. I was calculating, assessing whether I could leap
forward and grab a chocolate and then run away before the monk
had the chance to seize me and drag me into the darkness behind
him. He took another step backward. He was in the open doorway,
his trembling, watery, dangerous eyes now frankly sinister in the
shadow imposed by the doorframe. I made the leap—snatched a
single chocolate and then spun around and ran as fast as I could
around the side of the building to where my friends were playing
on the circular drive.

"You didn't go in there with him, did you?" my friend asked anxiously, seeing the brightly wrapped chocolate in my hand.

I shook my head, no, staring down at the chocolate, trying to dampen the disappointment of finding myself with the only flavor I didn't like, lemon crème.

"Here," I said, passing it to my friend.

"No." She shook her head vigorously. "No way."

I tossed the chocolate onto the ground, aware that I was littering but throwing care to the wind.

I didn't tell my parents about the monks. I didn't tell them about the many things that kept me taut with distress, scanning every horizon for threat. How could I since they were themselves sources of worry and fear? I was furtive in my attempts to make sense of the simmering currents and violent undertows of our home life, monitoring, assessing, ever hopeful there might be something I could do to make a difference. To tease kindness from my mother, fill her face with warmth and make her eyes twinkle with love, but mostly to calm her, to ease her pain. To find a way to reach my father—so that he might see me or notice the molten misery that ran beneath the bright surface and seeming normalcy of our family. To broker some kind of accord between my parents that would undercut the mismatch that left them each feeling betrayed, maligned, and desperately alone.

Now I remember that my father, too, would sometimes erupt, furious when my mother played the piano—threatened by her talents and artistic absorption, by signs of her independence—closing all the doors between the piano room and his study on the other side of the house. There, he would sit in his recliner and stew, flipping through medical journals or dictating patient summaries for his secretary to type up the next day.

And what of that strange storm-cloud look on my mother's face when my father would enter the house in the morning as we were leaving for school? *Thirteen-hour operation,* he would say, *difficult kidney transplant.* I see her again, my very young mother, and now, looking back, I can decipher that look—churning anguish, clamped down fury, agitated helplessness. We children proud—*our heroic, surgeon father*—our mother sequestering a parallel narrative—*philanderer*—while she kept to her side of their pact: at my father's service, running everything that involved the house and children, keeping her figure trim, always exquisitely groomed, master of the domestic arts. She prized beauty and perfection in all things, setting herself to rigorous standards—in her singing, piano-playing, and teaching; in the making of her home and her physical appearance; and in all the external trappings of her role as *wife* and *mother.* The strain of all that striving stifled her and the air around her. The atmosphere of her love was strident, demanding, and critical, nothing ever quite satisfying or meeting the mark.

My knowledge of my father's affairs is patchy, something my mother told me about only in her final months as she succumbed to pancreatic cancer, the fourth of the siege of separate cancers that first struck when she was twenty-four years old, living in England away from all family and friends and caring for her first infant. I only now fully clock how beset by illness my mother was her whole life—a fact that is at complete odds with her extraordinary vitality, endless accomplishments, and engagement with the world. Bowel cancer, breast cancer, lymphoma, and pancreatic cancer were the big diseases, but there were also other causes for serious operations, along with migraines and severe intestinal attacks and other sequelae from her many surgeries, radiation treatments, and chemotherapies. My mother never complained about any of these ongoing physical assaults and multiple hospitalizations. If you were to ask her about her health, she'd say, *Oh, everything's fine, that's way too boring to discuss.* About my father's infidelities, my mother gave me only a few bits of information, hinting that they were ongoing and various, involving flirtations with friends' wives, and a long-term relationship with his secretary.

As she lay dying, my mother also told me something else: that in her late thirties, she fell in love with a man with whom she shared artistic interests and felt a sense of true soulmateship. He was the teacher of an adult education class she took on the history of art. I remembered her talking about it, radiant with interest. I even recalled the man's name—the name she now whispered, her face softening for an instant with a kind of broken joy. *I stopped it before anything really happened*, she said. He, too, was married and had a family. *I couldn't break up the family—two families. The stigma, the impact on you children—*.

My mother had yearned all her life for understanding, connection, and succor. She'd pined for transcendent love as a little girl trapped in a home of poverty, abuse, and abject misery (far more brutal than the home I had known). And yet, bound by a sense of duty and crushing, internalized societal expectations, she cut off contact with this man, abdicating all claims to the possibility of a grand love. In her eyes, which had always flashed with intensity but were now dim with pain and focused on the near lip of death's chasm, I could see the cost of that long-ago decision.

* * *

The cul-de-sac backed onto a lane that ran behind our house. My friend Sally lived a twenty-minute walk away if you took the streets, but a brisk five-minute stint if you jumped over the high fence at the back of our garden that stood behind a towering stand of cypress trees. The fence was a deadly threat, made of corrugated tin, with a sharp, rusty upper edge. Sally, who liked to roam the streets barefoot and would occasionally cut her feet on the tin, once remarked with a grin, "I don't mind a cut foot—better than a severed artery!" We'd climb on the wooden crossbars and catapult over, landing in the lane that took you to Sally's house in no time.

Sally's house was risky and unexpected, under slow construction throughout the ten years of our friendship, since her father, a builder, worked on it only in his spare time. I remember rooms without ceilings, piles of tools, and hillocks of sawdust. Sprawled on the rough sub-flooring boards of the living room, we would squint through the construction dust and picture freshly painted walls and beautifully appointed rooms. We dreamed about the enormous swimming pool that was to be nestled into a dramatic rock garden and of the parties we would hold under summer starlight, the gardens hung with fairy lights.

Sally had a sewing machine and she taught me to use it. We once made tube dresses with shirred bodices, all the rage at the time. Mine was fashioned from a piece of discard fabric, red with little white flowers. I wore it for years. In the background, there was always the sound of the black-and-white portable television, which sat on a wheeled cart and could be moved from room to room.

Those were the days of the Apollo launches; all morning long, on the Saturdays I'd spend at Sally's, we'd listen to the countdowns. They were likely showing the same launch, over and over, or perhaps showing repeats of earlier ones. But there they'd be, when I'd walk by the small gray screen, the rocket strapped to its launching pole, dense fog pouring out from its base, and the voice from Houston control, *ten, nine, ignition sequence start, six, five, four*, intoning like a priest, and we'd pause as he got to *one*, craning to see, and then *zero. All engines running. Liftoff, we have a liftoff!* The thing would rise from the ground and penetrate the skies. The camera would pan to the amassed crowd dressed in American summer garb, some of them in bathing suits, gathered in the spectator area, hands shielding their eyes, faces open with wonder and pride, necks craned to track the thrust of the rocket until it disappeared.

We'd turn back to our sewing, or card game, or arts and crafts project, satisfied with the impressive goings on of the wider world, and with an accepting shrug that things like that—rocket launchings, admiring citizens who bathed in the glow of their nation's prowess—didn't happen here, not in good old Australia. Aussies were different. Smiley, unflappable, not given to airs, happy to hang with their mates, go down to the beach, fix up the old house like Sally's dad was doing—but rockets to the moon? Not so much.

It was said that life in Australia was backward, not yet fully thrust into the technological age. We felt ourselves to be far-flung and somewhat misbegotten, inhabiting the antipode, a place that had been a mystery to the Western imagination for hundreds of years: terra incognita, the unknown land. The example always given was color TV. We were used to the black-and-white screen, but as children, we hankered for the color version we'd never known. When color TV finally came to Australia in 1975, having already been commonplace in the US by the mid-1950s, it was cause for celebration.

Money was scarce in Sally's household, though the overall impression I had in that half-built house was of bounty: high spirits, that Aussie can-do attitude. Her father was a handsome, burly man, devoted to his family and his work, and her mother was charming, warm, and relaxed about life. For me, they inhabited a casual, sun-burnt realm that had a crisp and alien lightness, with an existential horizon that was beach-like—endless stretches of sand meeting a blue and untroubled sea. This kind of Aussie life was beyond my own reach. That forever under-construction home, half open to the sky, offered no hidden crevices or underground passages, no history to lament as was true in our Jewish home, in which there'd been talk about the Holocaust for as long as I could remember, always the resounding echo in the oft-repeated injunction—*Never forget.*

And then there were Easter and Christmas, the closest to real-life magical events I had encountered. They tumbled in my mind like thrilling, alternate realities. Easter egg hunts, with prizes and games at every turn, and copious amounts of interestingly shaped chocolate—bunnies and eggs—that could balloon to gigantic proportions.

Christmas—or Chrissie, as it was known—was the pinnacle. On Christmas morning, the neighborhood kids would run around our cul-de-sac, excitedly telling each other about their presents. For weeks, the anticipation would build. I'd seen the Christmas trees in their homes, which held an exotic allure, flashing with tin-sel and ornaments. Milk and cookies would be left out for Santa, who would appear in the middle of the night. Christmas fell at the height of Melbourne's summer, so the Santa we knew wore a tank top and football shorts, though he did ride a sleigh through the air, driven by the same reindeer known the world over. The miracle of miracles—Aussie kids woke up on Christmas morning to discover *piles* of presents under the tree. In our household, on the other hand, the only real present we were given was on our birthdays, typically a modest affair (though once, I was given roller skates, which thrilled me). Hanukkah was decades away from any kind of wider recognition or commercialization and consisted only of lighting candles. We were given a single chocolate on each night of the festival, which held its own dazzle for me, until I learned from my neighbors and school friends about the bacchanalian excesses of Christmas. After that, the chocolate seemed little more than a chunk of coal.

My Aussie friends went fishing and boating and attended family barbeques and picnics with truckloads of relatives—grandparents, uncles and aunts, a great slew of cousins. Once a year was the famed Melbourne Royal Show. The chief reason for going to the show was the loot—show bags stuffed with samples, candy, toys, and games. I understood intuitively that Jewish people *didn't do these kinds of things*—at least, not the Jewish people I knew, and, specifically, not my family. We sat around reading books, having what Sally later referred to as "intellectual conversation" (exotic, it turns out, to her), everything imbued with the recent history of the Jewish people, with words like *survivor* and *the camps*, along with a keen awareness of geographical upheaval, which was the coin of my realm.

When I used the word *Aussie*, I was not thinking about us, about me. I was Jewish. Jews came from elsewhere—elsewheres that were horrifying and involved persecution, fleeing, murder, death. Villages on fire, babies tossed against barbed-wire fences, incomprehensible numbers of people just like us packed into cattle cars and starved, beaten, enslaved. Separated into lines to the left, to the right, those on one side sent to chambers in which they were gassed, their bodies then burned in massive incinerators. We were people without extended families, people who didn't belong to any one country, people who, in fact, had never belonged to any place, besides the shimmery, mythical location we invoked once a year at our watered-down version of Passover, when we would raise our glasses and say, in unison, "Next year in Jerusalem." Jerusalem existed in the Bible stories I learned for a short time when I attended the secularized Jewish Sunday school. It was the place our people had belonged at the very beginning but then been thrown out of—and now we were back to the centuries-long narrative of persecution, expulsion, fleeing, murder.

We were supposed to yearn for our lost home, even though this home had existed thousands of years ago, all the while commemorating the misfortunes that had befallen our people. Our holidays did not involve trees laden with celebratory ornaments, piles of presents, or a jolly fellow whose entire existence was focused on delivering unimaginable pleasures to children. Children who got to write lists stating everything they wanted! Our holidays commemorated nightmares. Yom HaZikaron, the Day of Remembrance, invoked and memorialized a plethora of historical horrors. Passover chronicled the Jews' expulsion from Egypt, along with their years of wandering in the brutal desert. And on Yom Kippur, the holiest day of the year, known as the Day of Atonement, we were to fast—no food, no water—for twenty-four hours while cataloging and atoning for our own shortcomings and sins. True, there were other, more celebratory festivals, though even those often harkened back to persecution—Hanukkah, involving the Jews under siege by their Greek Syrian oppressors, and Purim, recalling the abuse of the evil, antisemitic Haman, adviser to the King of Persia. Even Succoth, a marker of gratitude to God for providing food for the exiled Jews as they wandered for forty years, invoked major travails.

My friends, with their Aussie lightness, carnivalesque holidays, and outdoorsy family doings, simply lived in another world. They, to me, were Australians. Being Jewish was something altogether different.

Of course, there was more to the Aussie reality than at that age I could know.

* * *

It was at the beginning of fourth grade, after I met Tessi, the new girl, that I came to understand that there were other truths straining behind the Aussie reality I'd gleaned from the lives of my neighborhood friends. The brightness and sunshine I experienced in their homes was obscuring something that the society I grew up in was calibrated to actively, criminally suppress.

It was because of Tessi that I got to sit in the front row to watch the moon landing. We were outside on the asphalt quadrangle, where the principal had wheeled the black-and-white television in front of a hundred chairs we dragged out from the classrooms. When Tessi had arrived two weeks earlier, I was assigned to be her mate, which meant staying by her side. That first day, watching her cross the room, I'd been struck by the stick-thin ankles poking up from her scuffed shoes. My eyes traveled north—knobby knees, the same ashen color, and long thighs revealed by a uniform that was too small. Her wide-set eyes looked oddly mirror-like, as if she were somehow hiding behind them; her wavy, unbrushed hair, sun-streaked blonde, swirled around her face as if in motion. Though I'd lived in Melbourne all my life, I'd never seen an Aboriginal person before. It was like they lived off in some other world, wholly distant from ours.

Sitting beside Tessi in that privileged front-row seat in front of the TV, I peered up at the flickering images of a strange rocky surface swimming in dim half-light.

"It's the second time," she whispered, leaning close.

"No," I whispered back. "No one's ever landed on the moon before."

"I mean the telly." The Aussie word for TV. "I only ever saw telly once before. In the jail cell."

"Look—it's landing!" I said, too riveted by what was happening on the screen to attend to what Tessi had said.

The next day, eating with Tessi in the shelter shed, a vast roof on stilts filled with wooden trestles and benches, I recalled her remark.

"What did you mean when you said you'd watched telly in a jail cell?"

I eyed her scanty lunch of limp white bread and a wrinkled apple. I passed her half of my whole-wheat sandwich slathered with butter and thick with tomato and cheese.

"After they took us, they put us in a jail cell. Kept us there two days. Me and my brothers."

Someone had told me Tessi lived in an orphanage. I'd imagined a car accident, her parents buried in a dusty cemetery on the outskirts—and no other family of any kind, not brothers, not sisters.

"What do you mean, took you?"

"Police. Priest too, maybe. Some kind of church man."

How could a little girl spend two nights in a jail cell? And be taken away—by the police? I felt a cloud of confusion and doubt.

"They do that, you know," she said, her voice flat. "Take us black kids away. When they took my cousins Jimmy and Petal, mum was snake mad. She did that—went to the police station, hissed at them. They said the kids were gone off to white folks. 'Better life for them,' they said. 'You people got a bad culcha.'"

"What's a culcha?"

"You know, our stories, dances. Our lingo."

Tessi passed an anxious glance around the shelter shed. "I don't wanna get hit," she said. "I'm not allowed to talk about this stuff."

Two months after Neil Armstrong stepped onto the moon, Tessi asked me if I wanted to come over to her place.

"I don't know where you live," I said awkwardly.

"Kawara House." She winced a little with the word *Kawara*—a name I'd long known, that had about it a frightening hush. It was the place parents threatened to send naughty children to scare them into good behavior—a place with frequent spankings, a diet of bread and gruel, and no mum or dad.

I stood frozen. She averted her eyes, fiddled at the waist of her too-short uniform.

"It's okay if you can't," she said, her lip twisting pitifully.

"No—I mean yes, I want to."

"Really?" There again, that look in her eyes, as if they were shiny, reflective shields.

My mother drove me. We curved along the treeless road, past an abandoned factory with shuttered windows and a block of council flats, then pulled up before a large ramshackle building.

"Okay, then. Have fun!" my mother said with false cheer, her eyes wavering nervously.

The elaborate iron gates must have been grand in their day; now, they were crusted with rust. It took some tugging to dislodge the catch and, true to some haunted-house tale, the gate creaked loudly as it swung open. Tessi came bounding down the front steps.

"Come on!" she said, grabbing my hand. "I'll show you around. Mr. Shelbourne's at a funeral—death in the family!" She said this happily, which let me know how she felt about Mr. Shelbourne, who I assumed was one of the grown-ups in charge.

We scampered across the wooden boards of what must once have been an elegant foyer and out through double doors at the back, which led onto a large concrete yard. Plain red-brick structures had been built on three sides, joining the old building. I glanced around; the place seemed completely deserted.

"They're at church," Tessi said in that way she had of reading my mind. "Except for Mrs. Shelbourne."

As if there were some haze of mental telepathy hanging over everything, a woman appeared in the open doorway across the concrete yard. She was tall and thin, wearing an old-fashioned dress with a floppy lace collar that looked like the spread wings of a giant moth. Her face was gaunt, her white skin tinged with gray, and as we crossed toward her, she turned and drifted back into the shadows.

"Don't mind her," Tessi said. "She doesn't bother anyone."

I followed Tessi into the girls' dorm, sixteen cots lined up in two rows along the walls, each with its own metal side table. No desks.

I pictured her doing her homework seated on the cot, scratching answers into her exercise book.

A back door opened onto a dirt yard sloping down to a fence where a straggly silver birch stood. Its dangly leaves and worm-like pods seemed inviting, in among the concrete and dirt.

"Come on—." I grabbed her hand and we ran down to the tree. Its foliage provided shade and a feeling of protection.

"I never had a school friend before," she said. "They don't like me to have friends. I think they're afraid I'll say things."

She did that twisty thing with her mouth that cut into me and made me sad.

"How come you're the only one who didn't go to church?" I asked after a while.

"Don't like it."

"Why not?"

Tessi didn't answer. Instead, she said, "You go off to the Jewish RI."

I nodded. On Friday mornings, during regular Religious Instruction, we Jewish kids, six in all the school, traipsed off for our own special lesson held in a storeroom stacked with cleaning supplies. An elderly woman, Mrs. Wein, was brought in to teach the class. The Bible stories she told us got mixed up in my nine-year-old mind with the unpleasant, virtuous odors of naphthalene and lye, as if they, too, were antidotes to possible minor perils—moth-eaten jackets or dirty floors.

"You Jewish, then?" Tessi asked.

"Yes."

"They told us at church that the Jews killed Jesus, and so that made me think—"

"Made you think what?"

"That Jews wouldn't tell me I wasn't allowed to remember my own stories. My songs. My Dreaming."

I was struggling to make sense of what she was saying. Her voice had changed. It sounded gnarly, as if it were getting stuck in her throat.

"I was five when they took me away," she said.

"Pardon me?"

"They took us away from Mum. My brothers and me. Stole us away. Mr. Shelbourne says that's rubbish. But I know it's true." Tessi tapped her temple. "I got the memory right here."

Her eyes were wide; I could feel mine widen too, with the astonishment of it—that a person, that my friend Tessi, might be stolen—pinched, as we said at school—like a pencil or a ring or a fifty-cent piece.

"Mum—I think it's her. I don't remember her face too well. She's on the ground, kneeling. Smashing her fists into the road. We're in a car, my brothers and me, I'm looking through the back window. Driving away. She's getting smaller and smaller, she's smashing and smashing, like her hands are hammers that will tear up the tarmac. The land is suffocating, Mum is suffocating. She's gonna rip the road off with her fingernails and all of us will fall through—back to the Dreaming."

I see it too, everything Tessi is saying, and feel the smashing within me, my own thrashing heart. Her face is a blank mask. Her fist opens then clutches, opens and again tightens, as if she's grasping at something.

"Mr. Shelbourne hits us. Any of our lingo comes out of our mouth and *whack*." Tessi swung her fist in a wide arc then slammed it into her other hand. "Mrs. Shelbourne—she leaves us alone. But she knows he does it, she's seen it."

She paused, then, seemed to be mulling something over.

"Are Jews allowed to remember stuff?" she said finally. "Songs and everything?" Her face was open, like a child asking about the moon.

"Why, yes, of course! We sing them in synagogue. Though the truth is, I don't really know what they mean."

Tessi's jaw worked slowly, like she had a bit of gristle in her mouth. "Do you think they'd let me come to your RI?"

"Dunno. I can ask."

The flash of joy in her face came at me like a slap, leaving me suddenly fierce. "I bet Mrs. Wein will let you. She's old but she's nice."

The following Friday, ducking around the school building to the RI room, I saw someone crouched behind the bank of dented metal rubbish bins. I pulled ahead of the others to go see. It was Tessi, hugging her knees, her eyes nervous and bright.

The faint waft of mothballs—I turned to see Mrs. Wein.

"Hello, girls."

I pulled Tessi up by the hand. "Can she stay?" I asked.

Mrs. Wein's brow ruffled.

"She doesn't like the regular RI," I added hastily. "The Christian one."

"Alright," she said, putting her key in the lock of the door. I noticed something odd in her face—like she'd hurt herself and was apologizing at the same time.

Inside, there wasn't a chair for Tessi, so I sat with her on the floor.

"Today, we begin our study of Hanukkah," Mrs. Wein said.

I heard Tessi whisper the word under her breath, *Hanukkah*.

Mrs. Wein launched into the story of the miracle of the oil. After the destruction of the Second Temple by the Syrian king, Antiochus IV, only a one-day supply of consecrated oil remained, but it kept the eternal flame burning for eight days. Tessi leaned forward, a beam of intensity in her eyes. Something seemed to ignite in Mrs. Wein, as if Tessi's fascination were like the shamash, the menorah candle used to light the others, setting Mrs. Wein's words aflame.

A vivid image leapt to my mind with such force, I let out a little gasp. Something soft crept across my lap—Tessi's fingers, seeking my own. The image filled me, blocking out everything else. A magnificent stone structure rising from a sea of sand; a slim tower, coated in dazzling gold. People dressed in jewel tones—azure and rose, threaded with silver—swarmed around the massive courtyard. Bells clanged, the air was thick with incense and the smell of ripe fruit. A feeling of exhilaration coursed through me: heady, tantalizing, unlike any feeling I'd known. I wanted to clutch at it, memorize it so I might reclaim it again and again. The vision froze, shimmered sensuously—and then, there was a sudden feeling of searing heat, and the vision began to burn, as if a flame had been set to celluloid, the image coiling to a molten mess.

My eyes snapped open. Tessi's face was startled as she tried to pull her hand from my finger-crushing clench.

"Sorry!" I whispered, releasing her hand. "It's just that I—"

Tessi nodded slowly, her eyes bright. "It's okay," she whispered back. "I saw it too."

What could she possibly mean? *I saw it too?*

Later, at recess, Tessi and I ran down to the dirt yard behind the shelter shed, muddy in winter, baked hard in summer. That day, it sent up wafts of reddish dust that clung to our legs. We crouched, and I reached into my pocket and pulled out a bag of diamond-shaped eucalyptus sweets. We each popped one into our mouths.

"What did you mean," I asked, "when you said in RI—I saw it too?"

"The ceremony."

"What ceremony?"

"Your teacher, she said *Hanukkah.* I never heard that word—but it sounded like something far away, something I know. I shut my eyes, listened inside me, and I heard a new word—different, but also the same. *Wominjeka.* Then I hear it again, this time in, well, in English I guess. 'Welcome ceremony.' And then—everything sliding away, like with you—" Tessi looked at me meaningfully, and I knew that she knew something of what I'd seen, as if by magic. "Only different."

"Different—how?"

"Everything in my eyes, inside me, went black and white. And I saw them—a whole lot of them. My people. Koori. Standing very still—so still, it scared me. Paint on their bodies. Holding things—flat shields, boomerangs, stuff like that. And over there—" Tessi waved now, off to the left, as if I could see the picture too, the picture she'd held in her mind as I was staring within at a blazing desert scene, at the gold tower of a massive domed temple. "Women. Sitting down. Marks on their chests." She passed her hand across her upper chest, under the collarbone. "Means they've had children."

I heard the break in her voice as she said the word *children*. Her eyes welled. I was thinking of Tessi's mother in the middle of the road, pounding on the tarmac, her children wrested away, stolen by a policeman and a church man. Was Tessi thinking about her mother?

"Me, there. But not there." She paused, struggling for words. "Not there ... taken away ... I want to see the dance, but I don't see it. They're so still, I think maybe they're dead, pretending to be alive. But then I figure it out. They're not real, those people."

"Yes, they are, Tessi," I said urgently. "They are real!"

"No! They're only a picture! An old photograph I saw—someone showed me, maybe. Maybe I remember it from Adnyamathanha." Her face clouded.

"From who?" I asked. "Tessi, what's wrong?"

"I don't know. Those words—Koori words—they came into my mouth, but I don't know what they mean! And I don't see them dance. I don't know the dance! It's just an old photograph!"

I didn't know what to say.

Finally, words came. "I know it's different ... I will never understand ..."

She reached for my hand. Our two hands curled together softly.

"I don't know ..." I said, struggling for words. "I saw something that frightened me, something I did not understand."

"Hanukkah?"

"Yes, Hanukkah. Very far away in time. I think I saw—the beginning. Where Hanukkah began. The Second Temple. It was beautiful." I recalled the splendor, trying, though failing, to recapture that extraordinary feeling I'd had. "Then it got—I don't know, pulled away. Like someone was destroying it."

"It was destroyed. Mrs. Wein said so," Tessi said.

"I mean—like someone was taking it away from me. It was like someone set fire—to the picture in my head. I know, it sounds weird."

"Not to me, it doesn't," she said.

"I wanted to know what happened next, but it just kind of let go of me. As if—" I hung my head, stunned by the feeling of shame washing through me. "As if someone, something, was just throwing me away."

Tessi's face was knowing and wise. Tears stung my eyes.

"Mrs. Wein said they found the oil," she said. "Magic oil. There was only enough for one day, but it lasted for eight." She said this as if she'd been reciting the story of Hanukkah all her life. "You should add that part in. You know, into your Dreaming."

My eyes closed, as if drawn shut by an invisible hand, and then I saw it: an ancient candelabra wrought in fine gold, covered in tiny carvings—vines and flowers winding around the curves. The candles in place, the shamash being lit, a powerful, sweet smell as the wick caught, like melting honey, and then, one by one, the eight candles also set alight, until the space around the candelabra sprang into view, a cavernous room made of stone, a huge crowd of people with somber eyes. *Hanukkah*—the sound of the word, rumbling and guttural, issuing softly from the lips of a thousand souls. *Rededication*. And in place of the ecstasy I'd felt earlier, there was something melancholy and sweet.

I opened my eyes.

"Did you see it?" Tessi asked.

"Yes," I said. "I did."

"Then I must close my eyes and see my people, too." Tessi screwed her eyes shut. "Help me," she whispered, a little frantically. "Help me to see it."

I had no idea what I was supposed to help her see. I closed my eyes too, hoping for inspiration.

"There's fire there too," I said, relieved that words had sprung to my lips. "A campfire. And stars—lots of stars in the sky. Dry earth—reddish brown." I grabbed a eucalyptus sweet from my pocket and thrust it under her nose. "And the smell of eucalyptus leaves that have been baking all day in the sun. Only now, it's nighttime. The dance is about to begin."

Something was happening to her face. Her tensed eyes relaxed, and it was as if she had come upon something unexpected and beautiful.

"Yes, I see it—."

I held my breath, watched the ripple of feeling cross her face. I wondered if Tessi's mother was there, in her mind's eye. I knew I could never understand Tessi's experience, the unspeakable tragedy that had befallen her, her family, her entire culture—the cruelty and barbarism directed toward her by church and government officials. It defied understanding, or belief, and yet it had happened ... to her ...

Tessi let out a low sigh. I had the sudden feeling I was sliding away from her, as if we were no longer side by side but separated by a growing chasm.

She opened her eyes, placed a fist on her breastbone.

"Not gone," she said, her eyes shining with an unearthly light—perhaps with the starlight from her vision.

"Here," she said, giving her chest a little thump. "It's all here."

At the beginning of the next school year, I scanned the faces as we lined up in the schoolyard by the Grade 5 sign, looking for Tessi. She wasn't there—and she never returned to Deepdene Primary School. For a while, I would find myself looking for her during the school day, expecting to see her in the shelter shed or by the water troughs. I became busy with new friends, and first love sparked—for a sweet boy named Mark, whom I'd think about dreamily in long afternoons after school. The months were an electric daze, and soon, I stopped seeking Tessi. How porous childhood is, the way things fill and seep and leak away.

It wasn't until 1981, with the publication of leading scholar Peter Read's landmark paper *The Stolen Generations*, that studies began to appear on the devastation wreaked on children and their families by Australian church and governmental authorities, who forcibly removed children from their homes for almost one hundred years, from 1883 until 1969. This state-sanctioned, criminal destruction of families, communities, and cultures—known now as the "Stolen Generations"—is, in the words of Read, a story of attempted genocide.

Now, in my own late middle age, the months pass differently. That hazy, buzzing timelessness of childhood has transformed to a dull skidding. I see Tessi in the eyes of children separated from their parents at the southern borders of this country I now call home. And I wonder, with an ache that passes beyond my own heart to the bottom of the world, about the generations that will follow, if any of this can ever be undone, or if the trauma will simply roll along forever.

- 2 -

Imaginary Life Buoy

Danielle Gold and I became best friends our first day at the new high school, falling into each other the way teenagers do. Our schoolteachers had heavy Eastern European accents—mostly Polish, though some Russian, Lithuanian, and Czech—as did the parents of most of my new friends. After the Australian public school, everything was strange at this Jewish school, including the symbol emblazoned on our powder-blue satchels: a lion on its hind legs, front paws held high, with the Hebrew words *chazak ve'ematz* and below, the English, "Be strong and of good courage." The words held special urgency, since Mount Scopus Memorial College was founded in 1949, a mere twenty-five years earlier, by Holocaust-survivor refugees. My own family had immigrated from South Africa, half a world away from murderous Europe, which in a deep, unspoken way, set me apart.

The thickest accent of all belonged to our principal, Mr. Ranoschy, a diminutive man, elegant in his thinness, whose intense gaze and baldness somehow went together, as if the burning in his eyes had incinerated his hair. He insisted on our pursuit of excellence, whether we wanted that or not. Our school had been entrusted with—encumbered with—the mission to rebuild a destroyed world here, in sunbaked Melbourne, the farthest habitable place on earth from murderous Europe. Mount Scopus was the anti-crematorium. Here, we were all phoenixes, rising from the pyre. Many of my friends' parents watched ferociously over their grades, unwittingly encouraging a corrosive perfectionism—the demand for educational success at all costs a thin papering over of trauma.

At Yad Vashem in Jerusalem, on a youth tour Danielle and I took together at the end of tenth grade, it hit me. The emaciated faces in the photographs of liberated concentration camp victims were the faces of my friends' parents. The skeletal bodies in huge piles, arms askew, with open dead eyes and grimaces of suffering, were the murdered bodies of their grandparents, aunts and uncles, cousins. For some, the small child corpses were their own siblings—their parents' first families—thrown up against electrical wire fences for sport. One schoolfriend's mother had recognized herself in a photograph here, on the wall at Yad Vashem, a gaunt teenager in prison rags whose sunken eyes held the awful knowledge she spent the rest of her life trying to strangle.

Danielle Gold was one of these second-generation kids. That day at Yad Vashem, I reached for her hand as we walked through those rooms. A moment later, I became aware that there was something cruel in my gesture—like throwing an imaginary life buoy to someone struggling to stay afloat.

For survivors of genocide, there is no old country to remember with longing, warmth, or hope. Families, generations strong in their home country, were stripped of citizenship, hunted, starved, tortured, enslaved. Since surviving at all was a statistical rarity, each of their stories was remarkable: improbable near escapes, plucked by the fates from a multitude destined for death, through extraordinary confluence of precise, highly unlikely events. After the war was time spent in displacement camps, then uncertain, extended wanderings, closed doors, and endless trials of one sort or another. I picture these malnourished young souls with haunted eyes—my friends' parents as teenagers and young adults—arriving on boats to Australia, disembarking on this massive island at the far end of the earth, the terra incognita with its swaths of desert and honey-mint eucalyptus, blistering summers, mild winters devoid of snow, lethal funnel-web spiders, and sweet-looking kangaroos capable of weaponized kicks.

Perhaps it was no coincidence that there were so many American TV shows in the 1960s and 1970s that cleaved to metaphors of people stranded in bewildering and sometimes threatening worlds, confronted by unfathomable practices and circumstances, life coming at them quick and furious as they scrambled to get a foothold and survive. America had its own masses of Holocaust survivors and other war refugees, some of whom found their way to careers in Hollywood, alongside other American Jews attuned to the realities of their European Jewish siblings. Shows such as Lost in Space, which we avidly watched as children. Or Gilligan's Island, My Favorite Martian, and a bit later, Mork & Mindy.

At Mount Scopus College, the atmosphere was giddy with possibility and hope. We were made to feel that, with hard work, we could do anything. That if we were "strong and of good courage" we would grab every opportunity available in this open, friendly, egalitarian society. We were to be doctors and lawyers, accountants, psychologists, physical therapists, and teachers, all of us working toward an unshakable place of security and respect in this far-flung country that not a single Jewish refugee could, in their youth, have imagined they'd ever find themselves. The giddiness had a double-edged feel—freedom tied to desperate escape. The glittering futures we pushed ourselves toward beckoned up ahead, but there was also something else. Behind the school's state-of-the art features—shiny new science labs, expansive assembly hall, the neatly mown sports fields we called "the Ovals"—something terrifying seemed to glower. We dipped into this dire other world in our Jewish Studies classes. A key moment in my own life was a school screening of the film Night and Fog, a documentary that included Nazi footage cataloging Third Reich atrocities. I was sitting next to Danielle in the little school theater, and as images of corpses being bulldozed into pits flickered across the screen, she leaned in closely. I couldn't stop thinking of the person operating the bulldozer. Who was he? What was he thinking as he went about his gruesome work? The film was a culmination of all the horrors I'd learned about in a school curriculum focused on a two-thousand-year history of one set of murderous or expulsive terrors after the other—the list was endless, arcing back to ancient Egypt.

Our teachers, charged with the mission of conveying the full extent of these soul-crushing realities, had fanciful names. Names that had nothing to do with the explorers, pioneers, British over-lords, and convicts who made up the Australian history we were not actually taught at our school, nor with the story of Australia's First Nations people, with their rich cultures and internally config-ured land, whose history at that time had been effaced from public consciousness. I remember one teacher, Mrs. Katzenellenbogen, remarkable for the heavy eyeliner she wore, which made her eyes seem to pop out of her face, and for her outdated, beehive hairstyle. I was repelled by the way she detailed the torture and execution of the first century scholar, Rabbi Akiva, by the Romans, her accent an added layer of heaviness: *Zey dragged ze metal combs viz zer razor-sharp teez sru ze flesh of his arms and legs.*

We were exhorted time and again to remember, to never forget, though I intuited that my friends' parents, ruined from within by what they had endured, had made it their business to slam their memories shut so as to continue living.

I took to spending weekends at Danielle's modest house, which was different from the homes of my other friends in the area. There was something open and raw about the atmosphere, as if the sar-cophagi of memory were not hermetically sealed. I felt the pull of stories vibrating with emotion too powerful to suppress.

Danielle's parents adored me. They spoke of me as a second daughter and treated me as one, delighting in my conversational patter. We sat at the kitchen table for hours, eating and talking— and smoking, which for me was a glorious, transgressive freedom. If my parents had found out I smoked, they'd have been apoplec-tic. Smoking was the ultimate taboo in our home, but Danielle's father, who went by the anglicized name Harry, thought it was just fine. He was a rakish fellow, short and trim, who wore a schmoozy nightclub-owner smile and always held a lit cigarette in his hand. Danielle would light up our first cigarettes while we were still in bed in the morning, two at once, passing one to me. She had a sardonic smile, and none of the hard-striving ambition-anxiety that vexed my other friends, whose families focused on education with an intensity that risked crossing into fetish. She was extremely smart and an excellent writer, but she didn't do that well in school. Her parents didn't worry. Her father worked in real estate, made a good living, and didn't seem to expect his daughter to go to college.

Danielle's house was often filled with her parents' friends, fellow refugees who would sit in the kitchen chain-smoking, drinking coffee and eating cakes from the European Jewish pastry shop on Acland Street, playing cards, and talking loudly in Polish. All of them had been in concentration camps. Danielle's parents had miraculously survived years of horror. Both had been in Auschwitz, though they didn't know each other there. Her father had also endured the long death march from Auschwitz to Buchenwald. After being liberated by the Russians at the end of the war, the two met in a refugee camp, each the only surviving member of their entire families. No parent, sibling, cousin, aunt—not a single other related soul. They were part of the group who attended the annual Buchenwald Ball, where they would sing the song Danielle's father had, as a slave, been forced to sing while standing for hours in the brutal night cold, thinly dressed in prison garb. After re-evoking this terrible song, the group would drink and dance late into the night, a brazen nose-thumbing to the universe. In Danielle's home, the thick sound of the Polish language matched the laden atmosphere of an ever-replenishing fog of smoke and coffee fumes, the aroma of chocolate, cinnamon, and honey rising from plates of rugelach and tortes. And laughter—raucous, untrammeled. Nothing like the restrained, formal dinner parties my South African immigrant parents hosted for my father's medical colleagues and other non-European friends.

One Sunday morning, I stumbled into Danielle's kitchen earlier than usual to get some coffee to go with my first cigarette of the day. Mrs. Gold was sitting statue-still in front of the window in a kitchen chair, her back to me. The room held a strange silence that raised goosebumps on my arms and made the air thin, as if the oxygen had been sucked away. She seemed unaware of my presence. A fresh pot of coffee sat on the stove. I helped myself, then leaned against the kitchen counter, sipping from my mug, gazing at Mrs. Gold's frozen form. The hair at the back of her head was flattened from lying in bed, revealing the black and gray roots beneath the blonde dye coating the robust curls I'd seen her set into place at night with large plastic rollers. Her early-morning routine included slathering large amounts of Lancôme cream on her face and neck, something I'd marveled at, knowing how expensive Lancôme was and aware that the Golds were not people of means. In my own, more monied household, such a face cream would have been seen as a frivolous extravagance. And yet, while Mrs. Gold was not indulgent in any other way, she applied the unguent with abandon, scooping up a great glob and smoothing it in until her face gleamed. I spied the open tub beside her on the kitchen bench, aware of the familiar scent, heavy as perfume. With the white early-morning light slanting in, I felt shunted into a time warp.

The silence was broken by the rise of Mrs. Gold's heavily accented voice.

"It was so, so beautiful," she said, her inflection guttural and unfamiliar, as if her voice were coming from some unrevealed place deep within.

She was speaking to me. She knew I was there.

"What was beautiful, Mrs. Gold?" I asked, my cigarette forgotten, burning slowly in the ashtray beside me on the kitchen counter.

"The snow. So beautiful. White snow, falling from the sky."

Her back still turned to me, she raised her arms high above her head, the way small children do. She craned her neck back to look up at the sky outside her window, a sky that showed the dawning Melbourne day, mild now, but holding the promise of intense dry heat. Her arms still raised, she flickered the fingers of both hands and slowly brought them down, tracing the movement of snowflakes.

"Before the war, when I was a child, in Poland. Near the lake. I had a beautiful jacket with fur on the hood. My brothers and sisters would skate on that lake. I was too little. I couldn't wait until I was older, until I could skate on the lake too. I sat in my mother's lap and the snow came down. So pure, so white. Everything white."

Now, she is facing me, though I have no sense of her having turned the chair around. I know that for some minutes I have been gazing at her, taking in every detail of her face, which I can still see in my mind's eye as if it is happening now and not forty-some years ago. I am looking into her broad face, the high, wide cheekbones that Danielle remarkably shared—remarkable since Danielle had been adopted at birth. In Auschwitz, Mrs. Gold had been a victim of Mengele's medical experiments, which had left her infertile. Now, Mrs. Gold's face is shiny with the Lancôme cream, silent tears stream from her bright eyes and her mouth spreads in a beatific smile, the smile of a small child. This child's smile hangs uneasily on the lined face of this woman in late middle age, existentially out of place in a way that triggers the queasy unease inspired by carnival clowns and children's toys in horror movies.

"You've no idea how beautiful the snow was," she said through her tears. "So pure, so white."

I had never actually seen snow, having grown up in temperate Melbourne, where people complain if the temperature drops to fifty degrees Fahrenheit. But I could see it then, just as she described, as if the roof of her house had opened to reveal a Polish sky in the thick of winter. Both of us seemed to disappear as shadowy figures reared up in my imagination—and there, I could see the child in the warm winter coat, the hood lined with fur, a child whose eyes were alight, naturally bright, not bright with haunting as Mrs. Gold's had been moments before. The smile of a child who is loved and cared for, who has known nothing but the unfolding marvels of the world, who has seen only loving faces, felt only the strong, protective arms of her parents and older siblings, whose days are rippled with singing, laughter, and light. Nothing unnatural about that smile. No, her smile was the most natural thing in the world. Large fluffy snow-flakes swirled down from a luminous white sky, frosting the pine trees, dusting the ice of the lake so that as the older children twirled and spun, flecks of snow danced at their heels.

The Poland of Mrs. Gold's childhood. So beautiful, before the war.

Toward the end of eleventh grade, Danielle came to school one day clearly shaken. We met as usual at the buses and I could see that something was wrong, but she brushed me off in an uncharacteristic way, which left me worrying about her all morning as I sat bored through chemistry, Hebrew, then math.

I found her at lunchtime, grabbed her arm and ran with her to the back of the Skolnick Oval, to the farthest edge, out of earshot of the other smokers.

We sat on the grass. I unwrapped my sandwich. Danielle left her lunch bag untouched. We lit up and she did her trademark sharp inhalation, then let the smoke out in a slow, narrow stream. Her enormous green eyes, set with perfect symmetry in her wide face, were the color of worn sea glass; her long eyelashes were always expertly coated with mascara. Her skin was creamy white and unblemished, her nose slim above a slightly unusual mouth whose upper lip had a little curl to it, the lower one jutting slightly forward, in line with a forwardly thrust chin that signaled something of her stance toward life. Tears slipped from her eyes.

"You know that bowl my dad keeps on his dresser," she said.

I nodded. It was where Mr. Gold threw his spare change and dollar bills for Danielle to grab if she needed money. Her parents were endlessly generous, and there seemed to be no limits when it came to her needs or wants. They lived without hierarchy, with none of the monarch-subject dynamics that marked my own home.

"I was going to get some change." Her tears were sliding, sliding down. "It was lying there on the dresser, next to the dish."

"What? What was on the dresser?"

Now she looked at me full on. "The census."

We'd discussed the census at my own family's dinner table—a civic responsibility, a symbol that we were an orderly society that took seriously the business of knowing its citizenry.

"I don't know why my dad left it there. I've never seen one before. They must have been careful, in the past."

"Careful?"

"To hide it."

Danielle had read through what her parents had marked on the census. In the section where you list children, she saw that in addition to her name and birth date, four other children had been noted, along with their dates of birth.

Born, June 17, 1936

Born, February 12, 1938

Born, January 26, 1940

Born, August 3, 1941

Had they been her mother's children, or her father's? She'd had no idea either had been married before they were in the camps. One or both must have had children—before.

Also noted were dates of death. For the first, October 15, 1941. For the other three—the same date, December 3, 1941. So, very likely, one of her parents had lost one child, the other, three. There was no instruction to state the cause of death, but in the blank margin of the page, beside each of the repeated dates, Danielle's father had written in his small, neat hand: Murdered at Auschwitz.

* * *

We were sixteen years old when Danielle told me she'd tracked down someone she wanted to see and asked if I'd come with her. I wondered if it had to do with her adoption. Perhaps she'd found her birth mother, or a long-lost biological sibling. But no, it was something else. She told me that, when she was little, the son of a family friend would babysit her on occasion when her parents went out for an evening. Starting from about the age of five, he would play games with her that filled her with dread and disgust. He would tell her to close her eyes and open her mouth and then she'd find something awful thrust into her mouth, something warm and terrible and vile, and he'd raise his voice to almost a shout, telling her not to move, not to make a sound, and there was something suddenly violent about everything, the world crashing in on her.

It was only when she was older that she began to understand the kinds of things he did to her, and then the rage and fear and helplessness came to a boil, and she decided to do something about it. She found out where he was living and made a telephone call, asking if he would meet her. He suggested a bar in the city—strange, since he would have known Danielle was only sixteen, but of course not strange, since the guy was not exactly a concerned adult you'd expect to take such things into account.

The bar was a bustling spot in gritty, bohemian Carlton, an inner suburb just north of Melbourne's central business district. We ordered lemonade and waited for the man to arrive. Danielle recognized him at once and went very quiet, reaching under the bar for my hand. He was a regular-looking guy, in his late twenties, I guessed. He ordered a drink—Scotch on the rocks—said he was happy to see her, then eyed us both up and down, approvingly. He seemed to think we were all going to be friends. I was in a flurry of anxiety, picturing the terrible things this guy did to Danielle when she was a little girl. Danielle was staring down at the bar. The room was a swirl of people talking too cheerfully, too loudly, the bartender sliding drinks up and down the bar, the rise and fall of laughter, the sound of ice clinking in glasses rapping at the inside of my skull. I lit two cigarettes, one for Danielle, one for me. When I handed her one, I saw ferocity in her eyes.

"I didn't come here so we could hang out," she said, her voice emerging from a cauldron.

The man adjusted his expression. He looked oddly polite.

"You did terrible things to me. I don't know, maybe I could turn you in to the police. You shouldn't have. You shouldn't have done those things to me."

The man looked around nervously, uttered a gentle *Shhhhh*, then urged Danielle to keep her voice down.

She took a sharp draw on her cigarette.

"Really? You want me to keep my voice down?" she said, raising her voice so that a few people turned their heads our way. "I'm not going to tell the police. But—hey, everyone," she called out, glancing around the room, "this guy here is a pedophile."

She looked him straight in the eye. "After today, I'm never going to think about you again. I'm going to flush you down the toilet. Because that's what you are, nothing but *shit*."

Danielle dropped her lit cigarette into his glass of Scotch. It sizzled and sent up a puff of Scotch-y steam. She grabbed my arm. "We're out of here."

The man looked like a kid who'd been slapped. He glanced around, as if hoping someone might rescue him. Danielle pulled me out in the street. We raced down the block, the cold wind lifting our hair, running recklessly, the way children run. We turned to each other at the same moment. I saw abandon in her face, her wide green eyes soft with relief. She laughed, and I pulled her to a stop, turned her toward me, my hands on her shoulders. I affected the heavy Polish accent of our school principal, the feared, revered Mr. Ranoschy.

"At Mount Scopus College, *ve are brwave, strwong, and ov good courage*," I said.

For a moment, Danielle's face turned serious, and I thought I saw her lip tremble. Then, we embraced, a long hug on the street in the cold night. I buried my face in her thick blonde hair, breathing in the familiar sage and rosemary scent of her shampoo.

We were seventeen and in our final year of high school. Danielle and I were walking down a busy shopping street, having played hooky again from school. We were charged up with a few tokes of hashish that turned Glenferrie Road into a boulevard taking us forward into a misty future shimmering with unnamed dreams. Arm in arm, we stopped in front of a butcher's shop and took stock of the offerings, laughing about what it meant to window-shop before a display of meat slabs ribboned with fat. I pointed to a giant pair of T-bone steaks and remarked that they'd make great snowshoes. This set us into a fit of stoned laughter, and we stumbled on down the street, flicking aside the disapproving glances of passersby.

We rounded a corner and Danielle came to a halt, radiating that sudden mood change I was familiar with, an instantaneous darkening. Before us stood a middle-aged man smiling broadly, though with an incongruent metallic look in his eye.

"Hello, Danielle, darling," he said, the Polish accent turning the word to *daalink*.

Danielle was stiff, she muttered a few perfunctory words, and we were on our way.

"What was that all about?" I asked.

"You don't want to know," she said, her tone matter-of-fact.

"Actually, I do."

She shrugged. "You know, stuff from the camps."

"I don't exactly know what *stuff from the camps* means."

"He was in Auschwitz with my dad. He's Connor's father."

Connor was an older boy from school—good-looking, popular, smart. He was dating a friend of ours named Lauren.

We were walking again, and Danielle picked up the pace.

"Why were you so curt?" I asked.

"He's a creep."

"What do you mean?"

Danielle sighed, as if the whole thing were just tedious.

"Okay, well. Here's the thing. We were on holiday at Mount Martha. Couple of years ago. Walking into town for ice cream with Uncle Moishe"—not actually Danielle's uncle, her parents had no surviving blood relatives. Moishe had also been with her father in Auschwitz. "That man walked by. He came up to us, just like he did now. Stopped in front of us, gave that smile. Moishe pushed him so hard he fell to the ground, then he kicked him in the stomach."

She said all this in a flat voice, as if she were reporting on something mundane.

"What the hell?"

"Dad pulled him off. Uncle Moishe was red in the face. We walked away. I turned around and saw Connor's dad getting up. He still had that smile on his face. Don't you think he has the weirdest smile?"

"Wait. Moishe is Lauren's dad, right?"

Danielle nodded.

"Did you ask your dad what it was about?"

"He doesn't like to talk about these things."

"Did you ever find out?"

"Yeah, Uncle Moishe told me. Connor's dad was a *kapo*."

Of course, I'd heard about *kapos*. Prisoner functionaries, often chosen from the violent criminal class rather than from the "religious prisoner" population, placed by the Nazis in a position of power over their fellow inmates and encouraged to be brutal.

"Oh," I said.

"Yeah," she said.

By the time we reached the Middle Eastern café we frequented, the effect of the hashish had worn off, so we ducked around the back to light up a joint. The smoke blew away her bad mood. In the alley, arm in arm, we smiled at each other as we passed the joint back and forth, falling into that liquid space where we were one.

Inside the café, we sat over glasses of heavy Turkish coffee and played a dozen rounds of backgammon. Danielle was a master strategist, and I didn't often win. She looked at me drily, her eyes perfectly deadpan, a little smile playing about her lips, threw the die, then expertly moved her pieces without pausing to think or to count out the places, just a quick flick of each across the board. She won ten games in a row.

Time had a sticky, warm gingerbread feel; I could almost smell it. We knew the staff, who sometimes joined us in a game of cards when things were slow. I looked around, aware of a feeling of intense well-being and connection. Slinging the die from their faux-leather shaker across the board, I felt tethered to Danielle by the intimate looks that passed between us, the two of us stalwart together against drudgery and convention, our eyes trained on a distant horizon, far from the constraints of our respective homes—mine with its beauty and bursts of engagement and that confounding, unpredictable atmosphere, and Danielle's with its fretful darkness curdled by insistent, heroic attempts to drown it out. Our truancy had a common goal: to swat away the life script being set down before us.

My heart breaks for Danielle, knowing the course that her noble, well-meaning flouting of expectation took. I intuitively knew how to sidestep the rules while keeping my eye on the prize. Danielle held a match to it all and then found herself lost, wondering where and when the sense of possibility had slammed shut.

A few years ago, I heard that Lauren and Connor ended up getting married—Lauren, the daughter of the man who had accosted Connor's father on the street, knowing him as a *kapo* from Auschwitz. Who knew what Lauren's father was remembering the day he kicked Connor's father in the stomach? And who knew what was behind the kicked man's strange smile, a lifeless half-moon hanging below expressionless metallic eyes? I tried to imagine the wedding: the two fathers, one walking his daughter down the aisle to give her to the son of the other, whom he would always revile, pondering the haphazard fates that had brought these two young people together in love.

When I heard about the marriage, I recalled an article I'd read about Heinrich Himmler's great-niece, Katrin Himmler. Raised in post-war Germany, she suffered taunts and rejection from the other kids because of her notorious last name. When she was eleven years old, she cried as she watched the TV series *Holocaust*, forced to confront the details of the family history her parents and relatives had kept hidden. Her great-uncle Heinrich was the mastermind of the Nazi concentration camp system he'd dreamed up to implement the "Final Solution." Her grandfather, who disappeared in Berlin in 1945, had been a committed Nazi who joined the party early on, in 1931, and in 1933 joined the SS. Not the "apolitical" soldier her grandmother had insisted he'd been.

As a young woman, Katrin fell in love with an Israeli man whose father had survived the Warsaw ghetto as a child by living under false papers as a Polish "Aryan." Dozens of his relatives were murdered. When she married, Katrin declined to take her husband's name, not wanting to bury the truth about her own family history. After her first child was born, she turned to her husband and asked: "What will we tell our son?" She wondered how she would explain to her child that one side of his family had set out to systematically murder the other side's entire people, and that her great-uncle had played a pivotal role in conceiving, building, and overseeing the vast system of Nazi extermination camps.

To address her own question, Katrin spent years researching her family history so that her son, and others, might know everything in excruciating detail. The result was an impressive tome: *The Himmler Brothers: A German Family History.*

I imagine Katrin Himmler was familiar with that mystical Jewish notion of *gilgulim*, the idea that souls cycle through many lives in a quest for growth toward spiritual perfection. Her son's very being was perhaps one answer to the question she posed at his birth. In marrying her Israeli Jewish husband, in together having a child, perhaps she managed to bring about a tiny shift in the cosmic order, the blood of their two peoples now mingled for eternity in ever renewing generations—freeing both sides, I would like to think, for at least an instant, from the tremendous burden imposed on all of us: that of being part of a race that endlessly inflicts horrors on its own kind, creating perpetrators and victims in bulging millions around the globe.

Photographs of Ms. Himmler reveal that she looks strikingly like her monstrous great-uncle, just as another of her generation, Bettina Göring, bears a remarkable resemblance to her own infamous great-uncle, Hermann Göring, whose odious legacy definitively imprinted her life. At age thirty, Ms. Göring had herself sterilized, feeling it was her destiny to put an end to the Göring gene line within her own biological control. "I feared I might create another monster," she said, citing her physical appearance. "I look more like him than his own daughter." If his looks could be so accurately passed on, she reasoned, why not, also, his murderous evil?

In keeping her name alive and writing the book about her family's history, Katrin Himmler dedicated her life to the "Never forget" injunction that marked my own upbringing. Bettina Göring chose to put an end to her piece of the family line through having her tubes tied, a personal, visceral enactment of finality, a primal way of declaring that what happened in the past could never happen again.

* * *

Danielle failed her high school finals on which, at that time in Australia, everything regarding one's future seemed to rest. The day the results came in the mail, Danielle called me in tears, her voice weary with defeat. We talked about her options, the best one being a year at technical college where she could earn her high school equivalency diploma. I made the trek to Jewish Caulfield South to meet at our café. We sat over glasses of thick Turkish coffee and played a few desultory rounds of backgammon.

I was leaving two weeks later to on a gap year, to study in Jerusalem. We hadn't talked about the fact that we were about to be wrenched apart after years of living in the conjoined way that young people who are best friends live, our souls washing in and out of each other, not always certain where one of us ended and the other began. Years of me living part-time in her home, with all its noise and activity—the brightly dressed, heavily perfumed women coming and going on the arms of their men whose teeth flashed with gold, the Polish gossip flying, and laughter always a bit too loud, desperation hanging high near the ceiling, pushed upward by the fog of cigarette smoke. It was all slamming to a close.

Danielle came to see me the day before my departure. My room was a mess of in-process packing. Danielle was sad and still. We didn't say much. She sat on the bed as I sorted through my belongings, hoping to fit everything into one suitcase and a carry-on bag.

We lingered by the front door, then hugged goodbye. I was hardly able to imagine moving through life without the regard of those heavily lashed green eyes that saw me so wholly, or without the lingering scent of her rosemary-sage shampoo. No more nights smoking in her bedroom and imagining our futures, talking about boyfriends and books we were reading, our conversation punctuated by the eruptions of laughter coming from the kitchen where her parents sat playing cards with their friends.

And yet something rattled loudly within me, something restless, eager to get away.

A slimy slug of guilt crawled through me.

I was escaping. Danielle was not.

* * *

A few years later, I moved to New York City to try to make my life there. On the day of my departure, as the plane climbed, I felt an inrush of extraordinary freedom. I watched the craggy coastline of Australia peel away, leaving a wide expanse of glistening ocean, its surface rippled white with froth. The hours passed, and soon the waters were swaddled by night. I peered into the blackness and felt the thrill of the unknown. I was crossing the world's largest ocean to remake myself, flinging myself into the land of TV shows and broad accents, of skyscrapers and American suburbs and a cold that bit into you and heralded such exotic shenanigans as Halloween and Thanksgiving. Heading to a city where people of all races crammed into subway cars that sped underground, a system built with brash spirit. I sat and waited for the sun to emerge, straining at the endless possibilities that rang in my ears like otherworldly chimes.

Danielle and I lost touch.

Many years on, my mother told me she ran into Danielle at a little costume-jewelry shop on some side street, where Danielle was working behind the counter.

"She looked very thin, and tired," my mother said. "When I asked her how she was doing, she looked so sad, it broke my heart. She said, 'It's been hard. Life didn't work out as I expected.'"

"Did you get her number?" I asked. My own heart leapt at the thought of re-establishing contact with Danielle.

"I'm so sorry, I didn't think to ask," my mother said, and when I pressed her for information about the shop, she simply could not remember a thing about it—not the name, or the side street, or even what part of town she'd been in when she'd walked through the door upon sighting some dangly pearl earrings she did not end up buying.

On my next trip back to Australia, I was determined to track Danielle down. I made a few phone calls but then got caught up in the intensity of my family visit. Before I knew it, I found myself on the plane back to New York. Pulling away from the shore, I felt a pang of mortification that I'd not followed through on my plan to find Danielle. I resolved to take steps to find her once I was settled back at home.

A few days later, my sister sent me a picture of the obituary she'd seen in the *Jewish News* announcing Danielle's death. I was unable to find out exactly how she died; everyone in that hyper-connected Jewish community seemed to have lost touch with her. I think of her death as a wafting away, rather than a passing, and wonder where she wafted off to, and if she was able, at the end of her life, to find some measure of peace. I picture her in her school uniform, down at the back of the Skolnick Oval, looking right into my face with her exquisite, expertly made-up eyes, reciting the birth dates of the children her parents silently mourned, all of them murdered at Auschwitz. She takes a long draw on her cigarette and slowly releases a narrow, perfectly straight stream of smoke that hovers for an instant and then disperses into the air.

* * *

Midway into the sequestered isolation brought about by the pandemic, I published a version of this chapter about Danielle in an online magazine. People from my growing-up years in Melbourne read the piece and wrote to me or posted about it on social media, sharing their own thoughts and memories of Mount Scopus and what it was like to carry the legacy from that particular Jewish community at that particular time. Many still live in Melbourne; others wrote from Israel, England, and the United States. There was even a man from Prague. I am not the only one flung far from that spot on the squiggly southern border of the island continent we grew up in, mostly first-generation Australians (and me not even that, having been born in South Africa).

One old classmate sent a photograph of Danielle and me taken at a party. There we are, at exactly the time I discuss, aged sixteen, looking cockily into the camera, Danielle holding a lit cigarette, me brandishing a glass of wine. We had our whole lives ahead of us. I imagined mine would be a grand adventure, and I was about to say that Danielle surely felt that way too, but I stop myself. As intimate as we were, I don't know how she had envisaged her future—whether her smooth bravado was a deep fact about her or rather sat thinly on her beautiful, sheeny surface. I learned that Danielle had moved away from Melbourne and lived on the Gold Coast for a time, working mostly in retail stores. In her late twenties, she became diabetic. There was a rumor that she didn't manage it well, perhaps had a drug problem, but in any case, her health seriously declined, and at some point, she became blind. Danielle never quite found her people, or her place in the world. Eventually, she returned to Melbourne and moved into a small apartment. When Danielle was in her early fifties, an old classmate learned she was living in a local nursing home and visited her with a friend. Danielle died a few weeks later.

The classmate sent me a picture taken the day of that nursing-home visit. In the photo, Danielle's face is oddly unchanged from when I last saw her, decades earlier, aside from the lines etched into her skin that look as if someone has clumsily applied aging stage makeup. There is something quizzical in her sightless gaze—and a glimmer of recognition. Her enormous green eyes peer out flatly, seeing me across time, even in their dullness, from beyond the grave she would soon enter. A faint smile hovers around her lips. I zoom in on her face and see it is not a smile but a shadowy grimace—of what? Disappointment? Resignation? Or perhaps simply weariness? She is being patient with her visitors, this is what I sense. She is waiting for the photograph to be taken, waiting for them to finish their visit. They are leaning down beside her wheelchair, these two middle-aged women I also knew in high school, who are fashionably coiffed and dressed, faces bright with makeup and the kind of staunch good cheer people don when visiting nursing homes, their smiles shellacked and eyes brittle with denial. I am struck by how white their teeth are. Danielle could not have known that a decade after the photograph was taken, I would be studying this snapshot, my heart filled with a grief so bulky it buckles my being.

The classmate also sent me something else. A video she made in tribute to Danielle that was shown at her funeral. The funeral was sparsely attended. Danielle's life had diminished, year by year, and at the end, she was keenly isolated. Her aged mother was at her graveside, her father already long gone. The short video mostly featured a slow panning across the spread of a photo collage Danielle had hung on the wall in her small nursing-home room, a display she'd taken with her through the itinerant years of her life. Cutouts from photos of her childhood and adolescence. Danielle as a little wide-green-eyed baby with her youngish parents—her mother radiant and loving, her father handsome, well-built, proud. And on through the years, Danielle with a variety of changing hairstyles and that look in her eyes I knew so well, languid, wry, farseeing, alongside the friends who'd moved in and out of her young life. Danielle, so beautiful and bemused, echoing with the slightly gulpy, almost-guffaw of her laugh, but also troubled and stormy. I recognize faces from the past, old schoolmates I long ago lost touch with. And, in this expansive, carefully curated photo montage of what I can only surmise were, for Danielle, what she thought of as the happy years of her life, not a single photo of me. Not one snapshot of the two of us together. I watch the video over and over, trying to lay hold of Danielle, trying to pretend I'm not shattered by the omission of me in the collage, trying to choke down the feeling that somewhere, within all of this, I carry some measure of blame.

~ 3 ~

The Jazz Band

It was a locked-door unit, which meant you had to have your keys at the ready. Doors really did clang open and shut, echoes, all day long, of the penitentiary. After a morning of orientation as a new clinical psychology intern at the psychiatric hospital in the South Bronx, I was taken to meet my first patient. The man, in his thirties, was locked in the isolation room and on twenty-four-hour suicide watch, so the meeting took place through the pane of unbreakable glass in the door. Clothed in a hospital gown, he peered at me urgently through the window, reached up and touched the glass with his hand. Instinctively, I placed my hand there too. I looked right into him. He looked right back into me. Later, I would discover what was behind the frantic look in his eyes; this gentle soul was in the grip of a psychotic belief that he'd been charged by God to save the starving children of NYC. He was planning to swoop above the city streets—delusion had granted him the gift of flight—and draw them to his bosom. Imprisoned on the ward, he was being denied the chance to fulfill his mission. At the end of my shift that first day, he was rushed to the ER where they stitched his sliced neck. He'd managed to break the hard plastic bowl serving as his toilet, using one jagged piece as a knife. Psychosis, I learned, can endow superhuman strength.

I was immediately hijacked by the vivid intensity of the psychiatric ward. All day long, I sped up and down the corridors, aware of the percussive sound of my high-heel pumps on the green linoleum, the glare of the fluorescent lights effacing all shadow. I was astonished at the openness of the patients I was asked to evaluate and then "treat," which I attempted to do in my bumbling, newly-minted-degree way, having little clue what this entailed. Supervision was its own befuddling affair—sitting across from seasoned therapists with their mysterious vocabulary and alternating emotional registers of assurance and criticism. Where was I supposed to begin? What, in God's name, was I supposed to do? *Just listen*, I figured, was as good a place as any to start. I quickly discovered this was something the people I sat with had had in short supply over the course of their lives. The patients often seemed to expect to be bludgeoned in one way or another, based on years of sorry, accumulated experience. Sitting and listening, I heard things I would never be able to unhear. To this day, when approaching the large garbage cans in front of our apartment building, I find myself thinking, more often than I wish were the case, of the teenage girl who recounted ghastly treatment at the hands of her family, including being stuffed for long periods into a full, stinking garbage can with the lid tightly closed.

My second patient was Marlena, a woman in her sixties, elegantly dressed and made up, her hair dyed blonde and set into a chignon. For months she sat in my office talking obsessively about her desire to end her life. Her husband, she said, was a hindrance: well into his seventies, she reported that he badgered her daily for sex. One description had him swinging from the chandelier in their two-bedroom apartment, attempting to ravish her against her will. We staff talked about the ways in which reality, on the psychiatric ward, was elastic. Subjective experience and facts did not always align. Careful consideration was given to what, in a patient's account, was *true*; part of the coin of our realm was to tease fantasy from fact, exaggeration from accuracy, distortion from clear-eyed clarity.

Such lines could hardly be clearly drawn outside of the psychiatric hospital. What made anyone think that subjective experience would be any different for our hospitalized patients? I marveled at the certainty I often saw around me in the faces, words, and actions of the hospital staff. In some ways, it was reassuring. Who would not want a doctor to baldly state what is and isn't the case, and which course of action is clearly the best one to take? But it unsettled me, at odds with my view of the human condition. What we called reality was itself dubious, shot through with vagaries. The psyche was a vexed business, human motivation and intention about as sticky as things could get. The boundary between sanity and insanity wavered, whether we were talking about patients, families, or staff. The longer I worked there, the more fluid these boundaries came to seem, human experience normal and crazy, both, no matter which side of the divide the person was deemed to occupy.

I struggled to find solid ground when it came to my role as therapist but managed to settle on an unspoken compact. Whoever entered my therapy room was to be heard, not just listened to, their voice respected and honored. The first principle was to understand that there was some truth in their disclosures, if not always literal veracity. I became versed in the different kinds of truth that emerged in the space of that room: the hazy, shifting certainties of memory; the swellings and bruisings of the heart; the encroaching calm, even salvation, of connection. My role was to do my best to make some sense of what was passing between us, aware I was holding power in a relationship that was inherently skewed. The whole thing was real and surreal, pulsing with intensity, suffering, injustice, love. This almost unbearably poignant occupation was alluring, yet baffling as hell—and just simply my job, what was expected of me as, twenty-six years old, I launched into the demands of adulthood.

Marlena seemed most alive when talking of her suicide attempts; she carried them around like trophies, buffing the shine with the edge of her silk sleeve. I tried to talk with her about what that meant, but then, she would refuse to engage, adopting a stony silence. The irony was not lost on me—that Marlena clung for dear life to her death wish—though it was outside the bounds of my power to untangle the puzzle. She fell in love with her therapists, and now she fell in love with me. It was a lethal love, as I was soon to discover. Judged to no longer be a present danger (besides, her insurance had run out), Marlena was discharged back home to her husband. Within a week, she was back in the ER, having accumulated her sedatives, swallowing the entire bottle. Her husband found her unconscious and called an ambulance. After detoxing, she was readmitted to the psychiatric unit and soon back in my office, not a hair out of place, wearing a tailored magenta dress. Her pale eyes were framed by blue eye shadow, her lashes thick with mascara.

Smiling, she told me this: "While I was swallowing the pills, I was thinking of you. Each pill, one by one—I was looking right into your face."

She seemed to think this awful declaration was a tribute—I suspect she had no inkling that what she was saying froze my blood. Upon her release from the inpatient unit, Marlena was assigned to me as an outpatient. We met twice weekly in my office. Somehow, the alliance held. As my yearlong hospital assignment drew to a close, I thought about which incoming intern might be best suited to take her on. One young woman seemed a good match, smart and soulful, with equal measures of humor and grit.

Some months later, I heard from the new intern that Marlena had suicided, finally achieving her morbid ambition. I imagined the young intern would carry this with her for a very long time, perhaps forever.

At the start of my internship, my father was diagnosed with Hodgkin's lymphoma, considered a curable form of cancer. I clung to the statistics—a 95 percent cure rate. My father was such a robust character; he would have the growths removed, undergo chemotherapy, and surely make a complete recovery. Being so far away from Australia made it all seem unreal. I was also in the habit of putting a fence around everything to do with my past. Besides, I was intensely busy, working at the hospital while also finishing my doctoral dissertation.

Toward the end of my internship, my father took an unexpected turn for the worse. He called to tell me he was preparing for a bone marrow transplant. He sounded weak and his spirit seemed beaten. I immediately called my sister and asked if it was serious enough for me to book a flight. I expected her to tell me no, the bone marrow transplant was sure to be a success. Instead, she hesitated, then said, "Yes, I think you should come."

I hung up the phone and booked the next flight to Melbourne, which left in the morning, then discovered that my passport had expired. I called the Australian consulate.

"When is your flight?" the consular worker asked.

"Nine thirty a.m."

"Come to the consulate at six a.m. Someone will be here to open up and issue you an emergency passport."

That afternoon, Simon and I went out to eat Japanese food. It had been three years since our first date. We'd met after I extricated myself from the mismatched marriage I'd entered into when I was twenty and hardly knew myself. With Simon, it was love at first sight; I felt as if the earth's tectonic plates were shifting beneath my feet. I could almost hear it, a booming, geological heave. Human life has its own cosmic wormholes, and for me, they come with sounds. The last time I'd had this sense of the seismic was several years earlier, sitting on the plane that took me from Melbourne to New York. Looking out the window as the plane lifted, I watched the rugged shoreline shear away, that squiggly line I'd memorized in geography class. I'd learned to draw an expert map of our island continent, perfected over hours of practice. Perhaps I'd known that one day I'd leave and wanted the shape of my homeland committed to memory. How odd I always found it that, from the plane, the line looked exactly the same as it did in the atlas. It amazed me when the abstract aligned with the real, the uncanny collision of two worlds made of entirely different stuff. The whirr of the engines as the plane torqued through the atmosphere held another sound within it, a stealthy creaking, as of roots being torn from the ground.

On our first date, I sat waiting for Simon in a café in Greenwich Village. I had driven in from New Jersey and ended up being a half hour early. I tried to read my book (Virginia Woolf's *To the Lighthouse*) but found the words were swimming on the page.

And then, Simon walked in and sat down opposite me. We talked about Virginia Woolf, and then moved on to other things. We were still talking as we made our way to the St. Marks Place movie theater, where we saw *Les Parents Terribles*, and then as we sat for hours at the Caffe Pane E Cioccolato eating spaghetti Bolognese, and then lingering over coffee and strudel.

It was one a.m. when I finally got into my car to drive back to New Jersey. I sped along the half-empty highway, the crescent moon rushing toward me, the streetlamps bright puddles in the black sky. I'd never felt so intensely alive.

It is now thirty-nine years since that night of endless, engaged conversation. Like many long relationships, ours has had its difficult times. The ongoing conversation, however, has never lapsed, and the electricity, granted by the cosmos, continues to course between us, and within.

I remember, those long decades ago, the night before I was to fly off to Australia to see my ailing father, looking across the table at Simon—the man I loved so wholly—feeling sunken in sadness that he and my father had never met.

After our meal, we walked west and took the long stairway down to Riverside Park. It was seven p.m. The park was full of people, some jogging, others pushing strollers or walking dogs, couples strolling, a few rollerbladers zipping by. We walked to the stone wall and looked out over the water. The river was flustered, churned to choppy little waves by a robust spring wind. We found a bench and sat looking up at the hilly part of Riverside Drive, where regal pre-war apartment buildings took greedy bites out of the deepening dusk sky.

It hit me, as it sometimes did—the power of New York City. Growing up in Australia, New York had not been on my radar. I would never have imagined I'd end up living here. Vast oceans separated me from my family, from everyone I'd grown up with, from everything I had known of life until I stepped on the plane that would carry me here, some five years earlier. Where had it all gone?

"What are you thinking?" Simon asked.

"The ocean."

"The ocean. What about it?"

"It's strange, that everyone I grew up with—in a way, they've disappeared. So distant." I checked my watch. "It's morning in Australia."

"Maybe I should get you a little Aussie flag. You could wear it in your hair."

"New York is so far away."

"Actually, no. New York is right here." He leaned down, looked into my eyes. "Like me. I'm right here too."

The next morning, I went straight from the consulate to the airport. Before I left, my sister told me by phone that, by the time I arrived, they'd know whether the bone marrow transplant stood a chance of succeeding. Such a long trip, forty-eight hours door to door, in a time before cellphones. I would be out of contact for two full days, during which time it would become clear whether my fifty-seven-year-old father would live or die.

On the long plane ride, I wrote to my father. I tried to imagine myself into his skin, to write my way into how it felt for him to approach death—the looming of that ultimate blackness, the slamming shut of consciousness, the one human experience that not even a fiction writer with her sleight-of-mind tools can conjure. *Dear Dad*, it began, innocently enough, then launched into how I imagined he must be feeling with the latest turn for the worse. As if finding words for his experience might ward off a bad outcome, excise the cancer, and return my father to the land of the living.

The skies stayed light as I crossed the planet; the hours passed in a wide-awake daze. I stared out the window to see clouds gathering and holding, the heavens opaque, then blowing clear to reveal we were floating in a deep-blue forever. My father lay in a hospital bed, the distance between us closing by the minute, waiting for the results that would either grant him reprieve or sentence him to death.

And then, we were landing. The plane dipped its wings and growled at the ground rushing up to slap against its wheels. There was a rumble and bump and shake, and we taxied, the white Australian light bleaching everything to beach tones. I blinked, waiting until the last passenger had disembarked to hold on to every second of possibility—that the verdict for my father would be *life*.

My sisters were waiting at the gate. From the instant I saw them a hundred yards away, I knew it was over. I put one foot in front of the other until I reached them.

"Let's get a cup of tea," my sister said. "Then we'll go straight to the hospital."

In the airport coffee shop, that same sister told me she was six weeks pregnant. It would be our parents' first grandchild. I asked if our father knew. She nodded, biting her lip to hold back the tears.

Less than an hour later, we were at the hospital.

Walking into hospitals has always filled me with an all-encompassing feeling of safety and well-being. As a child, we would visit my surgeon father at his hospital, and he'd show us around. He would stride through the hallways, greeting people left and right—cleaning staff, nurses, doctors, aides, and trainees—and we would stride behind him, as if the Red Sea waters were parting. It was clear that my father was an event, both a celebrity and a friend. He knew people's names, remembered whose wife had been sick, who was about to have a baby, who was studying for their boards in pediatric medicine. Excitement and optimism spilled from my father and splashed over everything; he made people feel welcomed—not merely by him, but also by life, as if he were an official existential salutation committee. I do not believe this was my mother's primary experience of my father, as is often the case in long marriages of fundamentally disparate natures, in which each partner's worldly charms fail to operate within the confines of the home.

Sometimes, when our mother needed a night off from cooking, we'd head across Melbourne to eat in the hospital cafeteria. As medical director and chief of surgery, my father had taken a small suburban medical outpost and turned it into a major teaching hospital.

To a child's consciousness, being able to have *whatever we wanted* in the cafeteria was a rare privilege. The offerings seemed exotic and exciting—not the refined, healthy fare my mother prepared. Here was stewed lamb swimming in thick salty gravy, and vats of wilted vegetables that tasted gooey-delicious-soft. Mashed potatoes with gobs of butter, and brightly colored puddings and Jell-O studded with tinned fruit, as well as slabs of heavily frosted cake. At those dinners, my parents were in good spirits. Our uneasy family dynamics lightened out in this shiny, illuminated world, all of us wearing our good manners and outward-facing personas. Here, we could embody our external family incarnation: well-presented, well-educated, each with our own talents and successes. We were inhabiting the "clean, well-lighted place" of Hemingway's short story, a place in which despair can have no purchase.

Everyone had something to say about my father—about his generosity or kindness, his expertise or inventiveness or oratory flair, his largesse of spirit or ability to lead and inspire. On occasion, outside of the hospital, I'd meet an elderly relative of a school friend and, hearing I was my father's daughter, their face would light up, the shirt might rise to display a slim, neat scar, and then, in a thick Eastern European accent, something like: "Your father saved my life! Look at this beautiful scar. And he wouldn't charge me. *Not a penny!*" My father had grown up speaking Yiddish, and so was able to converse with these elderly Holocaust survivors in their mother tongue. He would take them on as private patients and refuse payment.

At dinner parties, my father's colleagues also told stories about him. Like the time a construction worker walked into the ER with a piece of wood impaling his neck. The wood appeared to have missed a major blood vessel, but what would happen if it were removed? None of them had the nerve to pull it out.

"Call the chief," someone said. That was often the solution. *Call the chief.*

My father was paged and minutes later, he bounded into the cubicle where the unfortunate man was waiting for someone to take his fate into their hands. My father assessed the angle and placement of the projectile, talking encouragingly to the man, his hand firm on his shoulder. He communicated non-verbally to his staff, who seemed able to read his mind. The nurse rushed around gathering instruments and materials, and the junior doctors stood by to await orders. My father positioned the man, braced one foot up against the wall, and pulled on the stick. The bloodied spear fell to the ground and my father staunched the blood as the medical staff got the man onto the trolley to rush him into surgery, where my father successfully operated.

As I climbed the four flights of hospital stairs behind my sisters, I felt the span of my father's life, its shape suddenly altered.

My father had refused his morphine dose, wanting to be alert for my arrival. I agonized at the thought of our half-hour tea break at the airport, during which his pain was unnecessarily prolonged. The intensive chemotherapy had left him with an enormous excruciating blister on the underside of his tongue, which made it arduous for him to speak. When he saw me, he sat up in bed and broke into the welcoming smile he always greeted me with, eyes alight.

"How lovely of you to come!" he slurred, wincing through the pain, his tongue curling unnaturally, allowing me a glimpse of the awful slug-like blister.

The hospital gown gaped to show his pale shoulders, the muscle reduced and collarbone sharp. He'd always cut an impressive figure and even now, though terribly diminished, he was still imposing. I sat beside him on the bed, and we talked for a few minutes. He told me he was proud I'd been accepted to the post-doctoral fellowship associated with Cornell University, a name he knew. He valued academic institutions—he'd been part of them all his life, having taught and mentored throughout his professional career, beloved by students and professors alike. I'd had the pleasure of attending several of his lectures; he held the audience spellbound with his nimble mind, energetic wit, and wide-ranging intellectual command, drawing parallels with fields outside of medicine.

Now, looking drained, he told me he thought he might have to give up playing tennis, a game he loved. I didn't know what to say. Did my father not know that this was the end? Had nobody told him the results of the latest test?

"Oh, I'm sorry," I said, roped into the deceit. "Never mind, there'll be other diversions."

He slumped with exhaustion. He asked me to call the nurse so that he might use the portable urinal. I said I could help him. He gritted his teeth for a moment, aware of the awful change of roles, but also taking command of his dignity to rise above the whole she-bang—in fact, it seemed, to rise above death itself. He gave a wan smile, and I picked up the plastic urinal. He lifted the hem of his hospital gown and peed into the spout; a droplet of urine splashed onto my wrist, a tiny warm spot of wetness that lasted an instant before evaporating. It felt precious; this moment was precious, my father was precious, his life was precious and was about to be over.

His eyes drooped and his body sagged.

"Why don't you rest, Dad," I said, touching his arm.

He nodded, weary, fighting defeat for a moment and then resigning himself to it. I helped him settle back down in the bed. He grimaced in pain. The nurse, a tall young man, approached. I looked at him, full of pleading, and he nodded, moving the control on the IV to release morphine into the drip. My father's face soft-ened as the drug took effect.

I sat by his bed and watched as his breathing slowed and the look of pain drained away. I didn't want to wash my wrist. I wanted to never wash it again.

Given my father's taste for adventure and his way of acting with certainty and vigor, it had not been surprising when he told us he was taking flying lessons. "Can't wait to take you up, kids," he said, "as soon as I get my license." I was fifteen and excited by the prospect of adventure of any kind; I'd always loved roller coasters—how much more fun this would be!

A year or so after my father got his pilot's license, he bought a plane, a Cessna 182 that he named Whiskey Sierra Foxtrot for its license plate, WSF. My father's enthusiasms were contagious. My mother, more cautious by nature, and an artist by spirit, found my father's extreme interests trying; most of all, she wanted time and mental space to pursue her music and other creative endeavors. With each of my father's new passions, she would find herself yanked out from the calmer, more orderly life she fought to maintain. Now, she was being expected to go up in a tiny shuddering aircraft, which triggered migraines and made her vomit.

My father was ebullient when he announced he'd organized a trip to the rugged Flinders Ranges of South Australia. It would be Whiskey Sierra Foxtrot's first major voyage. To accommodate the six of us—my mother, father, three siblings, and me—he rented a second plane and engaged another pilot. Since my father was still inexperienced, he also arranged to have an instructor co-pilot with him, an affable fellow named Vince.

We were all in high spirits taking off. I had just finished my final high school exams. Within a few weeks, I would have my results in hand, and then fly to Jerusalem for a gap year. I could feel myself withdrawing from my family and from the world I had known in Melbourne, itching to cast myself into the unknown and start anew. This final family trip into the Australian Outback seemed a fitting prelude to my removal to a tiny country half a world away.

We stopped to refuel at Broken Hill, taking an hour to enjoy an Aussie high tea of scones with strawberry jam and clotted cream. We then reshuffled the planes. I went with my mother and middle sister in the rented plane. My father, brother, and eldest sister went in my father's Cessna, piloted by Vince, so my father could take a break. Then, it was full-throttle shaking into the skies, where I lost myself in the exhilarating cant of the plane as the landscape unfurled beneath us, rocky, unspoiled, whispering of the Aboriginal

Dreaming that had enfolded every crevice and peak for more than forty thousand years. The grandeur of the varied, endlessly stretching land tilted me into an altered consciousness; our plane had become a still point, the earth freed from its axis to rush headlong toward its own mysterious destination. We climbed higher, and my mood swelled with the ballooning sky, and then I was no longer there, not really. I, too, had taken flight, as I had that day long ago on a dark, rainy night, following my mother as she helped to carry an unconscious woman.

Time stalled as it raced, pitching me into another dimension where, settled in my spirit, I could breathe. All of life stretched ahead of me, as wild and propulsive as the landscape below and the wide skies all around. *This* is what I had been sensing through my long childhood years—this ability to be airborne and free.

The landing strip suddenly reared up. Within a minute or two we were bumping steadily along the ground. But as soon as we came to a standstill, Gordon, our pilot, leapt from the plane and stood peering up into the sky, his hand shielding his eyes. My father's small red-and-white plane was coming in for a landing, but nowhere near the landing strip we'd just touched down on. The plane plunged unnaturally, then jerked back up again. There was another older strip about three hundred yards away, littered with rocks and dangerously close to a ravine. It looked as if Vince was planning to attempt a landing there. The plane rose and then plunged again, down into the ravine. Gordon tore off in the direction of the ravine; my sister and I followed. My mother, who had found a shady spot under a tree to wait for the other plane to land, was sitting reading with her back facing us. We got to the edge of the ravine in time to see Whiskey Sierra Foxtrot careening through the brush, bouncing along the ground. An enormous tree ripped one of the wings off. The nose of the plane had been torn loose and lay on its side. The plane slammed into a thick stand of bushes and came to a stop, tipping onto its front end, where the nose had been. Smoke rose from the engine, along with the acrid smell of burning metal. Gordon was closing in on the crashed plane. I came to an abrupt halt, and my sister stopped beside me. No movement from the plane. We stood there staring at the utterly still plane as the smoke intensified, curling upward into the desert air. Very slowly, the door to the plane, now perpendicular to the ground, opened upward and we watched as my father pulled himself up and out of the plane. My older sister followed, and then my father clambered up onto the body of the plane to help pull my brother out. Co-pilot Vince hopped out last. My brother's leg was bleeding.

"Quick, run!" Gordon called out. "The tank—it could blow!"

They all broke into a run, only my little brother stopped and turned back toward the plane.

"Hey! Come back!" my father shouted, turning to run after him.

My brother clambered back onto the fuselage and disappeared, emerging a minute later hugging his prized camera.

"Are you *mad*?" my father yelled, an uncharacteristic look of panic in his face, grabbing hold of my brother's shoulder and running with him away from the plane. By the time they reached us, the panic had been replaced by a broad smile.

"Crazy kid wanted his camera," he said, his arm tight around my brother.

We stared at the plane, waiting for the tank to explode. The curling smoke fell and then extinguished.

Some years later, when I was already living in the United States, my father was flying with my brother and mother from Melbourne to Tasmania amid a storm. Visibility was next to zero. Navigating with instruments, my father got disoriented and found himself flying blind, nowhere near the land that was supposed to have appeared below. For over an hour, they flew that way, the little plane tossed around by strong winds, lashed by rain. Beneath them roiled the black waters of Bass Strait, one of the most dangerous stretches of water in the world. My father's panic mounted as he watched the fuel gauge edge lower, until finally it was hovering at zero. My mother later told me that amid her despair, certain they were about to meet a tragic end, she felt inflamed with fury at my father for endangering them all, particularly, of course, my brother, not yet twenty. Miraculously, just when things seemed irretrievably dire, the dense cloud parted. Land appeared. My father managed an emergency landing in a clearing and they all got out of the plane unhurt, then made their way in the drenching rain to a nearby farm.

My father's life ended in similarly alarming circumstances.

It has been thirty-six years since his death, but still, I find myself unable to write about those circumstances—it feels too raw, too tragic, too utterly avoidable. Most of us know of tragic endings that might have been averted. We comb back over facts that remain unyielding as rock, convinced we could have done something to change the outcome. Perhaps for a few minutes, magical thinking allows us to believe that if we clench our whole being around the wish, we will rewind time and avert the catastrophe, bringing the beloved back to life.

Five years before his death, my father was taken in by a consummate conman. The man knew just how to tap into my father's desire for male friendship and thirst for adventure, as well as his naïveté in the world of high-risk business ventures, which he expertly spun to his own sociopathic advantage. It was a drawn-out process, involving enormous drama. The outcome was that my father lost everything he'd worked so hard for—all his money, including property he'd cannily bought over the years, and more importantly perhaps, his jobs as chief of surgery, medical director, and clinical professor, along with his stellar professional reputation. The life he and my mother had so carefully and diligently built in their adopted country unraveled in a public and horrifying way. And then, when he was at his lowest point, he was diagnosed with Hodgkin's lymphoma—with its hopeful statistic of a 95 percent cure rate. With such a salubrious number, who thinks they will be in the 5 percent? Beaten down by all his losses, especially the loss of his honorable, glittering career, my father was unable to fight for his life. He quickly succumbed and was gone at the age of fifty-seven.

I look back now to that plane crash my family survived in Arkaroola. It really was terrifying, and yet we were all rather blasé about it—another good yarn to add to the store, since weren't we untouchable? Wasn't life all a bit of a hair-raising lark? Plunges into risk left us unscathed, grinning into the sunlight. We weren't afraid, no. We didn't live life by halves.

The constant, heart-thumping panic I'd felt since early childhood told another story, but I kept that hidden, eyes always on some new adventure, calmed by the vision of a new horizon, a new jumping-off point.

Now, the plane crash in the bush seems like a harbinger, signaling the perils that lay at the heart of my father's outsized appetites and penchant for risk. As we ascended, or bounced around in flight, or began the plummet back down, I would feel sickened by the noxious diesel fumes and gripped by fear, keenly aware of the flimsiness of the rattling plane, of the dangerous elements that could at any moment plunge us to our deaths. I was alert as well to the threatening atmosphere inside the cabin, the unnerving electrical arcing between my parents that trip-sparked out to the rest of us. Yes, my father was larger than life—a brilliant and intrepid man of action. I admired him enormously and put him on a pedestal, steadfast in my refusal to acknowledge the dark side of his flamboyant manner and pursuits. Only now can I fully confront the recklessness and obliviousness, which were perhaps responsible for the catastrophic unraveling of his life eight years after that plane crash, and for his premature death.

* * *

It's a shocking thing to look at one's dying parent while they yet live—the life in them so fierce, so *everything*, the horizon of the world as it must be, since there was no world before them, no self, no anything. How to imagine them ceasing to breathe, ceasing to be the person they so ineluctably are? What would that look like?

No land to stand on, no sky above, no sun no atmosphere no mountains or trees or grass or air. I wanted to grab hold of my father, *my Dad*, to feel his warmth, to shake him awake so that he might look into my eyes with his own illuminating gaze, one of the two beacons of *me*, so that he might smile and say something ordinary, some daily remark or endearment, or just remind me that he'd be bringing home roast chicken for lunch on Sunday after his tennis game. I wanted him to promise he'd go on *being alive* as long as I was alive, which is to say forever, so that I myself could continue to exist. Looking at my father propped up in the hospital bed with its cage-like rails, the IV pole standing beside him like a prison guard, hung with its plastic pouch of morphine, a fury rose within me—protective, angry, hopeless. My father was suddenly no longer just my very-own-dad, with his quirky individuality—his charisma and effusive enthusiasms, his quicksilver mind and childlike self-focus. Lying there, so frail in the slanting afternoon light, my father was also *World* and *Life* and *Being* itself.

His chest rose and fell, his breathing calm but shallow. I lost myself in the rhythm, casting my eye every now and then at the IV bag attached to the pole, taking a moment to watch the *drip drip drip* into the tube that ran down to his arm. Of a sudden, his eyes still closed, his breathing still the slow breath of unconsciousness, my father extended both his hands and mimed the motions of brisk handwashing, then clenched his right fist, as if holding a brush, and scrubbed vigorously at his other hand. My sister had told me he did this from time to time in his sleep, acting out what had been his daily routine for more than thirty years, scrubbing in preparation for surgery. His eyes fluttered, and he muttered something indecipherable under his breath. Then, his hands dropped, and the slow breathing resumed.

I couldn't take my eyes from his face. I knew I was committing these moments to my own eternal memory—knew that, very soon, I would never see my father again. My heart leapt into my throat. *But I've had no time!* I heard a voice inside my head. *No time at all!* Of course, I'd had time—twenty-six years of having my father alive. But I felt like time itself was being snatched away—as if I were about to be relegated to some sci-fi planetary realm previously unknown to man in which time simply did not exist. *No time to talk—to be together, to say goodbye, to say all the necessary things that remain unsaid.* In that moment, I felt gripped by the feeling that I'd never really, fully *connected* to my father.

There, my father, his muscles beginning to waste, no longer the powerful, invulnerable, larger-than-life figure he'd always been, the jazz band who walked into a room, the master of ceremonies to whatever might be going on. The force of his lungs was diminished as his thin chest rose and fell, the gentle expressions passing across his face formations of ephemeral cloud.

Again, he raised his arm, this time just one, extending it gently toward the window.

I leaned in close. "What it is, Dad?" I quietly asked. "What are you reaching for?"

His eyes snapped open, and he stretched his arm out further still, his palm extended toward the light pouring in through the hospital window.

He looked right at me, his brown eyes shining and lucid. "Life," he said. "I'm reaching out for life."

I wanted to clasp his hand, wanted to take hold of him and never let him go. But I didn't. It was a private gesture, though he'd generously included me. He was reaching beyond me, reaching for the light, for the world beyond the window where he would never again walk, for all the people and adventures and knowledge and action and contributions that were now, and forever, beyond his grasp. This man, whose enthusiasm and energy for living had defined him. Had he lived enough? Do any of us *live enough*? And what of his regrets?

His eyes glittered impossibly with understanding. I imagined he was staring into the questions roiling through my own mind, seeing not only all the living he would now not get to do but also those parts of living he wished had been different, things he wished he'd not done. Hurts inflicted, support not given, vows not upheld as honorably as they might have been. And a major misstep: succumbing to that virulent conman in what would be the last few years of my father's life. He lost almost everything he'd built, including his unimpeachable reputation. Did this make it impossible for him to fight for his life? Out of fear of further damaging his reputation, he'd refused the most aggressive chemotherapy treatment (might this treatment have saved his life?), wanting to avoid the hair loss that would mark him as ill.

It is only now, writing this, that I feel a spike of anger toward my father for what might have been his unnecessarily untimely death. But I squelch it right away, as I always have, preferring to indulge in protective thoughts, sadness for the way his life ended, and for whatever pain, sorrow, and trouble marked the fifty-seven years that were his.

My poor mother, I find myself thinking. I never felt angry at my father. I reserved the totality of my anger for her.

The nurse came to talk to our family. He explained that the end was near and was likely to be unbearably painful.

"We can, with your permission, make him comfortable," he said briskly.

My mother nodded. My eldest sister nodded. We other three—my brother, other sister, and I—sat immobilized and in silence. Within, I felt a shriek: *How do you know this is the end? There are miracles! He could "come through" as people do in novels and movies. Recover enough to try another bout of chemo, another bone marrow transplant. Too hasty! Too rushed! A day ago, there was hope—*

I said nothing, watched as the nurse approached the side of the bed where the IV hung on its pole. As he fiddled with it, the tube arced, and the needle dislodged from my father's arm. This jogged my father awake. The nurse said something nonchalant, I can't remember what, and issued a bland, professional smile.

"What are you doing?" my father, the surgeon, asked.

"Let's sit you up for just a moment," the male nurse said to my father, whose eyes showed bewilderment. "The IV has dislodged."

My father's eyes darted to his arm, then to the nurse's face, back to his arm. "But why don't you ..." His voice drifted off.

What was he thinking? What was he trying to figure out? What had he been about to suggest to the nurse? What surgeon's insight did he have about the patient's condition?

"This vein's a bit flat," the nurse said, businesslike, avoidant.

He was avoiding my father, allowing the truth of what was going on to slip away, all of us now complicit. Silent. Pretending. Lying.

A demon of pure panic rose in my chest.

"Let's try the other arm," the nurse was saying, his manner controlled, his voice pleasant. *Pleasant*, for God's sake.

My father was sinking into pain; I watched him disappear. He looked around the room—saw all of us, his four children, his wife, from whom he'd been estranged in recent years. She sat looking equally bewildered, her mouth tight, her eyes filled with anguish. The nurse busied himself with the needle, trying to find a usable vein.

My father tried to speak, seemed to want to ask a question, and then—*and then*—the look that will always haunt me: the dawning realization, and a final dipping of his head in acknowledgment, another quick look around at us, at me, and then, acquiescence.

He knew about these practices. He'd likely nodded *go ahead* on who knows how many occasions when a patient had been deemed near the end. Yes, *go ahead, make the patient comfortable.*

I wanted to scream. I wanted to grab hold of him.

Don't go, Dad! I'm not ready to have you go! You can be saved. We can save you! I can save you!

I cast wildly about the room, but nothing was happening to stop this—to stop this ending of my father's life. This willful infusion of a lethal dose of morphine that was being matter-of-factly administered by the pleasant nurse at my father's side, this man who was saying something practiced and euphemistic and perhaps even cheerful as he stood fiddling with the robot-bird-like contraption attached to my father's arm. Something about how this would make him feel better. That he should relax. *Really? Death* would make him feel better? He should relax so that—what? His dying might be more palatable? To whom?

There, again, that weird paradox, that failure to grasp what death really is, that strange sense I was keenly aware of almost thirty years later when my mother was also, finally, dying. That if we can only just *get through* this tough situation, everything will be better. I think now of my Auntie Gloria who only recently died, whose end came quickly. In the last week, she kept asking the doctors, "Why is this *taking* so long? How long will this take?" As if she were talking about a root canal or the removal of a stubborn wart. My cousin reported she was eager for *the process* to be over. As if after the business of dying, one will be able to get back—to normal life. Of course, this is not the least bit true for the person doing the dying, or for anyone else in the room, and yet we're all somehow in this together, as families are through thick and thin, good times and bad, so why should this be any different? Why should we not *get through this* together as we have *gotten through* countless previous challenges? Just soldier on, that's what we do, and things will get better, they always get better.

Except that the beloved person dies, and one discovers that, contrary to the weird experiential sleight-of-hand that thrusts us toward optimism, dead is dead. Gone is gone.

As the nurse had whispered would be the case, our father *drifted off*. We were told he would then *peacefully slip away*. That doesn't sound like the right way to say *stop breathing, transform from my father to an organic slab that will immediately begin to rot*, but that is what we were told, and we sat around silently and waited for this *slipping away* to happen. Vicious grief gagged me silent. My father's breathing became labored. My mother's face, a mask of layered emotions: disbelief, a strange pinching I can only describe as existential irritation, and helplessness tricked out as stoicism, a life-long habit that went all the way down to her bones. And beneath all of that, deeply sequestered, a billowing sorrow, pungent with anger, disappointment, regret. I didn't know then what I know now—that my mother was not the villain I had, in part of my being, taken her for. Many of her anguishes and complaints had merit; she'd been a victim of the times, of a lurid and life-destroying treatment of women she railed against as she also strove to fulfill the exploitative, demeaning demands she'd been made to believe were honorable and just, and in any case, her unavoidable lot. She sat there beside my dying father, fighting to keep hold of her dignity, keenly aware of all the ways she'd been deemed by others—by my father him-self—to have *let him down*. She sat there, aware of the estrangement of their final years, of his bitterness toward her. He, the revered, renowned husband, who had in critical ways broken the societal contract they'd both signed on to that my mother, at tremendous cost to her own happiness, had stayed true to. She sat there beside her dying husband, whose poor judgment had caused ruination not only for him but also for his wife, and in some deep and enduring ways also for his children—for me.

None of this had space in that room at that moment as my father's breathing went from peaceful to belabored.

"It's going to take some time," the nurse said. "Why don't you all go home, take a shower, get some rest. You can come back in the morning."

I didn't know what to do, what to feel, and in some ways, this instruction felt like a reprieve. I rose, touched my father's arm, let my hand linger for a moment, then turned and left the room. I noticed it was seven p.m. I had arrived from New York at eight o'clock that morning. My suitcase, in which I had packed a black suit, was still in the trunk of my brother's car.

My brother drove me to my mother's house where I got into the shower and let the hot water pour over me. Growing up with drought that went on year after year, I had been so trained to save water that I still can't indulge in a long shower without guilt. After a few minutes, I turned off the water and stood hugging my towel, breathing in the steam.

The telephone rang. I walked dripping from the bathroom and picked up the receiver.

He's gone, someone said.

Gone. Well, okay. But he was supposed to last the night, we were supposed to come back after a few hours of rest to be with him on his passage, though it's not really a passage, I knew that. More a slamming into a brick wall, like those safety tests for cars I've seen on TV, the dummy smashed to smithereens.

"Who was with him?" I ask.

"Actually, no one," the voice said. "Everyone was taking a break."

We'd all been taking a break. From what? From my father's dying? We'd been taking a break and my father died alone.

I've since learned that this is common. The dying are considerate, demure, perhaps not wanting the most final and primal of physical acts to be witnessed, uncannily arranging privacy for that last in-drawing of breath, while blood still flows, before spirit and soul are sucked away.

* * *

It hardly makes sense when I say it; my father died thirty-six years ago. Since that last time I saw him, so thin in the metal-barred hospital bed, I've not seen him bound into a room, nor heard his ebullient storytelling, nor treated to the sparkle of his intelligence and enthusiasm for life. He never saw me shed the bewilderment I felt as a child, invisible in the high-wattage beam of his world-guzzling, self-focused gaze. I wish I could tell my father that I've learned to acknowledge my own struggles and find guidance and help when I need it, that I no longer feel panicked and lost and alone, as I did in my childhood home. And that perhaps because of this, I can see him more clearly.

But I've also learned I was wrong about one thing—that dead may be dead, but it isn't necessarily gone. My father's history, his gaze and smile and bounding gait, his height and arm gestures and the fine breadth and shape of his hands all play within me, an ever-present magic-lantern show that is somehow *not* me but also *is*.

And I look at the screen and know that he is here in the little black shapes that take form on the page as my fingers click over the keys.

When the pandemic hit, I found myself conjuring my father's reaction. He'd have been fascinated and keenly aware of his Hippocratic responsibility. Had he lived, he'd have been ninety years old, and I picture him still vigorous, leaping from retirement to offer medical services, eager to be on the front lines.

We know implicitly that, when our own end comes, our deceased beloveds will again be lost—only worse, because now they'll be lost forever. Time only takes shape within the contours of being. While my consciousness exists, so too do my memories, thoughts, and imagination. When I die, I will kill them all again—everyone I've loved and lost who has continued to live within me. And when I die, I will eclipse those still-living beloveds I leave behind, snuffing out the psychedelic memories of the infants I birthed: my children's first words and quirky little ways, their laughs that changed as they grew, every new angle and crease on their faces. My daughter's child-sweet smile, or sorrowful eyes, my son's impish grin, or the way his chin trembles when he attempts to hold back tears.

Each one of us who goes is a library burning to the ground.

– 4 –

Dark Night of the Moon

Amanda lived in one of those pre-war buildings on the Upper West Side with meandering hallways interrupted by heavy metal fire doors you had to push open with the full weight of your body. I'd been in the US for almost four years and had a serious boyfriend and nice circle of friends but had not yet established American holiday traditions. When a rakish intellectual I knew named Paul heard I had no Thanksgiving plans, he insisted I come with him to his friend Amanda's.

"You two will be great friends, I know it," he said. "The thought of you together reminds me of a Matisse painting—*La Musique*. Two women with a guitar."

A fellow guest opened the door to Amanda's apartment and ushered us into a vast dining room dominated by a polished mahogany table, the kind I imagined was passed down through generations. The panes of a breakfront on the far wall caught the light of a half-dozen candles flickering in a silver candelabra.

Ten or more people sat around the table. Engaged conversation rose in the air, punctured by easy laughter and the gurgle of wineglasses being refreshed. My eyes were drawn to one woman in that magnetic, soul-connecting way that happens a few times in a lifetime, if one is lucky. She turned out to be our hostess—tall, with a dancer's posture, her broad shoulders squared, her elegant neck pulled upward toward the ceiling. In one hand, she held a cigarette, in the other, a glass of red wine. In my memory, the image glows, the goblet an enormous ruby, darkly catching the light, the tip of her cigarette burning orange as it arcs through the air, her eyes flashing with intensity, acuity, and mischief.

The food was a gourmet version of the usual Thanksgiving fare—cranberry relish made with cardamom, turkey stuffed with cilantro and prunes, pecan pie doused with Cointreau and topped with rosemary ice cream. I joined Amanda in conversation with an older woman who turned out to be a well-known literary journalist. They were discussing Flaubert. Amanda talked about authors as if they were her personal friends; insofar as they accompanied her in her daily life as an actor, writer, and reader, they were. She thought *The Golden Bowl* Henry James's finest and had read George Eliot's *The Mill on the Floss* multiple times. She had copious aesthetic and intellectual appetites and a developed point of view about every-thing, tossing off aperçus I found myself mentally squirrelling away.

That Thanksgiving, our wineglasses remained full. There was no one waiting on us, and yet I was left with the impression of being catered to by staff, as if in a Washington Square townhouse from Henry James's own day. At one point, I went to the bathroom and found my acquaintance, Paul, sauced and sprawled out in the bath-tub, which was filled with ice and spiked with bottles of white wine and beer.

"Cold as hell," he announced with a grin. "Dunno, seemed like a good idea at the time. It's gone soupy—." He stepped out of the tub and stood dripping on the bathmat. "Guess I should change."

Ten minutes later, he emerged wearing a pair of Amanda's jeans and a loose T-shirt.

"Rummaged in your closet, darling," he said to her in a vaude-villian stage whisper. "Lovely dresses, but none seemed quite right."

At one in the morning, everybody straggled out in various stages of intoxication. I lived twenty blocks south. It was the mid-1980s and being so far uptown, it wasn't safe to walk alone at that hour.

"Stay over," Amanda said, lighting up another cigarette. "There's a futon in the spare room."

We stayed up all night talking, so I ended up not needing the futon. At six in the morning, she put on a pot of coffee.

"Let's watch the sunrise!" she said. "We could go to Riverside Park and walk down to the river."

"But the sun rises in the east," I replied. "Don't think I want to walk through Harlem at this hour."

Amanda raised her cup of coffee to the south.

"Here, as I point my sword, the sun arises, which is a great way growing on the south, weighing the youthful season of the year."

"Hello?" I said.

"Casca's view of the matter. *Julius Caesar*, act 2, scene 1."

She poured coffee into a Thermos and added a generous portion of cream.

"Sorry," she said. "Don't even realize I'm doing it. Just plops out of my mouth."

I was to learn that Shakespeare was Amanda's constant companion, but far from her only one. She always had lines from something or other at the ready, along with moments from the lives of painters, photographers, dancers. Her charisma was theatrical but had the effect of deepening one's sense of authentic experience, flashing windows onto the human condition.

We grabbed our coats and headed out, walked the two blocks to Riverside Park, and took the long stairway down. The pathway was littered with fallen leaves, crunchy underfoot. I looked up. The bare branches of towering trees cut animate shapes into the lucent gray sky. Amanda, her face serious, reached out her hand. Our fingers latched into a clasp. A current passed between us. She nodded, as if acknowledging the sensation, and I nodded in return.

Looking back, I knew then that we were soulmates, that we had known each other already a very long time and would be connected forever. But I see something else now, as I squint back through time—a shadow broad and taloned, sweeping across the pale early-morning sky. Did I know that our forever would be shortened, Amanda's life snatched away too soon? Did I know I would spend the rest of my own life reaching for her and finding her gone?

* * *

A practicing Buddhist, Amanda was a devotee of a *roshi* who led a monastery in the Catskill Mountains, the Dai Bosatsu Zendo. It was a solace when, soon after I returned from my father's funeral in Australia, she suggested we visit the zendo as working guests. It just so happened they were about to celebrate Obon, a festival of lights that honors the dead.

The bus left from the Port Authority. It was peak hour. The terminal was a crush of humanity, people dashing for their buses, the panic splashing off them. As if on cue (NYC, circa 1987), a drunk with stinking clothes staggered through the crowd, while a gaunt woman of indeterminate age sat in a corner, nodding slowly, her eyes slits. We stood in line for our bus. Ahead of us were a family of Haredi Jews, the young man with long sidelocks, his pregnant wife behind him with a toddler in a stroller as well as five other children of differing heights. In front of them stood a group of women wearing the bonnets and homemade dresses associated with the Amish.

Once we broke free of the highway and found ourselves on country roads lined with wildflowers and trees in new leaf, I breathed a sigh of relief. I was happy to be leaving the jangle of the city behind.

The monastery sits within the Catskill Forest Preserve, fourteen hundred acres of meadows and woods. Cultivated gardens fan out from the zendo buildings. The main house, built in traditional Japanese-monastery style, consists of sparsely appointed rooms with broad windows, latched open in fine weather, allowing fresh air and birdsong to circulate. My work duty, which began at four in the morning, was to sweep the floorboards of the long passageways. I lost myself in the repetitive motion and the stillness of the early morning, aware of the slow bleaching of the sky as the sun rose.

Other guests and resident Buddhist monks went about their tasks, everyone in silence, as the air filled with nature's sounds— maples and lindens swishing in the breeze, the clear peeps of warblers and melodies of the hermit thrush. After work, we attended zazen meditation, seated on cushions in the main hall as the sun climbed up from the horizon. When the gong sliced the air, we rose and made our way to the eating hall for a breakfast of brown rice, vegetables, and tofu, which we ate from delicately glazed bowls. After breakfast, our time was our own until dinner.

That first day, Amanda and I went for a long walk through the woods and found ourselves talking about our college days. I learned that, as a sophomore, she had met a Frenchman and followed him to Paris, leaving all her belongings in her dorm. "I won't be coming back," she told her roommate by long-distance telephone. "Be a sweetheart and give my stuff away."

The affair with the Frenchman was short-lived, though her affair with Paris was to be lifelong. She moved into an apartment on Rue de Vaugirard with a group of young women, one of whom was a dancer who aspired also to act.

"Poor darling, she seemed to have no talent," she said. The light fell through the trees onto the cleared path, creating shifting, dappled shapes. "She was diligent, by god. She took class after class. Well, that dancer—Jessica Lange—ended up being one of the most celebrated actresses of our day. Ferocious commitment is a magical elixir—in the arts, it can be the Midas touch."

For three years, Amanda studied acting and mime, became fluent in French, and made Paris her own. Then, when the spirit moved, she returned to New York. She did a slew of plays in little black box theaters and off Broadway, with one shining moment on Broadway. A second Broadway offer followed but so too did a new affair with another Frenchman. Having accepted the role, she skipped out on it to return to Paris, short-circuiting the more prominent acting career she might have had.

The pathway we were on narrowed, and I slipped behind her as we walked single file through a thicket of trees.

"God, Amanda. How could you?" I called up ahead.

"Young love—fearless and foolish. That's what makes it *such fun!*" she called back. "Just like Art. If you're in, you're *in*."

The path widened again, and she came to a halt.

"That reminds me. I have something for you," she said, rummaging in her tote bag.

"If you could go back, would you do it differently? Maybe skip the Frenchman that time around, and make good on your commitment to the play?"

She flashed her eye-twinkling smile. *"Never regret thy fall, O Icarus of the fearless flight. For the greatest tragedy of them all is never to feel the burning light."*

"This one, I know," I said. "Oscar Wilde."

Amanda handed me an envelope. Inside was a postcard, a line-drawing of a girl outside in the thick of night with a long-necked butterfly net. The girl is reaching up with the net, attempting to capture the bright moon hanging in the sky. Beneath her are the words *I want! I want!*

"That's just what I'm talking about!" I said. "What about you? Reaching for the moon?"

"That Broadway play was god-awful. Can't even remember the name of it. I was cast as the airhead love interest—an ornament."

"It would have been a good career move," I said.

"You know the difference between careerism and Art," she said. "As far as I'm concerned"—and now I could see that thing she did, that flicking away of anything that was inconvenient—*"Living* is just as much *Art* as anything else."

The Obon festival took place on our third night, by the expansive lake. We walked from the dojo in the early evening, a hundred or more participants. The cicadas started up as we fanned out along the shore, barely covering a quarter of the lake's circumference. A dozen monks, women and men, all with shaven heads and wearing maroon robes, floated among us, handing out paper lanterns on which to write something to commemorate the person we were honoring. My father's death was so fresh. I anguished about whether his spirit had yet had time to leave this earth. If I could only find the right state of mind, then maybe I could help my father's spirit settle.

Silence fell gently over the gathering as we turned our attention to the lanterns. I leaned up against a tree, glancing over at Amanda, sitting under her own tree a hundred yards away, just as she raised her eyes to find me. A gentle smile grew on her face. The words I needed came to me and I transcribed them onto the thick rice-paper casing in my best handwriting, wrapping around all four sides. I looked up to see that she had also completed her inscription for her own father, who had died when she was a child, and we rose to get candles. We lit the candles and placed them inside our lanterns, then set them onto the lake's still surface. Within minutes, a hundred lanterns were drifting on the water, flames flickering through paper skins inscribed with messages for the dead. I watched as mine floated out into the center, in among dozens of others crisscrossing in their calm, fluid motion, each on its own path, as if knowing its way.

The sky had gone from transparent gray to a black dome, bored through with countless pinpricks of light. The chanting began, a chorus rising. Amanda and I looked out over the lake as the lanterns drifted, sending their quivering messages through the portal of this world into another.

After the ceremony, we walked around the lake and then cut through a bank of trees to enter a woodsy area that blotted out the stars and the bright sliver of moon, plunging us into shadow.

"I love the waxing crescent," she said. "Just beyond the dark night of the moon."

We walked in the heavy shadow that swept all of nature into a perfect singularity: the soil and groundcover, sleeping birds and scuttling beetles and towering tree trunks, and we two women, stirred by the incantations honoring our fathers, hers long gone, mine freshly in the grave.

She knew the terrain and I followed, losing track of time until my tired legs told me we'd been walking for a long while and the sky gave off the feeling of midnight. A clearing opened, releasing the light of the stars and moon, revealing a pergola encircled within by a bench. We climbed the steps and sank onto the bench.

My mind drifted back to the lake. The ceremony had been both as sturdy and flimsy as the paper lanterns themselves. The few words I had written in my best handwriting were meaningless dots, I knew that, and yet my heart had broken as I wrote them. Amanda had also written words for the father she had last seen when she was nine years old, the ordinary day he'd kissed his daughter good-bye before going to the golf course at the country club. After hitting a hole in one at the eighth, he had a heart attack. I saw from the set of her face as she penned her words that her father's death had long since settled into a groove, one she was now sliding into with a certain ease. My own emotions felt dangerous in comparison, as if they might leap out of me and set their bare teeth into some unsuspecting innocent.

I opened my eyes to find that she was studying my face. She was framed by the wooden slats of the pergola and flecked with starlight. I suddenly felt a curdling of anxiety.

"You have them too, don't you," she said. "The dreams."

At the sound of her words, an image swam into view, as if from a photographer's bath of developing fluid.

"Yes," I said. "I'm walking on a hard, wet street."

"Cobblestone."

"And the sound—"

"—of boots, the soldiers chasing."

"Brown uniforms, and the—"

"—fence."

I see her in the white half-light, her face smoothed by shadows.

"When did you start having those dreams?" I asked.

"Can't remember. Very young. You?"

"Five, maybe."

"I knew it, there, by the lake," she said. "It suddenly made sense."

She told me she why she believed we knew each other so deeply and had from the start. I sat quietly as she unwound the story of a young Jewish opera singer in Germany in the early 1940s and her best friend, a gentile, who risked her life to hide the singer from the Nazis in her basement.

"I was the Jewish opera singer," she said.

In this life, I am Jewish. Amanda was of Protestant background. The story she was telling reversed these threads.

"Yes, and you risked your life. When they broke down the door to the basement, I began to sing. We died together."

"How sad," I said, taking her hand. "Are you absolutely sure?" What a strange question, I thought, hearing it fall from my own lips. As if there was the possibility of certainty about anything, let alone regarding matters of past lives.

"But *we got to come back!*" she said, leaning in close. "To do it all over. To be together, to be here. To give your father a beautiful send-off. Don't you see? It's all part of the great cycle."

A concept came back to me, learned in youth—*gilgul neshamot*, cycle of souls, the mystical Jewish belief in reincarnation based on the work of the sixteenth-century mystic, Rabbi Isaac Luria. The idea is that each person has a unique purpose to fulfill in the sweep of humanity. As part of God's compassion, each soul is given many opportunities to complete the tasks on this earth that only they can achieve. Linked to the idea of *tikkun olam*—repair of the world— each individual's role is sacred; the world will not be repaired until each soul has made its unique contribution. The soul, then, might be attached to numerous physical beings in the course of its cosmic journey. Amanda seemed to be talking about exactly this notion— she even used the word *cycle*.

That night, I lay awake, peering up at the pale sky through the high window in my monastery room. Images swirled. Shadowy faces, the looming shapes of bushes and trees, the air heavy with the breath of a hundred people—footfalls swift with the intent to remain undetected. My heart raced—that familiar panic. I'd been here so many times before, and each time, the terror was fresh. I found myself bolting upright in bed. Amanda—she was there, in my terrifying, wide-awake half dream. That's where I'd seen her eyes before, those eyes I knew and loved so well. Amanda, amid all that frantic effort to flee. I'd dreamed of her all along.

* * *

Amanda's mother, Patrice, was a confusing force of nature who specialized in bouts of outlandish indulgence and impassioned cultural tutelage, punctuated with periods of withdrawal and dismissive attacks. A first marriage had ended badly, leaving her with a young child, Amanda's much older half sister, and financial struggles, a single mother on a journalist's wage. When her daughter was eighteen, Patrice married a wealthy businessman and, at age forty, gave birth to Amanda.

Patrice was in her mid-seventies and somewhat infirm when I first met her, though her forceful intelligence was undimmed. Her chin-length hair was dyed espresso brown, with thick bangs that hung close to her piercing eyes. Her aura of pungent sophistication was somehow as profligate as her Chanel suits and the strong perfume that announced her presence. She imbued everything around her, including inanimate objects, with electric intent, which could slip for her into malevolence. If she bumped into something, for example, and bruised her knee, she would castigate the offender. "I'm so *sick* of being *persecuted* by everything," she might say, giving a vicious slap to the wall or table or chair.

That first visit, Amanda's mother entertained us with stories of her housekeeper, a young Swede named Christine, who according to Patrice was endowed with superhuman strength.

"When she vacuums, she moves the furniture lickety-split—heavens, see those couches?" She pointed to two enormous leather couches. "She lifts them up, one in each hand, as if they were crackers!" She riskily set aside her walking cane to do a little prance, her flattened palms above her head.

Gushingly warm to me, Patrice was oddly impersonal with her daughter, while also clearly attached, in the way of a barnacle. She asked me what I did for a living, and I told her about my new career as a consultant.

"Can't you get Amanda a nice job like that? She's *on the stage*, as you know, but that's not much of a livelihood."

This was how Patrice introduced Amanda to others: "My daughter—she's *on the stage*." It made me laugh. I pictured Amanda alone in a darkened theater, facing empty seats, left standing there, always *on the stage*. Later, I said, joking, "Will someone let that poor woman go home?"

Some of the stories from Amanda's childhood were amusing, others harrowing. She and her mother would get into terrible fights that continued into her adult years. When Amanda was fifteen, she faked an appendicitis attack in a fit of theatrical attention-seeking and was rushed into surgery. The operation revealed a healthy appendix. Amanda's mother was advised to get her daughter psychological help. Her response was to have her fifteen-year-old committed to a psychiatric hospital, where she spent several terrifying months, during which her mother refused to visit.

For the first few weeks on the ward, Amanda was combative. She insisted there was nothing wrong with her, accused her mother of child abuse for locking her up, and was labeled "uncooperative." She soon realized that, if she kept that up, she'd be there for an eternity, so she became a model patient, saying and doing what was expected of her.

"It was a performance," she said. "I figured out the script, and then followed it to a T."

Beneath the skilled dissimulation, she was seething. Finally released and back in their suburban mansion, Amanda unleashed her fury. One story—I never knew exactly how much of what she told me was fact—had her chasing her mother around the kitchen table, wielding a knife. I do know that her mother maintained a virulent hold over her, well into Amanda's adulthood. She indulged Amanda's cavalier attitude toward making a living—as if the dreariness of financial responsibility was not worthy of an artist—while dangling money strings to control her.

On a later visit, Patrice insisted we join her at her country club for lunch, adding that she'd booked us for an overnight stay at the club's guesthouse.

"There's something unexpected about that guesthouse," she said on the phone. Her tone was vaguely ominous. "It's gonna be a gas for you girls."

Amanda warned me about what I could expect from the lunch: unapologetic members of the wealthy WASP class who'd only recently allowed Jews to join their club.

It was, indeed, an odd get-together. Patrice's country club friends were, true to stereotype, wearing twinset sweaters or silk blouses, pearl necklaces, and glittering rocks on their fingers. Several eyed me curiously as I approached. One asked me questions about "my people," both titillation and distaste in her face. After lunch, Patrice and her friends retired to the games room to play cards while Amanda and I took a walk on the grounds. Later, we joined the ladies for iced tea and cake.

"It's moody, up at the guesthouse," Amanda's mother said with a mischievous smile. "Some say it's haunted."

"Oh, mother, don't," Amanda said, also smiling, though there was something weary in her eyes. "You'll just scare her."

"How silly," her mother said. "Nothing scary about *ghosts*, for heaven's sake. They've just gotten there before the rest of us." She waved her hand dismissively. "You know that better than anyone, darling. What about all of Shakespeare's dearly departed? Hamlet's father, the one in *Macbeth*, and lots in *Richard III*."

"Not the best examples, Mother. Hardly Casper the Friendly Ghost, any of them. Hamlet's murdered father. Banquo, also murdered. And the ghosts that open *Richard III* are a parade of all his victims."

"Well, dear, why don't you give some examples of the nice ones?" Her mother's smile was brittle.

Amanda stiffened.

Her mother turned to her friends. "You know my daughter is *on the stage*." Then, to Amanda: "*Do* recite something for the ladies."

The women turned to Amanda expectantly. Amanda's irritation hardened to rage. I'd never seen her like this, her mouth tight, her dancer's supple posture turned rigid.

"Mother, please," she said. "We've talked about this."

"Don't be a stick in the mud," Patrice said, her own eyes hardening. I felt it then, a steely, red-hot battle of the wills.

Something wavered in Amanda. I saw it as a clenching of the muscles in her cheek.

"Alright then," she said. "Shakespeare gave us only one friendly ghost. It appears in *Cymbeline*."

She'd clearly decided to back down, and I wondered if she was swallowing her pride to spare me unpleasantness.

"Let me think." She looked downward for a minute.

When she raised her eyes, her face was transformed. Amanda was gone, and in her place—the ghost of Sicilius Leonatus from Shakespeare's *Cymbeline*, father of Posthumus, who visits his son as he lies in miserable bondage under the watch of two jailers.

"*The crystal window opens; look out; no longer exercise upon a valiant race thy harsh and potent injuries.*" She paused and looked at Patrice, who gave her an impatient nod.

"*Peep through thy marble mansion; help; or we poor ghosts will cry to the shining synod of the rest against thy deity.*" Amanda's voice was in full actor boom, but her delivery was hollow.

"And?" Patrice asked, glancing around the table, her gaze like a net, scooping up the admiration of her friends.

"*Away! And, to be blest, Let us with care perform his great behest.*"

"As you have performed mine!" Patrice said triumphantly.

I saw a flicker of defeat in Amanda's eyes. "We really must go and settle in," she said to her mother.

"Come and find me to say goodbye," Patrice said brightly. "I have the car coming at seven."

We wheeled our bags along a path that skirted the lawn. We walked in silence. I'd not seen Amanda like this before—deflated, weary, annoyed.

We came to the front of a building that looked run-down and incongruously gothic—four stories high, including a pitch-roofed attic. A cylindrical tower rose in the center, its roof a patina-green cone. We dragged our rolling cases up the stone stairs to a double front door; patches of naked wood showed behind tongues of peeling blue paint. We rapped with the brass knocker and when no one answered, we pushed the door open and found ourselves in a vast foyer with an impressive, curved staircase.

"Hello?" Amanda called out.

No answer, no signs of any staff or guests.

"I wonder if we're the only ones staying here tonight?" I asked.

Just then, a man appeared—tall, with a fleshy face, pot belly, and an absurd-looking handlebar mustache.

"Ladies," he said. "You *are* the only ones who will be staying here tonight. We don't get many guests these days." His voice was thick with insinuation.

"Will there be any staff through the night?" Amanda asked.

"Well, there's me. I'm down the hill, in the roadhouse. Nothing to worry about. There hasn't been an incident here for a while."

The guy was messing with us.

"You're in the Blue Room, I see," he said. "Let me get you the key. Down that hallway, all the way at the end." He retrieved the key from a hook behind the reception desk and handed it to Amanda.

"And if there's anything you need—"

"Thank you, we'll be fine," I said, eager to get away.

We dropped off our bags and then headed back out to continue exploring the grounds.

Later, we said our goodbyes to Amanda's mother—air kisses at cheek level on both sides—who had a driver waiting to take her back to her apartment in the city. She was distracted, as she typically was when without sufficient audience and adequate staging for her entrances, exits, and monologues. Unexpectedly, she took notice of me, or rather my hair, which was long and dark. She raised her manicured hand, a jewel flashing, and took hold of a swatch of my hair.

"That must be marvelous, tossed across the pillow." She lingered with the thought. "I'm sure your boyfriend loves that."

She let my hair drop. I could see Amanda's eyes fixed on her mother's face, expecting, I think, that her mother might turn one last time for a kiss or sign of farewell. She didn't, though—her attention had already flown from us to somewhere else. She concentrated on getting into the car and then was gone.

The club closed early on Sundays. Passing by the main building, we saw that it was shuttered for the night. The parking lot was empty. Back at the deserted guesthouse—no sign of the peculiar man—we realized we'd made no plans for dinner. We scrounged in our bags for snacks, turning up a bar of Toblerone, a bag of cashews, and four little pouches of pretzels from the plane.

"The four key food groups—covered," Amanda said. "Protein, carbs, fat, and chocolate!"

It was early October and, as night fell, the temperature fell. The heating had clearly not yet been turned on. We sat on the queen bed, under the blankets, nibbling our rations and sipping on tap water. There, in the elegantly appointed room, with its high windows, and chandelier sprouting from the ceiling, I felt cozy and appreciative of this latest sisterhood adventure.

But then we heard a loud creaking and the sound of something falling. In the silence, I heard my own pounding heart. We looked at each other for a moment, and then, we were up from the bed. Amanda grabbed an enormous bureau and tried to slide it toward the door. I went to help her and pushed with all my might. It felt like it was made of granite.

"I wish Christine were here," I said. "She'd pick it up in the palm of her hand, like a cracker!"

Amanda dragged the chest while I did my best to assist. I saw the muscles in her arms at work—all those years of horse riding, swimming, dance, acting, mime. To me, she was dauntless, powerful, indestructible. She slid the chest into place against the door. I wedged the back of a wooden chair beneath the door handle. We appraised our barricade.

"No one's going to get through that!" she said.

We jumped back into bed. It was late, and we were tired.

"I've written a story," she said. "Would you read it?"

"Of course."

She retrieved a wad of typed pages from her bag and handed them to me. I settled against the pillows.

The story, titled "The Dancer," pulled me in from the first sentence. It opened with a description of a professional ballet dancer exiting a cattle car at the gates of Auschwitz, drably dressed, and carrying a battered suitcase. She is sent to the line on the left, the one condemning its number to immediate death by gassing, perhaps because she is already so thin. Her hair is shorn, she is made to strip naked. And now we see her standing in line for the gas chamber, under the guard of numerous SS soldiers. She catches the eye of a young guard and imagines she might coax from him some shred of humanity. Slowly, she assumes the pose of a plié and then, still holding his gaze, raises her arms, gives her naked body over to the dance sequence in which Giselle is raised from the dead by kindly spirits. Her limbs elongate and her body arcs as she dances. The soldier is mesmerized, and though she has broken eye contact now to immerse herself in the dance, an observer would see that the soldier's eyes have softened and even hold a sheen of tears. His posture remains rigid, but he, too, has given himself over to the dance. The line of the condemned is moving forward and the dancer breaks free from the ranks, veering off the path to give full flight to her motion. The soldier follows her with his gaze. He is no longer there, no longer a guard in the concentration camp. Joined with her artistry, they are together.

An order is barked, the sound of a *thwak* ruptures the air, and the dancer is felled. Another *thwak*, then a third, and three welts grow in parallel lines on the white skin of her back, blossoming with blood. The dancer rests for a moment on the ground and then slowly, gracefully, pulls her body upward and rejoins the line, still dancing, never ceasing the dance. The soldier's face has turned stony. His eyes no longer follow the dancer but fix on the condemned children before him, huddling together, their faces frozen. The dancer is now only the dance—she, too, has disappeared. No one is watching, not even the guard who struck her down with his whip. No one pays her any attention as she stretches and coils, giving her physical all to each careful position of her muscles, from calf to thigh, torso to shoulder to fingertips. She is in search of perfection and in each moment, she finds it. At the end, the children behind her in the line notice her, and the expressions on their faces change. Their eyes shine as they fix on the sinuous shapes made by the dancer's body. They follow her into the gas chamber.

I set the pages down on the table, the tears sliding down my face.

"Amanda," I said. I found I had no words.

"I know," she said, her face soft. "It's okay. I found the words for both of us."

I hunted in my bag for a tissue.

"I never did tell you about the children," she said, taking my hand.

"What children?"

"*Our* children. The boys—they're waiting for us. Up ahead."

We turned off the overhead chandelier, leaving only the bedside lamp lit; it cast a dull glow that seemed more responsible for creating shadow than for giving off light. Looking into her farseeing eyes, I had the sensation that time was shuddering, that the present was being shaken and might at any moment fall away.

"The two of us, *back then*—"

"—you the Jewish opera singer, me your gentile friend—"

"Yes. We both had babies. Little boys." Fright filled her face.

"Maybe now's not the time to talk about this," I said. "I'm already scared."

She shook her head and gripped my hand more tightly. "Trust me on this," she said. "It's important. If I don't tell you, maybe it won't happen."

"What won't happen?"

"Those baby boys, they're going to come back to us."

My heart thumped. I glanced over to where the back of the chair was jammed beneath the brass door handle, the massive chest surely blocking any possibility of a forced entry.

"They took your boy, that day. The soldiers passed him from one to the other. He was quiet as could be, didn't utter a sound. Everything about you was frozen. One of the soldiers took the shot."

I could hardly tolerate what she was saying. But she'd asked me to trust her.

"I knew it was my turn next, and I could feel my own baby in my arms. He also did not utter a sound, and I held him tightly, and more tightly still, and then everything went black."

A sob flew from my throat.

"This is the thing. I had a dream—last night. About the boys. When I woke up, I knew that the boys were going to return. And just like *back then,* they're going to be almost twins ..."

"You mean, we'll have babies at the same time?"

"Almost exactly, yes. They'll be brothers, just like we're sisters. Isn't that *wonderful?* In my dream, they were already here—I saw what they looked like, had a sense of the kind of people they're going to be. My son with a shock of black hair—and dark, dark eyes, almost black. He looks like a Russian prince. He'll be serious, an old soul. And yours—a sunny pixie with fair hair, and a spirit light as air. That one is always going to be smiling."

I had a sudden vision of a sunny day, and two little boys walking ahead of us, holding hands. I saw only their backs, bright halos hovering about their heads.

– 5 –

I'm Dying, Egypt, I'm Dying

Simon and I could hear music coming from the house as we wheeled our overnight bags up to the front door. It was a run-down house with a screened-in porch, surrounded by windblown vegetation and close enough to the beach that we could smell the salt. A pair of seagulls caterwauled overhead. Inside, we found ourselves among a welcoming crowd of composers and musicians. I was drawn to the piano, where a small group gathered around a young man intently playing the tune of "Happy Birthday" in a classical-music style.

"Beethoven!" he declared, his fingers thundering up and down the keyboard.

At the crash of the final chord, someone called out "Mendelssohn" and he started up again, this time with a quick riff from Felix Mendelssohn's overture to *A Midsummer Night's Dream*, segueing into the "Happy Birthday" melody while keeping the overture's harmonies and embellishments riffling through. Next came Schumann, then Berlioz, Shostakovich, and Wagner. Philip Glass was the finale, after which the performer jumped up from the piano bench and bowed to cheers and applause.

Over the rowdy crowd, our hostess called out a general introduction. I'd met Sandra, a composer, through mutual friends, and she'd invited Simon and me to spend the weekend at her parents' house in East Quogue, Long Island. The group all knew each other from workshops and theater groups—composers, musicians, singers, actors. Several people came over to introduce themselves.

"New blood," one young man said—tall and lean with dark wavy hair that fell to his chin—reaching out his hand. "Don't mind us. We're rabid."

In the kitchen, a large farm table was laden with food—platters of cheese and pâté, crusty baguettes, elaborate salads, and an enormous basket filled with tangerines, fresh figs, dates, and walnuts in their shells.

"Help yourself," our hostess said. "Coffee and tea—over there. Bar—living room."

Breakfast and lunch followed this buffet style, with people wandering in and out, the table seeming to magically replenish itself. Toward evening, a crew took over the kitchen. Dishes of steaming food were brought into the dining room, where we all filled our plates then found a seat in the double living room with its stuffed couches and chairs. Music was always erupting. Someone would start a round or improvise a musical-theater number appropriate to the conversation, the piano coaxed into every possible style—classical, country, blues, jazz. I was in a state of blissful wonderment.

After that first lunch, we followed a group heading down to the lake to row. It was a sizable lake with a long pier, along which six rowboats were tied up and bobbing on the water. The air was filled with birdsong, sweet with honeysuckle and rosemary that grew in the overgrown garden. A boat was approaching, rowed by two young men, both extremely handsome in a mirror-image way: one blond with dark eyes, the other dark-haired with blue eyes.

The blond man fixed his gaze on me; his face broke into an electric smile.

"Darling, we *must* become acquainted," he said in a plummy British accent as they pulled up on the muddy embankment. "My name's Anton, and this is my partner, Will."

Anton was wearing a T-shirt and shorts that emphasized his impressive build. He stepped out of the boat and took my hand. Will stepped out behind him—slender, his eyes soulful, wearing his reserve like a gently billowing cape.

Within minutes, Anton and I were deep in conversation on the hiking path. I must have subliminally noticed his limp, since it was quite pronounced, but I didn't consciously take note of it. It came as some surprise to me later that night, when we were all involved in a game of charades, to see that Anton was dragging his leg behind him as he cavorted in his attempt to get us to guess the book title. Raised in London, he had lived for over a decade in New York. He was a classically trained actor involved in the NYC downtown theater scene. I'd later have the pleasure of seeing him onstage— and it was remarkable how his limp seemed to disappear, though it was in fact always evident. He'd had polio as a child and endured a dozen or more excruciating surgeries and treatments, all of which had failed. I learned this years later from Will. Anton never talked about it. We became fast friends from that day on, and I was invited into his vital circle, at the center of which was Will, beneath whose seriousness I would discover a brilliant, creative soul.

That first night at the country house, playing charades, my professor boyfriend, Simon, mischievously slipped the title *The Critique of Pure Reason* into the grab basket. The actor with the cascade of dark hair picked the title on his turn, standing for a long moment in contemplation. Hoots of "Come on! Get on with it!" rose. He leapt to a witty performance—became a little "critter" prancing on its back legs, holding up clawed hands. Someone yelled out the word, and the actor clipped it short with fingers against palm to get *crit*. From there, it was a jump across a scattering of inventive mimes for someone to land the title, accompanied by well-earned applause.

Anton slapped Simon on the back.

"Of course that was you. You *are* dastardly. But you're useful among these musicians. You elevate us."

Back in New York, it felt as if Anton and I had always been friends. We had the easy rapport of childhood playmates, and an intuitive, emotional intimacy. We took to spending a lot of time together, long dinners and lunches and movies and plays, and prolonged ambles around the city. Anton had a trio of close women friends—the other two were actors. The four of us would sometimes hang out. I have a lovely photograph of us, Anton in the bottom center of the frame, the other two on either side of him and me above his head, a female halo of admiration and love.

We gathered at each other's small apartments, often at Anton and Will's, where the evening inevitably veered into music. Will was a composer and seemed always to have a new song; his wistful lyricism and blasts of pure emotion typically brought me to tears. I would feel eyes turning my way, as if whatever group was gathered had a standing bet—how many minutes until I would start sniffling and reach for a tissue.

One afternoon, Anton and I were out in the city, rushing down the subway steps in the hope of catching the train that had just pulled up to the platform. He paused to catch his breath midway down the stairs. He was super fit—I'd never seen him out of breath like that. He hung his head, drawing in long, heaving lungfuls. The ping sounded—*Stand clear of the closing doors*—and the train lumbered out of the station.

"Never mind," I said, as he looked up with that New York City just-missed-the-subway expression. "We'll catch the next one."

He nodded, then took the rest of the stairs carefully, dragging his lame leg behind him.

"Hey, you okay?" I asked.

He gave me his familiar self-deprecating smile. "Of course, darling. You know, the damned virus, finally getting to me."

The subway was a cavern of echoes, a press of humanity and ricocheting sound. We waited for the next train, then hopped on. Anton sank gratefully onto the bench. I squeezed in beside him, happy for the rare opportunity at this hour of a seat. We rode in silence. Something niggled at me—yes, the way he'd said, "the virus." He didn't seem to have a cold—no coughs or sniffles. Now, in the relative calm of the speeding underground subway car, my mind pulled free and attempted to land on the meaning I knew was eluding me.

We came to our stop and disembarked. He was walking normally now—normally for him—a graceful, lame loping at a normal city pace. We exited onto Broadway, back in our shared Upper West Side neighborhood.

"What did you mean, about the virus?" I asked, taking his arm, pulling us both up short.

"Oh, darling, it's not a big deal. *Everyone* has it these days."

My heart clutched. "What are you talking about? Are you really telling me—"

"Now, now, let's not get sentimental," he said.

"Anton, really? Sentimental? Are you telling me—you have *AIDS?*"

"I suppose it has moved there, my love. For the past I-don't-know how long, it's just been HIV."

He parted the collar of his shirt to show me an awful sore beneath his collarbone. Suddenly, as if an invisible veil had lifted, I noticed his face was thinner. And was there a gray pallor to his complexion?

"I'm starting on the drugs." His voice was measured. "They're experimental, but you know ..."

Those experimental drugs, early-stage AZT, ended up being attack dogs that grabbed Anton by the throat and drained the life from him. The decline took perhaps six months from that day we emerged into the cool sunlight on Upper Broadway—but even as I lived it, it felt like sped-up time-lapse photography, everything moving in fits and starts but at a barreling pace.

I pretended to take on Anton's casual approach toward "the virus," but inside, I was distraught. This vital, beloved, larger-than-life man, bursting with youth—not yet thirty-four—had been hit with a death sentence due to a single amorous evening a decade earlier, before he met Will, with whom he'd spent the last nine years.

He went about his daily life as if nothing were untoward. Auditioning, landing a role, working his part-time day job, spending quiet evenings with Will or small groups of close friends. One Wednesday, I arrived at their apartment, bearing the Entenmann's orange loaf cake Anton loved, to find a hastily scribbled note on the door. *At the hospital. Can you meet us there?*

The AIDS ward was the horror that has since been evoked in movies about the epidemic: room after room of young men, emaciated and covered in sores, eyes dim with suffering, their rooms hung with abandonment and despair. No visitors anywhere. Doctors and nurses wearing gloves and face masks, propelling themselves forward with an urgent air of overburdened mission. Anton's room was the only one filled with visitors—Will, of course, and several other friends who'd been with him at home when he'd taken a sudden bad turn, coughing up blood, struggling to breathe. Now, he was settled, propped up in bed. In the six days since I'd last seen him, he'd transformed. His skin was fully gray, and black under the eyes; fresh sores had appeared on his face and neck. His flesh was wasting away, his cheeks hollowed out. There was no sign of his formerly impressive biceps and pecs.

I gulped back the sob that leapt to my throat. "Entenmann's orange loaf cake," I said, plopping the box on the hospital table. "We're going to need paper plates and forks. I know I called this stuff *junk*, but I take it all back—it's delicious. You've won me over. Greet your fellow addict!"

"Darling, when have I ever been wrong? Face it," Anton said, smiling, but he didn't rush to open the box as he usually did. "I'm a man of impeccable taste."

Something trembled in his face, something foreign to his essence, to the man I knew and loved. Later, I realized what I had seen: a shuttering of desire.

For two weeks, the doctors and nurses pumped him full of medications and administered IVs and then Anton returned home, though from then on, it was the wild pendulum swings of a handful of passable days and then horrible symptoms, with trips back to the hospital. On one of the relatively good evenings, he and I went to the movies. Beside me in the darkened theater, he was beset by a furious itch on his arms and legs. Frantic bouts of scratching alternated with his own steely attempts to refrain, and more than once I leaned over and suggested that perhaps we should leave.

"Makes no difference, I'll only itch at home. It takes my mind off it to be here. Let's stay."

I reached out my hand, which he forcefully grasped.

Deeper into Anton's decline, Will called for a party at their apartment to celebrate Anton's birthday. All the friends made a showing, bringing plates of food and bottles of wine. They lived in a one-bedroom apartment on West End Avenue. The living room window opened onto the building's central air shaft, and the bedroom window faced a brick wall. It was a small home without much natural light but radiant with happiness and filled with creative activity.

As usual, Will ended up at the piano. Anton rose from the couch and hobbled, without his cane, across the room, positioning himself behind Will, his hand on his shoulder. Effortfully, he leaned down and whispered something into Will's ear. Will nodded, then pressed his fingers into the gentle chords that heralded a song of his—"See How a Flower Blossoms"—that Anton particularly loved. Will sang beautifully, his voice raw with knowledge and yet resonant with a child's pure yearning. He swayed over the keys while Anton stood behind him, his clothes billowy on his skeletal frame, his hand resting gently on Will's shoulder. Just at the moment I felt entirely overwhelmed by grief, Anton turned and looked directly at me, his cheekbones jutting sharply through his papery gray skin.

Isn't he wonderful? he mouthed, his face lit with joy.

The next time Anton had to go to the hospital, Will carried him to the elevator, then out to the taxi. By the time I got there, Anton had lost consciousness. It had been a long and tumultuous few months and Will's stamina was threadbare, frayed by around-the-clock care and his efforts to keep up a hopeful front. When I took Will's hand, his whole body sagged, and his shoulders gently heaved. I didn't know what to do, so I just sat there, holding Will's hand, looking at the ruined face and body of my beloved friend Anton. The nurses were attentive and kind, and often remarked how good it was that he had a steady stream of visitors, but there was nothing much either they or the doctors could do. They clearly agonized over the dying patients who were ever replenishing the ward, most of whom had been abandoned by their families, their own friends either desperately ill themselves or else already dead from the scourge. As I made my way down the corridor, I'd see their gaunt faces through windows and open doors.

A week passed, then two, as Anton declined further. He was still able to sit up in bed for an hour or two at a time, and since it was Academy Awards season, he asked us all to come to the hospital so that, according to our tradition, we could watch the Oscars together. Anton had mentioned daily how much he missed his beloved dog, Cuddles, a furry white tail-wagging mop of a creature. Pets were banned from the ward, but Will and I decided to smuggle him in. I would carry Cuddles in my large canvas tote bag. We'd ride the elevator and Will would position his body as cover.

The evening arrived. The hospital elevator filled up on the ground floor. Cuddles chose the moment the doors closed—likely set off by the *ping*—to jostle around in my bag. Will turned to me, moving in close to try to hide the movement. We talked loudly about the award nominees, predicting who was going to win. Exiting the elevator, Will stuck close to me, in the hope of hiding the fact that I was carrying a bag with a life of its own.

We'd been given permission by the staff to take over the Family Room at one end of the ward. There was no competition for the room; I'd never seen anyone in it but our group of friends, who were

a steady presence on the ward. Now, the room was bursting. A male
nurse had installed Anton in a hospital chair. The sores were in full
bloom on almost every square inch of his exposed skin, a red-and-
white cravat was tied around his emaciated neck.

"Darling, come in! The party has begun!" he called out, his voice
thin but steely.

I could see how very tired he was. I held up the customary
Entenmann's box and he pried loose a piece and took a tiny bite.
He had trouble swallowing. Discreetly, Will raised a napkin up to
Anton's cracked lips and waited for him to spit up the mouthful,
which he disposed of in a covered plastic bucket.

"I've brought you something else!" I removed Cuddles from my
canvas tote bag.

"Cuddles, *darling* …" Anton said quietly, his eyes filling with
tears. "My precious little darling." He held her to his face. Cuddles
wiggled in an ecstasy of licking and full-body tail wagging.

Just then, one of the nurses walked in. I froze. His eyes landed
squarely on Cuddles, who was emitting whimpers of delight. Anton
was lost in the purest happiness. The nurse's eyes lingered for a
moment on Anton and Cuddles, then he turned to Will. "Hey, can
you keep a tally of the winners? I have patients without TV. Want
to keep them up to date." He surveyed the room with pleasure, seeing us all there, surrounding Anton and Will. "One more thing, you
guys. No need to keep it down. If a cheer goes up, we'll know that
someone deserving took the statue."

The next day, Anton, hooked up to the IVs that were keeping
him alive, announced that he wanted to go home. We all talked
it over. The doctors were consulted, who told us he could be discharged, though it would be *against medical advice*. Will you hire a
twenty-four-hour nurse? we were asked. Who is going to take care
of him?

One of Will and Anton's acting friends was also a nurse. No
problem, he said. He could teach Will to change the IVs and he
would drop in once or twice a day to check in on everything. Within
twenty-four hours, Anton was back in the compact apartment

where he'd spent so many happy years with Will. His mother flew in from Canada, along with his sister, a single mother, who brought her two-and-a-half-year-old son with her. We set up the apartment as a functional hospice. Anton had requested a large TV, so Will arranged for a short-term rental. We set the VCR up on a loop, showing Anton's favorite movies (*Brief Encounter* and *Cabaret*).

Anton's mother had brought some of his favorite foods from Canada: frozen meat pies and a vegetable pastry pocket, similar to the pasties I'd grown up with in Australia.

"Can't I make you something more nutritious?" I tactlessly asked one mealtime, as I was heating up one of those frozen meat pies in the oven.

"For heaven's sake, darling," he said, "what difference does it make?"

He took a few bites. I stood at the ready with the bucket, which I grabbed as soon as I heard the first gag, getting it into place just in time. It all came up, as usual, and I felt a splash of sick on my hand. I found myself quickly rifling my body-awareness memory to recall if I had any little scratches or open cuts on my hand. We'd heard of doctors and nurses contracting the virus through an open wound. At some level, we all knew of the dangers and yet had put them from mind; we were simply taking care of our ailing friend. Now, though, it occurred to me that this might have been reckless. I went to empty the bucket in the toilet, then took a few minutes to vigorously scrub my hands with disinfectant soap.

For six weeks, we took turns being on shift at the apartment, dividing up the time into six-hour stretches. Will was often alone with Anton through the night. With our jobs and other commitments, we did the best we could.

Simon, who had a heavy teaching load and a long commute, had not seen Anton for several weeks when, toward the very end, he came for a visit. It was only when I saw Simon's face as he entered the bedroom that I realized how terrifying Anton must have looked.

He was lying in the bed, his head and neck propped up by pillows. Gaunt was no longer an adequate word to describe how he looked. His eyes were enormous in his shrunken face; they glimmered with ebbing life. He'd insisted someone tie a fresh cravat around his neck whenever he was sponged down; it hung loosely against his protruding collar bones, resting on the open sores. His face flickered with recognition when Simon entered the room. Laboriously, he reached out one long bony arm and, in a suddenly bafflingly strong voice, boomed:

"I'm dying, Egypt, *dying!*"

Simon almost leapt from his skin. It took us a moment to realize Anton was quoting Mark Antony from Shakespeare's *Tragedy of Antony and Cleopatra*. Simon took Anton's hand and held it for a long moment, blinking back tears.

Anton gently released his hand from Simon's clasp and reached out to Will, then continued with Mark Antony's speech, his voice waning, his eyes lighting up one last time.

"*Only I here importune death awhile, until of many thousand kisses the poor last I lay upon thy lips.*" Anton scanned the room. "Oh, *do* come on," he said, managing a wry smile. "Why all the *gloom?*"

The last two weeks, we all slipped into that waiting game that is part of attending to the dying. Day and night disappeared. We existed in an eternal present that hung like a bright, shining star about to implode.

One early morning, as I sat by Anton's bedside, his eyes snapped open.

"So, darling, what's the plan?" he asked, his eyes showing that flickering, inwardly focused light I've come to associate with the slide into death.

"What do you mean?"

"You know, a baby. What's the story with that? You told me once you were dying to have a child."

I flinched at the word *dying*.

"Funny you should mention this," I said slowly. "We've actually started trying …"

"Oh, that's just wonderful! I'm *so* happy for you."

He sank back into hazy semi-consciousness.

A few days later as I sat by the bed, Anton's eyes opened once more.

"I'm so happy about the baby," he whispered.

I laughed. "Well, I don't have one yet!"

"But you will. And soon, I can feel it." His voice trailed off and his eyes closed. But then, he managed a smile. "Who knows, darling, if we get the timing right, maybe I'll reincarnate. It would be a joy to have you as a mother."

"I'd love nothing more," I said.

"Make sure it happens," he said. "If you don't, I'll come back to haunt you. That's a promise."

Anton died in Will's arms. After they took away his body, I set up a bed for myself on the couch. Unable to sleep in their bed, Will crept out in the middle of the night and curled up at the bottom of the couch. Quietly, he told me about Anton's last moments. We held each other's hands and cried.

* * *

Two weeks after Anton's death, I took an over-the-counter pregnancy test, which lit up with two strong pink lines. I was over the moon. Within a week, I found myself waking up with an intense appetite. Food was suddenly exciting, and I'd start planning all the things I was going to eat that day.

During Anton's memorial service, I wavered between intense grief for his loss, and gratitude about the pregnancy, muttering to his parting spirit. *This **must** have something to do with you! The timing—it can't be a coincidence. Can you hear me? Are you passing something of your spirit into me?*

The doctor was happy with how the pregnancy was developing. The day Simon and I saw the heartbeat, we were electrified. After the appointment, we took a long walk in Riverside Park, too awed to speak. At the three-month mark, I told everyone I was pregnant. A few days later, I was in a restaurant, at a friend's birthday dinner, when I felt something wet between my legs. In the bathroom, I discovered an ooze of bright-red blood. Too stunned to think, I returned to the table and sat there frozen, unable to say anything, even to Simon. The meal over, I pleaded a headache, left the restaurant, and burst into tears. In the taxi, I was seized with cramps that quickly turned excruciating. Simon helped me up to our apartment and called the doctor. By this time, the blood was gushing. It got all over the sheets, and the floor. I limped to the toilet in time to see a huge clot bulge out between my legs. I could not stop crying. I cried all night long. My fitful sobs seemed to come from some deep, unknown place within. The pain was unremitting, and Simon was alarmed by the amount of blood. The doctor told Simon what to watch for through the night and instructed him to bring me to his practice the next morning.

Will came over that evening for an hour and sat by the bed, neither of us saying much.

The next day, the ultrasound confirmed that there was no longer a fetus. I squeezed my eyes and peered in my mind's eye at the horrible sight of the clot in the toilet bowl before I flushed it away. Swimming up in my memory was the form of an early-stage fetus, about an inch long, such as I had seen in my textbooks when I was studying physiology. My sad little lost baby that was never to be.

The doctor told me I needed a D&C. He administered a local anesthetic, placed me in the stirrups, and turned on the medical vacuum device. The pain was intense. I gripped the nurse's arm so tightly that later, when the procedure was over, she showed me the bruise growing on her forearm.

Back home, I felt empty and bereft.

Really, Anton, I said. *What was that all about?* Maybe, I thought, you're not yet ready to reincarnate. Maybe your spirit needs more time.

I was told to wait three months before trying to get pregnant again. Your body needs to heal, the doctor said, from the trauma of the miscarriage and subsequent medical procedure.

No way, I was already thirty-four, a ticking-away number that flashed with exponentially increasing fertility problems, not something I was willing to play around with. Simon and I were preparing to spend the summer in California, where he was doing a six-week seminar. Since I could work from anywhere with my consulting job, I was able to accompany him. We settled in quickly to the faculty housing on the moody Santa Cruz campus, set in a mixed landscape—forest and open fields by a craggy coastline, jutting cliffs that cut down to the sea. Two weeks later, I discovered I was ovulating. Our lovemaking was particularly tender that night, and afterward, I lay on the bed with my legs held up against the wall for a full two hours.

"Seriously, it makes a difference," I said, an hour in.

"I know, you've read studies," Simon said warmly.

Looking into his eyes, which even after eleven years together startled me with their intimate, farseeing intelligence, I felt the purest joy and knew that deep within me, fertilization was taking place.

* * *

In the early stages of a desperately wanted pregnancy, Charlotte Brontë died of hyperemesis gravidarum, the condition marked by intense nausea, inability to eat, and relentless vomiting. I suffered from the same condition. In the grip of the illness, I ceased to exist as the person I knew myself to be. The *self* I had always taken for granted simply dissolved.

Charlotte Brontë's case was cruel. Having lost both her beloved sisters, she finally acquiesced to marry her father's curate, Arthur Bell Nicholls, who had long pursued her. Charlotte, felled by grief for her sisters, unable to find succor or happiness in any of her former pursuits, yearned for a child. Once she made the decision to marry, she found herself falling in love with Nicholls. Soon, she was pregnant. For a brief time, Charlotte was truly happy. Within weeks, she succumbed to nausea and continuous vomiting. Charlotte became emaciated and delirious, unable to maintain the epistolary correspondence that had been her lifeblood. I thought of her in her final months, exiled from her own being. At the end, in a lucid flash, she intuited her fate. Her last words to her husband were: "I am not going to die, am I? He [God] will not separate us. We have been so happy."

The violent vomiting overcame me in the fourth week of my pregnancy, the day we arrived back in New York from Santa Cruz. On my third visit to the obstetrician, I'd undressed and was sitting on the examining table, shivering in the thin examination robe, where I waited for over an hour. When he finally came in, he confessed he'd kept me waiting, rather than other patients who'd come in after me, because I was "so nice"—he knew I would not make a fuss. In that hour, I'd already vomited twice and was readying for the next go-round when the doctor, whose name I've happily forgotten, leaned close to my face, and screamed, *BOO!* And then again, *BOO!!* I startled right up off the table, the robe coming loose to reveal my nakedness. I grabbed at the robe and rushed into the adjoining bathroom to heave. When I returned, the doctor had a grin on his face.

"It's psychological, you know," he said. "A psychiatrist friend of mine told me you can startle a patient out of the vomiting."

"I see. Well, it didn't exactly work, did it."

"He didn't say it would work the first time." He shrugged.

I wasn't startled out of the condition, which properly educated doctors understand has a physiological basis (recent evidence suggests genetic changes in two hormone receptors may be involved). For most normal pregnancies, the nausea and vomiting abate after six to eight weeks. With hyperemesis gravidarum it is severe and lasts longer, in my case into the sixth month, when we moved to Chicago, where Simon had a half-year visiting professorship.

We'd rented an unfurnished apartment, so the day we arrived, we went straight to a used furniture store stocked with discarded items from Marriott Hotels. I waddled from room to room holding my extended belly, which had begun to ache—the long journey in the car, I assumed—and picked out everything we needed: beds, couch, table and chairs, side tables, lamps. Within a couple of hours, we had what we needed, and arranged to have it all delivered later that day. I was just entering my third trimester; only three more months to go.

The next morning, my abdomen hurt so badly, I had trouble getting out of bed. That night we were attending a lecture by a colleague of my husband's—on the history, ethics, and views surrounding circumcision. A lapsed Jew, I was trying to decide how I'd feel about doing the ritual circumcision were the baby to be a boy.

On the walk to the nearby lecture hall, the pain in my belly worsened. I had trouble focusing on the lecture, shifting in my seat throughout in an attempt to get comfortable. Silly to have overtaxed myself setting up the apartment, I thought. On the walk home, I had to stop every few minutes, doubling over in pain. Back home, I collapsed into bed, then called my mother in Australia. I told her about the pain. So far away, the telephone wire echoing, she tried to reassure me.

"How well I remember it," she said, having herself suffered through terrible pregnancies. "It's normal to have aches and pains. Take your mind off it. Put your feet up, read a magazine."

Sensible advice, probably, but I called my friend Barbara in New Jersey, an experienced mother of two, to ask her opinion. I described the increasingly intense pains.

"Hang up the phone this minute!" she said. "And call your doctor. Now!"

I called my doctor and described my symptoms.

"You need to come to the hospital," she said.

Forty minutes later, I was hooked up to IVs, pumped full of steroids, and wheeled to a delivery room. Turns out I was in full-blown labor, the contractions coming every five minutes, my cervix dilated.

"At twenty-four weeks, the lungs are not yet fully developed," the doctor explained calmly, walking by my side as we rapidly wheeled. "The steroids will give a push to the development."

I'd had trouble taking in everything they warned me about, though the part about the baby's probable brain damage lodged in my mind like a bullet. They had me on intravenous magnesium sulfate to slow the labor; it burned viciously as it dripped into my forearm. They were setting up for a high-risk delivery—the preemie experts were on hand. I swallowed back sobs.

In the delivery room, I gazed up at the lights, everything blurry. The oxygen mask slapped to my face put me into a self-enclosed cave; my breathing was loud in my ears, and I felt like I was inhaling the hospital's own brand of clinical hope. I drifted into a delirium and found myself thinking of my father. The nausea plaguing me plunged me back to the days we used to fly with him in the tiny aircraft, sickened by the smell of the diesel fuel, my mother throwing up in the front seat. How I felt plundered by nausea and intensely dizzy, spinning wildly. A surge of terror made me wonder if we were going into a nosedive and I found myself gripping my belly, fearing not only for my own life but also for that of my unborn baby.

I cracked open my eyes. Seeing the blurry lights overhead, I knew I was not flying in the plane with Dad, who had been dead already for seven years. I was in the hospital in Chicago, a city where I knew only my husband, whose worried face was now hovering above me in the delivery room I was not meant to have come to for another sixteen weeks.

"What's happening?" I managed to ask.

"They seem to have slowed the labor down," Simon said in the deliberate, hyper-calm voice he uses when under duress.

My arm was seared with pain all the way up to my shoulder, where the magnesium sulfate was being infused. I directed my eyes to where it ached; it looked like someone had taken a thin Sharpie to my skin and drawn a long black line the full length of my inner arm. I was having trouble breathing. I tried to gulp in air, but it wouldn't go in.

Simon followed my eyes to the black line. "Magnesium sulfate burns the vein," he said.

Panic swelled in my chest and ballooned through my body. The last thing I heard before blacking out was beeping and the sound of running feet. When I awoke, I was back on the regular ward. My arm still burned but thankfully, the oxygen delivered through the mask was flowing in and out of my lungs.

I opened my eyes to see Simon's anxious face relax into a smile.

Twelve hours on the magnesium sulfate had caused respiratory failure, so they'd had to stop the drug and restore my breathing. Miraculously, against expectations, the IV medicine had stopped the active labor, though I was still having contractions every fifteen minutes or so, which was apparently a fantastic result. I was to remain in slow labor for the rest of the pregnancy.

"Everything's changed," my doctor said. She explained that I'd need to be on complete bed rest for the rest of the pregnancy. "No getting up, no flexing of any muscles in your body, not even wiggling your toes. Muscle contraction can set the labor back into high gear."

I returned home, hooked up to a fetal heart monitor that transmitted information over the telephone line. If the contractions increased beyond four an hour, I'd return to the hospital for more IV treatment. The aim was to get to thirty weeks, when risk to the baby decreases dramatically, since development is more or less complete. Anything beyond thirty weeks would be considered a bonus.

I got used to lying in bed and not moving, occupying myself with reading, doing some work, and watching TV. A co-worker sent a porcelain bell in the mail. I'd ring it to summon Simon. I tried to keep it to a minimum, but I rang the bell often enough that he started hearing it in his sleep.

I was at the hospital almost weekly, requiring additional doses of magnesium sulfate to keep the labor at bay. Miraculously, I made it all the way to thirty-seven weeks. Then, when the contractions accelerated, the doctor cheered into the phone.

"Come on in! Time to welcome that over-eager baby to the world!"

The labor was oddly relaxing; I was finally able to relinquish worry. I let my body take over, giving in to the waves of pain and letting them carry me to that otherworldly place that felt like a joining with the earth. At the height of the pain, everything went still, and I found myself aware of Anton's presence, as if his spirit were pouring down, joining, somehow, with the bright hospital lights overhead.

Darling. I could almost hear his voice. *It's all a great passage, don't you know?*

Passage? What do you mean?

We're all just passing through—.

"The baby is crowning!" Deborah, my doctor, said.

My eyes were slits. I could see my husband's face, a blur behind the doctor's bent head.

"Come on," Deborah said. "One more strong push."

Aren't you just wonderful? Anton was beaming at me. I could feel the force of his electric smile. *Your daughter—I will know her, I can promise you that.*

But you're gone! How will you possibly know her? And how do you know it's a girl?

I'll know her from within! Have you forgotten? That was the plan, all along!

With a heaving push, the earth's wrenching, everything went silent, and then—the first cry.

"It's a girl," Deborah said, passing her to me. I took her in my arms, saw the blinking new eyes, peering from the beyond.

"My baby," I said, "my baby, my baby." I looked over the rim of the unknown into my infant's ageless, mystified gaze.

* * *

Our daughter's brown eyes were deep and knowing, almost from the start. I have a photograph of her when she was not yet two, looking into the camera with a wisdom and seriousness of purpose that is both uncanny and comical in a child still in diapers.

As it happens, she grew up to be an actor. Sometimes, looking into her eyes, I sense Anton—even imagine I see a trace of his lively, ironic smile, passing like a fugitive half shadow across her face.

~ 6 ~

There for the Taking

Eight years after that visit with Amanda to the country club, she and I both gave birth to our boys, born six weeks apart.

For six years, Amanda had been trying to have a child—not with a partner, since she had none, but with medical intervention. Time was passing, and her doctors announced that at this point, her odds of success were almost nonexistent.

My own daughter was four when I found out I was pregnant again. When I told Amanda, she embraced me closely.

"Womb to womb," she said. "Pheromones—" She closed her eyes. "Let's pray to the female gods of fertility."

She took several deep breaths—breathing in the pheromones, I supposed—then said, in a barely audible whisper, "Our sons—I can feel it. We're finally going to have our sons."

Sure enough, with the next round of fertility treatment, Amanda got pregnant. The doctors were amazed.

She was one of those healthy, glowing pregnant women; she loved every minute. She went into labor on April 25, the day before my own birthday. At eleven p.m. that evening, she called from the hospital. She'd already been in labor for hours and the delivery was not progressing. Despite the tremendous pain she was in, her voice was cheerful.

"They're telling me I'll need a caesarian," she said. "Don't you think I should have them hold off an hour? Then he can be born on *your* birthday!"

"Absolutely not!" I said, rocking my own six-week-old son in my arms. "Don't mess around with those things. Besides, let the child have his own birthday!"

They wheeled her into the operating room and her beloved baby son was born—with serious dark eyes and a shock of dark hair that curled in toddlerhood. He looked like a brooding Russian prince. Before he could talk, I would jokingly plead with him not to hold me responsible for the revolution, for deposing him and the rest of the czar's family. "I had absolutely nothing to do with it," I would say as he appraised me warily. "I promise!"

My son's hair, when it grew in, was fair and curly, and through-out his childhood, his trademark expression was one of glee, his little nose always crinkled, his ear-to-ear grin so tight that he was two years old before I realized one time, watching him sleep, that he actually had full lips! We raised the boys side by side—long week-ends together, occasional trips away, the two of them comfortable and intimate as brothers, our families joined.

One afternoon, when the boys were approaching the age of three, we were strolling down Riverside Drive alongside the park, beyond which the Hudson River glimmered in the sunlight. Amanda's son reached for my son's hand, turning his head slightly so that I could see his strong profile. My son also turned—smiling, of course. They both faced forward again, and I watched as the sunlight danced around the edges of their curly hair, making them angels with gleaming halos. I turned to see Amanda watching me. I'd never seen such calm in her face—her features, usually mobile, were utterly still. It was as if I were seeing a snapshot of her soul.

She gave the faintest nod. I reached for her hand, and we walked together in silence, our eyes on the little boys before us, walking forth into their lives.

* * *

It is twenty years since that moment on Riverside Drive. Reading over the passage above, I hold on to the moment I have re-conjured. I am fully there—breathing in the air, cooled by the canopy of leaves and by the breeze rippling over the river. It is late, I go to bed, and slip easily into sleep.

When I awaken, my heart is pounding. Nightmare shards scatter, leaving only an engulfing panic. Amanda is gone. I know she is gone, but I cannot reckon with this fact. I reach for her constantly, summon her image, try to remember what it was like to feel so wholly seen.

It is hard, these days, to reach for the moon, the way I once did—*I want, I want*. It was only after she was gone that I understood that she was tethering me: to her, to the earth, to myself.

* * *

When her son was seven years old, Amanda had a stroke. Emergency surgery revealed an aggressive brain tumor, *the size of an orange*, the surgeon said after removing it. The tumor returned and was cruelly cured with what they call "whole brain radiation." Her brain was destroyed by the treatment.

I've tried many times to write about Amanda's brutal final years and I find, quite simply, that I cannot. I have discarded a great many pages, not been able to write a great many more. I can only bring myself to put down the following spare paragraphs.

Early in what would be her final years of incapacitation, she became so emaciated, there was no recognizable sign of her former self. Even her eyes—especially her eyes—held nothing of the woman I had known: wide staring hollows in the skeleton of her face, black pits of suffering, devoid of life's spark.

While she was still able to walk—at a snail's pace, with a walker—I took her to eat at the restaurant a half block from her apartment. She refused to take a taxi.

"I'm going to walk, damn it," she said in the newly flat voice I never came to recognize. Her radiation-damaged brain had swapped out her trained, expressive voice, full of inflection and nuance, with a husky, robotic monotone. It took us forty minutes to cover the distance.

At dinner, she ate two main courses and two desserts. She was always ravenous but unable to keep on any weight.

I left her for a few minutes to run downstairs to the bathroom, where I shut myself in a stall and wept. I heard two women enter the bathroom and busy themselves at the sink.

"My god, did you see that woman? She looks like a concentration camp victim."

"She's not long for this world," the other said.

The gods were not to grant her the grace of a final sinewy dance, such as she had bequeathed, in her story, to the dancer. There, in the restaurant's basement bathroom, I couldn't stop crying. I knew she was waiting for me upstairs, the woman I no longer knew, who yet held memories of the intertwined decades of our lives, facts she would recite in that strange, flattened voice that had nothing to do with *my* Amanda. I could barely bring myself to unlock the bathroom stall and climb back up the stairs.

Some months later, when paralysis set in, she was moved temporarily to a godforsaken nursing home in the Bronx, to await a better placement. It was not easy to find a spot in a decent nursing home, though thankfully, one did materialize some months later. I cannot describe the conditions of that place—to say the management was criminally negligent is not an understatement. But I do wish to describe one visit. My daughter, sixteen years old and already committed to pursuing acting, came with me. They allowed us to enter her room after making us wait a full two hours. I suspect Amanda and her room had been in such an appalling condition of neglect that it took this long to make her barely presentable. She was propped up in an ancient hospital-chair contraption, her limbs in peculiar arrangement, like a bendy doll left askew. Her eyes flickered with recognition.

"Darlings," she croaked in a monotone, even more machine-like than before.

I don't remember what we talked about. It wasn't really talking, of course, rather a sludging of words that felt to me like despair contorted into thick auditory form. Now, something she said comes back to me: that at night, she managed to float through the walls and visit some of her fellow inmates. Yes, that's what she called them, *inmates*—one man in particular, and when she mentioned his name, she gave a wicked chuckle. She also told me she spent a lot of time thinking about her childhood home—that in that moment, she was thinking about the kitchen utensils, wondering if she still had her grandmother's marvelous metal whisk with the wooden handle.

A long silence set in. My own amorphous terror filled the room.

"Darling," I said to my daughter. "Why don't you do a monologue for *tante?*" Amanda had been fluent in French and loved all things *français*; since she was our children's only godparent, we'd settled on *tante*, the French word for auntie, as her moniker.

"Oh yes, I'd love that," Amanda said, straining to turn her neck in the direction of our daughter, who stood up and took a moment to settle into her actor's internal space.

She announced the monologue, something from *Romeo and Juliet*. As I watched her perform, I felt she was bringing the full force of her artistic spirit to every line. It felt like this would be one of the most important performances she would ever give. Toward the end, I watched as the tears began to slip from my daughter's eyes.

"You need to build it more slowly," Amanda said in her dry, altered voice, struggling to raise the one hand that still had some potential for motion. "You started at a high wattage. You need to leave yourself space to expand. Let's try it again." Ever the consummate teacher and artist, even in her tortured, addled, utterly diminished state.

My daughter, thirsty for direction and creative engagement, who'd always been in thrall to her beloved *tante*, took the note and restarted the monologue. Amanda narrowed her eyes and craned her neck. Everything she had left within her trained on my daughter's performance.

The monologue over, Amanda's eyes closed and her face relaxed into a smile.

"Yes," she said. "Yes."

* * *

The grief is vicious. It feels like my heart has been boiled in water, hardened and ruined. I avoid a great many places in New York, the city I have lived in now for two-thirds of my life, since I cannot bear the memories attached to them, though it doesn't make much difference; the memories are within and ignite in any case. The pandemic is raging, I've hardly left my home for months, and now, I trip upon a memory that comes back to me like a song, spilling happiness.

It is the last play we saw together, not long before Amanda's stroke—Vanessa Redgrave in a one-woman show based on Joan Didion's book, *The Year of Magical Thinking*. It is a grief-soaked piece about the year after the author lost both her husband and her grown daughter, her only child.

After the show, Amanda and I walked silently, arm in arm, each lost in our own thoughts while utterly together, filled with the power of the performance and everything it had stirred in us. The streets were dense with people, all of us bathed in the thousands of New York City lights that obscure the moon and turn the night sky to a glowing white membrane. We both had young children to get home to, so we walked for only a half hour. We reached Fifty-Ninth Street, where she would take the Number 1 train uptown and I would get on the A train to Brooklyn, where Simon and I had moved when our daughter was a baby. We stopped and faced each other, reached for each other's hands. Her face was lit from within—how her intelligent eyes gleamed with life, how generous her affirming smile.

"Another superlative evening at the theater," she said, giving a flourish to her pronunciation of *the-a-ter*, mimicking the way her mother, Patrice, used to say it. "And *no one* I'd rather have seen it with."

She studied my face for a moment, her eyes serious and mischievous.

"Don't say it," she said, her smile hovering.

"But I do! I wish we were neighbors again! That we could see each other *every day*, that—"

"No, no, no," she said in her mock-teacher voice. "Let's not bemoan what we don't have—let's celebrate what we *do* have."

"I know," I said. "But—"

"Tsstsst—" She snapped open my own palm and pressed it against my mouth.

"We were together all evening, and we're together right now—*that is all ye know on earth, and all ye need to know.*"

She threw her arms around me, planted an exaggerated, loud, smacking kiss on my cheek, then spun around, and headed toward her subway entrance, doing a little hip-wiggling salsa dance. I stood and watched her, waiting for her to turn around and give me her quick dazzle-smile, but something distracted her—I saw her tugging on her coat pocket, as if the zipper were stuck, and then she disappeared down the stairs.

* * *

Amanda's son was seventeen when his mother finally died. She'd been in a nursing facility, several hours' drive from where her son spent his high school years living with a family with whom he'd formed a close connection in the early years of Amanda's infirmity.

I arranged a memorial service, which took place several months after her death. I chose an off-kilter place uptown, not far from where she'd lived in the sprawling apartment I'd first entered more than three decades earlier. It was a party room above a small store-front Greek Orthodox church. I'd booked it online, so I only met the person in charge on the day of the event. That person turned out to be the priest, a man in his seventies with a full beard, who shuffled to the door in slippers and an ancient smoking jacket. He chain-smoked through our encounter.

I was jangled by nerves from the moment I woke up that morning. I felt as if I were about to unravel, as if the universe were rattling the bones in my ears. I knew Amanda was gone but also knew this to be hardly possible. I felt a dogged commitment to the memorial service, as to a bureaucratic rite of passage, like taking the SATs. But I also felt a tender devotion. An insight flashed within—something about birth and death that I couldn't quite lay hold of.

The priest wanted to tell me about the history of their little storefront church. I listened as best I could, coughing from the smoke that billowed around him. I found myself obsessing about the caterers—would they arrive on time? Had I ordered enough food, or instead overdone it? Surely fifty mini-éclairs were too many? And does anyone even like spinach dip these days?

The food showed up on time, a perfect spread. Minutes later, everyone arrived, forty or so people, filling the room and spilling warmth and good cheer. I had not seen most of them for some years. I excused myself and went to the bathroom, where I sat on the closed toilet and did my best to meditate, trying to tune out the stale bathroom odors as I filled my lungs with air and then slowly breathed out, over and over, counting, until I could feel the calm taking hold.

By the time I asked the group to quieten so we could begin, the shakiness was gone. I felt centered, present, ready to speak.

I found myself mostly addressing my words to Amanda's son, who sat in the front, alert and utterly still, his eyes little-boy bright. I spoke about the day Amanda and I met and gave a brief account of our friendship.

Afterward, a small group of us headed downtown for dinner. I walked with him.

"Thank you for arranging this," he said. "You know, it really was something to hear everyone talk about my mother. It means a lot to me to hear what she was like."

"Do you remember much about her? From before?" I asked.

He hung his head a little as he shook it, *no*.

The dinner was boisterous; lots of talking and laughing. Amanda's son sat with my kids. We had seen little of him in recent years. He lived far away. And I suspect our home was a difficult reminder for him of a great many things associated with his mother and her terrible decline.

After dinner, we walked along Riverside Drive, headed toward the subway where we would be going in different directions. I was walking with my husband; Amanda's son was up ahead with my daughter and son. My daughter ran ahead for a moment to speak to someone else. I watched the two boys. Earlier, they'd been talking about which colleges they planned to apply to. One of them must have said something amusing; they laughed at the same time, turning to look at each other. I saw their faces in profile—two youths on the cusp of manhood, both tall and lean, one with curly dark hair, the other with curly light hair, framed by the milky white light of a streetlamp. I realized there was another source of light pulsing down. I turned my head upward to see the sky holding its dusk, the light dull but true, readying to slip away. And there, the moon, flat white against the deepening gray, unusually low-slung, there for the taking.

~ 7 ~

What Do You Do
Once You Have Seen God?

When our daughter was nine and our son was four, we decided to pack up our lives in New York and move for a year to Pátzcuaro, a moody colonial town in the south-central mountains of Mexico, having spent the previous two summers there. My husband had a Fulbright fellowship to study beliefs among the Indigenous Purépecha people. I had a grant to work on a book, which allowed me to take a year's leave from my consulting work. Our family culture was one of moving around, exploring different countries and languages. The ongoing series of displacements was, I suppose, creating its own sense of belonging—to a movable, outsider kind of life, an external, exploratory roaming. The day I became a US citizen, after twenty-seven years in the country, I realized it was the third citizenship I'd held, spanning three continents—Africa, Australia, North America.

I fell in love with Pátzcuaro at first sight. It was a long trek from New York: plane to Mexico City, taxi ride across the sprawling metropolis to the central bus station, then a four-hour ride to Morelia, the capital of Michoacán, and another hour in a rickety local bus to our destination. This was a ride through exquisitely shaggy countryside, passing roadside food stands with bright-blue tarpaulins stretched above the tables as shelter, under which were family clusters with mothers tending babies, the men smoking and talking. We passed lean-tos and the ever-present half-built

dwellings; donkeys and horses and goats; and American trucks
from the 1950s and 1960s in various states of disrepair, everything
functioning into an absurdly old age.

When the bus lumbered around the corner and I caught my
first sight of the town's main square, Plaza Grande, the splendor
knocked the breath from me. Massive trees towered crookedly above
tailored lawns and stone walkways, all surrounded by impressive
colonial-era buildings, scuffed at the edges. Rising from the large
pool of water in the center of the square was an elaborate pedestal
bearing a bronze statue of Vasco de Quiroga, the Spanish benefactor
of the region. In 1538 he swooped in to remove his vicious prede-
cessor, who had tortured and murdered the last Tarascan emperor,
and whose brutality had caused the local population to flee. De
Quiroga encouraged the Indigenous Peoples to return to the area.

The colonial invasion felt raw to me from the start, alive in the
faces of the people. The mood of the place struck me: serene and
without angst, so at odds with the edgy ambiance of New York
City, with its blaring ambition and clawing struggle, where I'd spent
the previous twenty years of my life. As a newcomer in Pátzcuaro,
I felt an odd disjunction between the easygoing daily life, the calm
wisdom that shone from people's eyes, and the layers of displacement, of conquering and enforced subjugation. But in the sense of
rootedness and connection—families cleaving together, involved in
shared, ongoing endeavors—I also intuited a strange, peaceful truce
with awful historical truths.

My own history involved being culturally and geographically
displaced in more ways than I could clock, the generational expul-
sions and wanderings coursing through my veins. Born in South
Africa, to parents who were the children of Lithuanian and Latvian
refugees, I had grown up in a close-knit Jewish community in
Australia, lived for a time in Israel, and then moved to the United
States, where I married a man whose mother was Icelandic and
whose father had been raised in the Protestant Midwest.

We enrolled our children in a local school in Pátzcuaro, a
cabin on stilts in the middle of a little wooded area, built of planks

cobbled together. When a new neighbor asked my daughter how her New York school was different from this one, she replied, "In Brooklyn, the light doesn't come through the walls. I guess they're made of brick."

Here were our kids, of mixed heritage and being raised a kind of default no-religion, since we'd never figured out what we were going to do on that front, beginning the school year in Spanish, among children from a world entirely foreign to us. Since our children's Spanish was still rudimentary, they struggled. Our four-year-old son's teacher told us our son spent much of the day sitting under his desk.

"I'm escaping," he said, when I asked why he was doing a thing like that. "Maybe she can't see me under there."

His teacher tried to coax him out.

"The only time he's happy," she said, "is when he sees his sister in the schoolyard."

Our daughter, shy at the best of times, withdrew even further than him.

"We're doing what we can," her teacher said. "I'm sure she'll be fine once she picks up the language. Children are sponges—just give her a few weeks."

Change had never been easy for our daughter; all this newness was perhaps too much.

"You can sit in the schoolyard," my daughter said. "It will help. I can look out the window and see you."

Okay, I thought, whatever it takes. I was reading an extraordinary book by Amos Elon about the intellectual history of German Jews from the mid-eighteenth century until the beginning of World War II. I was happy to read on the bench in the clearing that served as the playground, under a sprawling jacaranda tree, its riot of purple bell-shaped blooms scenting the air with honey. My focus was half tuned to my daughter, who I knew was struggling up in her stilt-borne classroom, the unfamiliar language sticking like barbs in her throat. The other half of my attention flowed to what I was reading. The book begins with the image of a thin Jewish youth standing in line to enter the city of Berlin. It is 1743 and the boy is the brilliant Moses Mendelssohn, who would go on to become one of Germany's greatest thinkers, but because he is a Jew, he must enter the city at the gate reserved for cattle. Considered subhuman by the Germans in charge, he is subject to the same entry tax imposed on the cows.

Day after day, sitting under the jacaranda tree in this quiet Mexican town, the bright sun shining down, I turned the pages, on through two centuries of both persecution and intellectual flourishing, until, toward the end, I encountered an extraordinary detail.

During World War I, Jews could, for the first time, serve as officers in the German army. It was the dawn of the twentieth century and Jews had finally been integrated and accorded equal treatment. One of these Jewish officers, Hugo Gutmann, unwittingly influenced history. Casualties were high among regimental dispatch runners, whose task it was to get messages where they needed to go, often in the face of extreme danger. Ahead of a particularly dangerous mission, Gutmann promised his runners that, if they got the message through and returned home alive, he would see that they'd be awarded the Iron Cross for bravery. Two runners indeed succeeded, but when Gutmann appealed to his commander to award them the Iron Cross, his request was denied, saying that the runners' success was not particularly exceptional. Gutmann spent hours arguing his case and, in the end, prevailed. He pinned the Iron Cross himself to the soldiers' chests. One of these soldiers was Adolf Hitler.

Some twenty years later, the German government was in violent disarray when Paul von Hindenburg, then president of the German Weimar Republic, well into his eighties and likely suffering from dementia, was pressured into appointing a new chancellor: the fanatical head of the minority Nazi Party—just for a short time, just to establish order. According to one account, the matter of the Iron Cross came up. Surely Hitler couldn't be the dangerous clown he appeared to be—after all, he was a war hero. He'd been awarded this highest medal of bravery. Since the fanatical clown declared martial law the day after he took office, it was not, of course, to be only a short time that he'd be in power.

Here, we find bookends to two centuries of German Jewish life: Moses Mendelssohn, marked as a cow, and six million Jews, slaughtered as cattle, whose deaths were orchestrated by the man who'd had the Iron Cross pinned to his chest by his commanding officer, a Jew.

I thought about my own parents, Eastern European Jews, who had never felt at home in South Africa, in Nazi-sympathizing Afrikaner territory. After a long and difficult journey for my mother, traveling alone with three young children (our father had gone ahead to find employment and a home), I landed in sunburnt Australia, my own parents carrying the sound of immigration in their accented speech. Then, as a newly minted adult, I sent myself across the oceans to live in the United States where, to this day, because of my Australian accent, people ask me where I'm from.

And yet, sitting in the schoolyard in that remote Mexican town, the people Amos Elon brought to life felt like *landsmen*, and as I followed their tales, I found myself feeling like I was winding my way home. It was gloriously mild and sunny, and I would frequently look up from the book to observe the play of light falling through the leaves onto the dry dirt. At recess, my daughter would bound down the stairs for a hug and sit nearby to eat her lunch, stealing glances my way. Then, a quick goodbye before steeling herself to return to the classroom.

At the end of the second week, however, the principal emerged from his office and crossed the yard wearing an unyielding expression.

"I'm sorry," he said. "This is a place for children, not adults. You're going to have to leave."

In my own faulty Spanish, I tried to explain my daughter's difficulty—that she was shy, and everything was new: the language, the town, the culture, the kids.

"No." He shook his head firmly. "I'm sorry. You need to leave."

I gathered my things, my heart in my throat. At that moment, the recess bell rang, and kids spilled from their classrooms, first among them my daughter, who caught sight of me walking dejectedly toward the exit at the far side of the yard.

From the landing of the rickety wooden staircase, she called out, "What are you *doing*? Where are you *going*?"

Normally reserved and impeccably behaved, she was suddenly oblivious to decorum, impervious to the eyes that turned her way.

"Darling, I need to go now," I called up to where she stood on the landing, looking tiny and defenseless. "I'll be back later to pick you up."

"*No!*" she cried, sending a knife through my heart. "You *can't leave*!!!"

Her teacher's face was kind; she nodded encouragement to me, signaled that I should leave, taking hold of my daughter from behind, clasping her closely.

"Bye, darling, I love you!" I said in as calm and supportive a voice as I could manage, given that my heart was anxiously leaping about. "You'll be okay, I promise!"

All of me wanted to rush up the stairs and whisk my little girl away, back home to drink hot chocolate and do a fun art project. But I knew that would not be the right thing to do—the easy thing in the moment, certainly, but not a good strategy for inculcating resilience in a sensitive child, for teaching her to feel strong in the face of a challenging world. I knew I needed to convey to her that she really *would* be okay. We had come to live here so that our children could experience this new culture, learn the language, be the kinds of people who could take on worthy challenges and then rise to them.

"Don't go!" she cried, the decibels rising. "*Don't leave me!*"

I put one foot in front of the other, pausing at the gate to give a final weak little wave. All the way down the long dirt alley, my ears echoed with her cry.

She's courageous, however, and my daughter went back the next day and the day after that, her face determined, if gloomy.

I decided to send an encouraging note in with her lunch, to help her get through her day. I quickly realized I'd have to expand my range to keep my daughter's interest, so I started including recipes and jokes, along with aphorisms and ironic asides about life in a foreign country. She's since told me that looking forward to those lunchtime notes sustained her until it was time to come home.

As our daughter struggled to find her place in this culture we'd thrown her into, I found a new sense of home in the pages of Amos Elon's book, sitting now in an outdoor café on the Plaza Chica, our new little puppy, Sparky, whom we'd found in a nearby village, in my lap. Elon's wild collection of thinkers, scientists, and activists seized my attention, their work and reflections jostling in my imagination like so many spinning lassos. Most were assimilated Jews; many felt more German than Jewish, some having converted to Christianity, like Abraham Mendelssohn, the son of Moses, whose famous composer son, Felix, baptized at the age of seven, penned some of the greatest church music ever written. And yet there was, for many of these people, some tug deep within, no matter how far they had removed themselves from their Jewish origins—*dark urgings of the blood*, as Martin Buber put it—that was inevitable and primal. I closed the book for a moment and looked across the square to the towering Templo de San Agustín with its worn clay brick, now a public library, aware of a new and almost electric inner attunement—yes, those dark urgings, I could feel them in my own pulse.

Amos Elon was my guide. I learned from him that the German Jewish political theorist, Hannah Arendt, used to say that her own best friend was a woman named Rahel Varnhagen, a Jewish writer who'd run a famous literary salon more than a century before Hannah Arendt was born. I thought about that friendship, traversing the life-death boundary, between two strong, iconoclastic, intellectual pioneers in those eras of soul-crushing constraint for women, and of repression and persecution of Jews. I thought about Hannah Arendt in 1933, whizzing through the darkness on the night train to Prague. She and her mother had been arrested by the Gestapo for her pro-Jewish activities and they'd spent eight days in prison. Released to await trial, they knew they had to flee. She left everything behind—family, community, home—turning within to her "best friend" Rahel Varnhagen for solace, inspiration, and advice.

I once set out to write a story that took this moment as its source, giving it the title "On the Night Train to Prague." But I could only take it so far. I would see Arendt sitting on the train as it speeds through the night, her entire life slammed shut, the world undone in ways she could scarcely comprehend. Staring out into the night, thinking about her lover—incomprehensibly, she'd been having an affair with the Nazi-sympathizing philosopher Martin Heidegger—her own philosophical thoughts whirling in frightening disarray. I wanted to know her better, more deeply, wished to commit her thoughts and feelings to the page, and to paint the surrounds of her circumstances (the word *commit*, here, rings with the sense of a crime).

Stop! I could feel my mind shutting down, screeching to a halt. *No!*

For some reason, I felt acutely that here, I had no right to tread. With a billowing sense of loss, I put away the pages I had written, leaving Hannah Arendt to her privacy as she sped away those many years ago (*no, it's all happening, it's happening still*) on the night train to Prague.

Since then, there have been other stories I fell into that felt like mine, but that I walked away from because I felt I had no right to them. The one that incurred the greatest sense of loss involved Joseph Roth, a Galician Austrian writer born in 1882, best known for his magnum opus, *The Radetzky March*. This never-completed novella of mine, "My Friend Ernst Toller Has Hanged Himself," written while we were living in Mexico, imagines a rather fantastical version of the events leading up to Roth's untimely death on May 27, 1939.

An assimilated Jew, Roth served in the Imperial Habsburg Army during World War I. By the end of his life, he considered himself a Catholic. Once the highest-paid German-language journalist, he left Berlin when Hitler rose to power in 1933 and spent the last six years of his life mostly in Paris. As a Jew—who only fifteen years earlier had served in the German army—he was banned from writing for German publications, and was therefore deprived of his livelihood, reduced to living on the pittance he could make churning out novels for expatriate Germans.

Roth lived almost his entire adult life in hotels. In late May of 1939, Roth received a letter in his Paris hotel, telling him that his friend, the playwright Ernst Toller, had killed himself. Toller, also a Jew, had fled Germany through literary connections and was living in New York. The night Roth got the letter about Toller, he spent the evening drinking heavily; he collapsed and was taken to hospital. Four days later, was dead. Literary scholars speculate that Roth deliberately drank himself to death, no longer able to tolerate what was happening in the world. In private letters, Roth prophesied Nazi horrors he would not live to fully know about, though he knew enough—Kristallnacht had taken place six months earlier.

I imagined Joseph Roth's despair, imagined words had finally failed him—no longer any still point from which he could describe, assess, or interpret, no place from which the vantage of *voice* meant anything at all. As I reached for the story, my own vantage point was swallowed in the vortex. And while the story I had in mind was vividly alive, it turned to ash the moment I tried to bind it to the page.

The Roth story I crafted in my mind went something like this. After a day walking around Paris, struggling to come up with a new novel he might serialize for a few francs (all he could now command), Roth heads back to his hotel, despondent and worn out. He can no longer write with his former wit and ease: the world has taken that away from him, along with everything else. Paris has yet to be occupied, but he knows that the end of the world is fast approaching, as he had written to his friend, the playwright Stefan Zweig, six years earlier, in 1933:

> You will have realized by now that we are drifting toward great catastrophes. Apart from the private— our literary and financial existence is destroyed—it all leads to a new war. I won't bet a penny on our lives. They [the Nazis] have succeeded in establishing a reign of barbarity. Do not fool yourself. Hell reigns.

On his way back to the hotel, Roth stops at the liquor store to spend the last of his money on two quarts of whiskey. The bottles are heavy. He pauses to look through the windows of the café bar on the ground floor. Sometimes he sits at the bar late into the night, but tonight he wants solitude.

He pauses at the desk to pick up his mail. The clerk hands him the usual small bundle, tied with twine. The top letter shows the handwriting of an old friend he's not heard from in a long time. His stomach lurches. So much bad news, it comes in every batch.

Upstairs, Joseph pours himself a drink and then opens the letter. His eyes hover over the first line, seeing the words and yet failing to take them in.

> I am heartbroken writing this to you, Joseph. Our dear friend, Ernst Toller, has hanged himself. He was in New York, as you know. I've been told he received a letter informing him that his brother and sister were sent to a concentration camp. The letter was found on the floor.

Ernst Toller, a well-known German playwright, had in 1919 been a key player in a serious, if somewhat absurdist, political coup. For six days, he was president of the socialist "Bavarian Soviet Republic," a political circus that left many people dead, including ten innocent hostages executed in cold blood (Toller supposedly tried to prevent these executions), and hundreds of citizens caught in the crossfire of hastily assembled armies populated by factory and other workers. The Soviet-backed communists overcame the smaller, inadequately trained forces of the socialists, establishing a feuding rivalry between the two sides that some historians argue could be associated with Hitler's rise to power; had they united, they might perhaps have managed to secure a dominance in parliament. (Of course, there were multiple other factors in play, such as the easy exploitation of President Hindenburg's toothless authority.) The Republic was quickly routed. Many of its leaders, and over a thousand communists and socialists, were executed, with scores more imprisoned. Toller himself spent five years in jail. To some, he was an inspiring hero in the ongoing fight against fascism, though much of the populace was left with an intense hatred of socialists. During his imprisonment, Toller wrote many of his important works. But even for this rash, seemingly indomitable spirit, the world had become too much to bear.

Roth struggles with the image now gripping his imagination: his beloved friend, Ernst Toller, alone in a hotel room, fashioning a noose, finding a place to secure it, and then climbing up onto a chair and kicking it away.

Holding the letter, trying to absorb its contents, Joseph hears a knock at the door. This is unusual. No one comes to his room, and were someone to venture a visit, the clerk would've called up to announce their arrival. But Joseph is in no state to think anything through. He takes three steps forward and opens the door.

I am standing there, in the hallway. He sees me, a woman in her early thirties. Pale skin, dark hair and eyes, with the prominent features stereotypically associated with Jews, and the look of someone who is not from Europe.

After arriving in Vienna as a young man, Roth had dropped his first name, Moses, eager to dispel his Jewish and Eastern European origins. He'd worked to erase the Galician accent that marked him as a peasant and had fabricated origin stories for himself—that his father was an Austrian railway official or a Polish count. In fact, his father had been a grain buyer who suffered a psychiatric breakdown, abandoning the family when Joseph was very young, to live in Poland under the care of a "wonder rabbi." In my imagined encounter with Roth, I find myself using this given name, Moses. He does not seem to flinch. I sense he has noticed my uncommon accent, not British, but close. He sees distress in my eyes, but also, I imagine, the warmth that I feel toward him, and something steady, though I sense he also tunes into the propensity I have for stormy emotions. (I recall that he once described himself in a letter to Zweig in a similar way.)

"I don't know why I'm here," I say in my heavily accented French. "I only know I had to see you."

"Where did you come from?" Joseph asks. Not the usual locution—*where are you from?*

"I'm from Australia." I hesitate. "But that's not exactly where I've come from."

I can see that Joseph is aware of something uncanny about the situation—about my presence, about me.

"May I come in?" I ask.

Joseph stands aside, and I enter.

"Drink?" he asks.

I nod, and he pours whiskey into a tumbler with the hotel name embossed at the bottom in red.

"I've read your books," I say. "Pretty much all of them."

He shows surprise, wondering if it is possible that I read German. He can have no idea that one day, many of his books will be translated into English. I note disappointment in his face.

"I haven't tracked you down because I'm a fan. Truly, I'm not stalking you."

Stalking, what an odd word, Joseph thinks. For him, there is something preternatural about me; I seem different from any women he's ever known—in my manner, my facial expressions, the way I move, as if I exist in a new and utterly strange way, from another time and place.

"Fräulein," he says, "I have no idea who you are. You haven't introduced yourself."

I give my name.

"I've not heard that name before," he says. "It sounds Hebrew. Is it biblical?"

"It *is* Hebrew," I reply. I want to say "Modern Hebrew" but stop myself, knowing this would only complicate things, aware that I am standing with Joseph Roth in his hotel room in May 1939. The State of Israel has yet to be founded, nine years ahead in the future, not an event Joseph Roth will live to see. "But no, not biblical."

"So," he says, gesturing that I take a seat.

There are two chairs in the room, and a tiny café table like those downstairs in the bar, along with a single bed, a small desk, and a short square bureau. The room has a sink and a shelf for supplies. Joseph tracks my eyes as they come rest on the two bottles of liquor removed moments earlier from the string shopping bag now lying shrunken on the table.

"I've been wanting to come for a very long time," I say. "I want to ask you something."

He looks at me kindly, raises his hand and nods.

"How did you do it? Write about everything that was happening, and yet manage to go on?"

I see in his face that the question at once surprises him but also feels expected, as if it is exactly the right question—obvious, but not unwelcome.

"I saw it as my duty," he says. "What else might I have done?"

I remember Joseph's wife, Friedl, the woman he married when young who suffered a psychotic break, four years after their wedding. For the rest of Roth's life, Friedl's suffering would weigh heavily on him. The financial burden of paying for her sanatorium plunged him into poverty from which he never recovered. He would not live to know that in the end, the Nazis would remove her from the sanctuary he had funded and exterminate her in a gas chamber as part of their eugenics program.

"Besides, I had responsibilities. Writing has always been my livelihood."

"It was different when you were in Poland," I say, thinking of the books he wrote about the Jews of the Polish shtetls, who lived in dire poverty: one a blazing, agonizing novel, another a nonfiction account of his extensive travels in the region. Both shone a light on an ignored, unknown people.

"There was still hope," he says, grief in his face. "The words had a purpose."

"And now?"

He gives me a long, appraising look.

"You know the answer to that as well as I do," he says, his eyes deep with mourning. He drains his glass and pours another, noting the lowered level in the bottle.

"I understood quite early in life that we writers have little choice about what we see. And that means seeing it all. Not *both sides*, but *many variants*. You know what I mean."

I nod, since I do know what he means.

"How charged I felt when I read Keats's journals. He ached to the tips of his fingers to *get it all down*. How mortified he felt, to think he might not get to describe *everything* before he died. A premonition, since he was to die so young. He was not to know that there was a gift in this. That he would only ever know and understand the experience and visions of youth. The vital, hot sun, giving life to all the beauty on this earth. Ah, the nightingale's song …"

Joseph stares across the room, his eyes resting on the window, which shows the waning light.

"Yes, he understood something of mortality—but his was a sweet melancholy. He died before he ever had to encounter the Devil."

Joseph appears to have forgotten I am here; he seems in conversation with himself. "When I was young, and first experienced those ecstatic fits of artistic creation, I remember wondering—*What do you do, once you have seen God?* All artists must wonder this when they first taste their own creative power. It's in every word of Keats, since he never lived to have it taken away.

"How little I knew, then, thinking that the greatest grief would be not knowing how to live in ordinary reality. As if *flatness* were the worst possible curse …"

Joseph turns to me. I see he is, in fact, keenly aware of my presence. Could it be that in this moment, he is feeling a sense of duty toward *me*? I see he feels compelled to convey something.

"What I never thought to ask myself," he says, "is what do you do once you have seen *hell*? Once you fully grasp that man is both God and Devil, you understand that in some sense that they must be one and the same."

"You mean—that there *is* no God?"

"Not exactly."

I recall that Joseph was thought to have converted from Judaism to Catholicism, late in his life.

"Do you see the Jewish God and the Catholic God as one and the same?" I ask.

"Well, of course, that is the point, isn't it?" he says. "Jews do not really have a concept of the Devil. That's where they get it wrong."

"Is that why you converted?" I ask, my voice a whisper.

I know I am treading on intrusive ground, but he does not seem to mind. I realize that Joseph is open to anything I may ask—that I have license to go wherever I please. This makes me a little giddy, though I am also aware of the dread, knowing the strange reality I am in, knowing that while I may have been granted this privileged license with a man I admire beyond reckoning, I am actually powerless to intervene in any meaningful way. All I can do is have the conversation—perhaps not nothing, but in the scheme of things, not so very much.

"Well, yes," he says, looking a bit startled, as if he'd never thought of it quite that way. "It was not such a conscious intent. There was a contradiction, for me, in the fact that though there is no conception of the Devil in the Jewish faith—God has no adversary besides the human beings he supposedly created—the Jewish God is ferocious and unforgiving. Look at what God makes of family. Cain and Abel, for a start. Abraham and Isaac. We're supposed to think well of Abraham for being willing to murder his son—and to see God's sparing of Isaac as an act of mercy.

"Catholicism recognizes our barbarity—takes it out of God's hands, puts it where it belongs. Within human beings. We slaughter not because God has commanded us to, but because we are vile. The Devil is within us. There is no godliness without the shadowy presence of the Devil. And yet, there is ever the chance of redemption."

I could hear what Joseph was saying in words, but something else was going on. He was not speaking to convince *me*, that seemed perfectly clear. Who, then, was he trying to sway?

"And yet—" I say.

He smiles. "Yes," he says, his eyes piercing but also warm. "And yet—"

"Do you believe, then, in the Sacrament?"

He shakes his head, as an old man might shake his head, wisely and with indulgence, knowing I am too young to have any inkling of what he means.

"No, I do not. But it is a lovely idea, no? The idea that grace is possible through the hallowed life of a spiritual being far wiser, more compassionate, than any of us have any hope of being. In this way, we can help each other. Each of us in his or her own way. We see what we see, we do our best to give it voice, to—I don't know, *get through*."

Joseph takes quick, short sips from his glass but then remembers the letter he has just opened. For a moment, my sudden appearance had made the news of his friend's death unreal. My gaze falls on the letter, and he sees my eyes fill with sorrow.

"Is *that* why you've come?" he asks, suddenly cognizant of the irrational fact that I know what the letter contains.

I nod, but when I next speak, it has nothing to do with the letter. "But I also wanted to talk with you about Heinrich Heine."

"You've come to talk with me about Heinrich Heine," he says, nonplussed.

Roth had a lifelong literary relationship with Heine, who died long before Roth was born. Both were Jews who considered themselves Christians. Both had written about the oppressed Jews of their age, illuminating their dignity, despite degraded conditions. Both had intuited something terrifying in "the German character" that would, they prophesied, wreak havoc not only on the Jews but also on the world.

I nod, though I had no idea this was the reason I'd come until I heard Joseph echoing back my words.

"He died thirty-eight years before you were born, but I sometimes get you two mixed up. He saw things before they happened, the way you have. One day, people will wish they'd listened to you both."

"May I ask what exactly you are referring to?"

"Something Heine said—*Where they burn books, they will, too, in the end burn people.*" My eyes well with tears.

Joseph sets down his drink, really listening now.

"He also said this." I pause for a moment, wanting to make sure I accurately recall Heine's words.

> 'German thunder is certainly German, and is rather awkward, and comes rolling along rather tardily; but come it surely will, and when ye once hear a crash the like of which in the world's history was never heard before, then know that the German thunderbolt has reached its mark. At this crash the eagles will fall dead in mid-air, and the lions in Africa's most distant deserts will cower and sneak into their most royal dens. A drama will be enacted in Germany in comparison with which the French Revolution will appear a harmless idyll.'

"I know," I say, nodding, as if he's said something, although he hasn't. "You said much the same thing yourself."

I find it suddenly too hard to look into his face, recalling a rare photograph I once saw of him that seared into my imagination. Roth is on a train platform, wearing a trench coat and a weathered fedora, seated on his suitcase, writing in a notepad. There is no indication he knows he is being photographed. I imagine the picture was taken by his lover of two years, the writer Irmgard Keun, with whom he traveled around Europe. Perhaps they were in Poland, where he visited an endless string of villages filled with desperately poor Jews, fervent in their religious devotion, almost delirious with hunger, people he brings to vivid life in his book, *The Wandering Jews*. In the book, he describes entire villages of redheads, a strain likely descended from some intercession of Celts, or Viking marauders. Hasidic Jews with frizzy orange beards and springy tight side-coils requiring extra work to tame into prayer curls. Little red-headed girls helping their mothers cook what food there is to be had, root vegetables mostly, almost never the sound of a chicken being slaughtered. And reed-thin boys, young scholars who rock for hours over broadsheets of the Talmud. From within this milieu, Roth found his unforgetta-ble novel *Job*, discovering on his journey through Poland that the biblical character was alive and flailing all over the unyielding coun-tryside, crouched in villages surrounded by hostility, the stench of pogrom conflagrations in their nostrils.

There he sits in that photograph, on his battered suitcase, for all eternity, gazing away from the camera into the literary space of his notepad, squinting to see what he was born to see. The sight of him there moves me unspeakably to a grief that involves love and loss, connection and beauty and trauma, and ultimately a kind of help-lessness that is knowing and wise and bereft. Joseph Roth, sitting on that train platform, was embedded in his historical moment, one of particular brutality and horror. My own historical moment is of course entirely different, bleak in its way, but with a level of personal safety and privilege that would have been inconceivable for Roth, or his friend Ernst Toller, to imagine. The photograph is repro-duced in the frontispiece of one of Roth's books. I have spent long moments gazing at it, trying to see through the page, into Joseph's experience. As I looked at that photograph, I was always gripped by a propulsive feeling that, from within my own undeserved context of peculiar safety and plenitude, it is my responsibility to keep the light shining on him, to connect with him in that moment on the train platform and then later—here, in this moment, as he sits in his hotel room in Paris, downing glass after glass of the alcohol that will poison him to death.

Opening almost any page written by Roth reveals he was a master of the lightning-fast picture, painted in words. Here are a few snippets:

> On Sundays the world is as bright and empty as a balloon. Girls in white dresses wander about the streets like so many church bells, all smelling of jasmine, sex, and starch.

> I have never seen the mother except in a blue dressing gown. She is very quiet, I think she was born in slippers, and I'm sure she has a shuffling and embittered soul.

In *The Radetzky March*, he describes a disagreeable nobleman, riding around in his barouche:

> ... small, ancient, and pitiful, a little yellow oldster with a tiny wizened face in a huge yellow blanket ... he drove through the brimming summer like a wretched bit of winter.

Roth could not have known, sitting on his suitcase, that one day the young woman now in his hotel room—me, that is, visiting him from a future that is also, on the page, an eternal present—would spend long moments gazing at the photographic image of him on the platform, waiting for him to look up from his notebook into the lens of the camera (perhaps, seeing Irmgard, his lover, he will smile—I've never seen a photograph of Joseph Roth smiling), to look directly at me.

In the hotel room, I see that Joseph does not read any of this in my face, though he does intuit that I am wondering, *Why have I come? There is nothing I can do, nothing at all.*

Joseph picks up his glass, downs its contents in one gulp, and then pours another.

This is part of the story I have tried to write so many times. The story feels like mine, and yet I also know that it is his story, and *not* mine. Sometimes I am able to purloin and sometimes not; I am not always this conflicted. I rise, give Joseph Roth one last wistful look, then turn, and leave the room. *Leave it be*, I say to myself, under my breath, though not without a deep sense of personal loss. *Just let it alone.*

I've heard those words before and uttered in just that tone: *Leave it be*. And now, I recall where.

In the first novel I wrote, *A Mind of Winter*, Marilyn, a protagonist, is a World War II photographer who spent months in London during the siege, documenting the devastation wrought by Nazi bombers. After a brutal bombing, Marilyn comes upon a child, perhaps five years old, standing before the ruins of his home. He is the only survivor. He toys at the ashes with his foot, worrying at a scrap of twisted metal. The sky glows with uncanny beauty, the horizon streaked mustard yellow and bloody purple by poisonous gases set alight by the sunrise. Luminous cloud glides overhead and a tentative beam of light angles through, illuminating the boy, who suddenly freezes, as if awaiting the eye of Marilyn's lens. Peering into the viewfinder, the scene before her comes into focus. She sees it: his world, our world, the violence and grief of it all. The cloud is moving, in a fraction of a second the light she needs to capture all this, to *say it*, will be gone. Her finger hangs over the shutter release. The camera has been an extension of her since she picked up her father's Leica when she was not much older than the boy before her, his foot still in the ash. She hesitates. It is the most beautiful frame she has ever made—*stolen* is the word that comes to mind— the most awful, and everywhere around her is the acrid miasma of truth. *Take it*, a voice whispers in her ear. *Take the shot*. The sun moves in its wide arc and the colors start to leak. The purple fades to magenta, then pink, the poison leached away, leaving a trail of fairy dust. *Don't let it escape.* She hears the final, stabbing sound of the shutter.

She knows the moment it is done that the picture is extraordinary, that she has never taken—will never again take—a photograph like this. She sees it in full Technicolor, a premonition, on the cover of *Life* magazine. A wave of nausea passes through her, and she lets her hands fall. The camera thuds against her chest, its leather strap slapping her neck painfully. She presses hot tears away with her fists. In that moment, she cannot know that the photograph will make her famous, but she does know this: that the viewfinder will never again offer her peaceful solitude and escape from trouble as it had almost the whole of her life, right up until that awful, ecstatic moment.

I suspect I knew in some secret part of my being that one day, the words on the page would no longer serve me as they once did— no longer a space of learning and growth, refuge, inspiration, and solace. Writing had been for me a horizon of adventure, providing the coordinates of exploration, the ground I walked on and the air I breathed, my anchor to both the world and me. But I, too, would one day find myself stranded in a wasteland that no effort would allow me to transform.

In fallow times, when writing has evaporated, I've anguished over the question of whether words had failed me, or I'd failed them. Is artistic endeavor like religious faith? Do you have to believe in order to believe? One of life's cruel tautologies—faith persists only for those who already have it. Lose conviction, and it's all snatched away.

Marilyn trod where the gods felt she had no right to go—something she intuited as her finger hesitated over the shutter. What caused her to hesitate? Did she feel it was not her place to show this scene to the world? Or did she sense she was pillaging—taking something from this child in his private, unspeakable devastation, orphaned, standing before the ruins of his home, the ashes partly made up of his incinerated family—to turn this moment into something else, into something that served *her*?

And yet, writing for me has been a form of prayer. Praying for those who have suffered, for the unhealable wounds of history, for the victims of the worst that humans inflict on each other. And a damning of the perpetrators who have appeared in my writing: the Nazi brute who raped the teenage Jewish girl he kept enslaved, the camp guard who snatched a dreidl—as a toy for his own daughter—from the fist of a two-year-old child before she was thrust into the gas chamber. Of the German soldiers who made a mascot of a seven-year-old Jewish boy, who watched as they shot his parents, siblings, and his entire village into a pit they'd been forced, themselves, to dig.

The prayers are inadequate, and the damning a sham, and yet it is all I have to give. So, I have sat in silent contemplation for hours, days, months, spilling my devotions onto the page. *Dear Lord, through my words, give them peace. Through my sentences, striving to get the story right, to speak the truth, grant me, in my anguished solitude of black letters snaking across the page, some peace of my own.*

Thinking about Arendt and Roth now, I am aware that their lives could not have been more different from mine—by comparison, a paradise of safety, opportunity, and ease. And yet, as I tried to imagine their experience, the texture of their consciousness and grief, it was as if I could hear my own footfalls. Unthinkable, uncanny, unreasonable.

A thought now floats eerily to mind. Was it their story I felt I had no right to voice—or my own?

* * *

Four years after our sojourn in Mexico, our kids now aged eight and thirteen, we again packed up our Brooklyn apartment, heading off for a year in Paris. This time, my professor husband had a sabbatical, while I had another yearlong grant to write a new book. Margot, the mother of one of the kids in my son's class, invited me to talk to her book club, a group of expat women who met once a month, having recommended they read my recently published book of short stories, *Awake in the Dark*.

At the meeting, the women ended up discussing the theme of intergenerational secrets. What should parents tell their own children, or not tell them, about the traumas they have suffered? And what do adult children have the right to know about their parents' pasts? How much of our identity is determined by our own family histories, reaching back through generations? Margot, a Canadian economist, living indefinitely in Paris with her family, was sitting beside me. An intelligent, forceful woman, she always had something interesting to say. Now, she was uncharacteristically quiet. I knew she was Jewish; I wondered if the Holocaust theme of the book cut close to home.

After dinner, Margot and I decided to go for a walk and headed to Montmartre. It was a beautiful fall evening. When we turned the corner and the Sacré-Coeur Basilica appeared on high, it looked as if it were floating in the sky. We curved around, up the steep path, our breath heavy with the effort. Finally, we reached the cathedral steps and paused to look at the city spread out below.

"Thanks for coming to the book club tonight," she said. "It meant a lot to me, personally."

I'd written the book for the kids I'd grown up with in Melbourne, whose parents had, against all odds, survived the Holocaust. I wondered if Margot was also a child of Holocaust survivors.

"Tell me about your own family history," I said. "I know you grew up in Canada …"

"Actually, I grew up in a small town," she said. "My family had lived there for generations."

So, her parents were not Holocaust survivors.

"I always felt different from my parents, going all the way back to—I don't know, when I was very small. It was just a feeling—I never thought about it much. Then one day, my younger sister said something that made me realize she felt the same way."

"Did you feel like you were cut from a different cloth?"

"It was more specific than that," she said, turning to face me, a steely look in her eyes. "I'd always had strange and frightening dreams. Even before I could talk. I would wake up screaming. The same thing with my sister. My parents didn't know what to do. They were calm people—they weren't used to such strong emotions."

It was beautiful up here. I picked out the landmarks—La Défense, the Eiffel Tower, the trees of the Bois de Vincennes.

"We never actually talked about our nightmares. But we had an understanding. We shared a room, and if one of us woke up upset, we'd get into bed together and go back to sleep. But we did talk about how we'd leave our town when we were old enough. We didn't feel like we belonged there."

Where was the Jewish background? I knew Margot and her family were members of a synagogue in Paris and celebrated the Jewish holidays.

"How did your family end up in Canada? I don't know much about Canadian Jewish communities."

"Oh, my parents weren't Jewish. My sister and I converted when we were teenagers. When I was nine, I learned about World War II in school—not much, and it was sanitized, but they did tell us about concentration camps. When the teacher said the words *gas chambers*, a peculiar shiver went through my body. A feeling of, I don't know, like I was being taken over by a ghost. That night, I asked my sister—she was only seven—what her scary dreams were about."

Her voice was gentle.

"Turns out we were dreaming the exact same things. Dreams about being chased. Running fast, at night, in the dark. Cobblestone streets."

Cobblestone streets. I, too, had had such dreams from as far back as I could remember.

"The terrible pounding of boots—soldiers behind us, wearing brown uniforms."

My own childhood dreams ... and Amanda's ...

"By the time we got to talking about the train, the details got more specific."

"The train?"

"The cattle car. The other people in the car. Those dreams were identical. The same visual details, and sounds. And people—we both knew who all the people were, the people who were with us."

"Who were they?" I asked.

"Our parents. Mother and father. And grandmother. And—" She drew in a quick breath. Her eyes glistened. It was clear that for Margot, this was all still raw.

"A little brother and sister. There were others too—" She shook her head. "That's when we realized—these weren't just scary dreams. In fact, they weren't dreams at all."

"Not dreams?"

"No." Margot said the word *no*, but she nodded an affirmation, a *yes*. "They were memories. All of it had happened. It had happened to *us*."

The air had turned chilly. It was late, almost eleven p.m. Paris glittered below.

"When we converted—we did the full orthodox protocol—it didn't feel like a conversion, since we both felt like we'd always been Jewish. It was more like we were just reclaiming our rightful home."

"Reincarnation," I said.

Margot nodded. "Exactly." Her face was glowing with a serene smile. "That was a very long time ago, you understand. Since then, we've found out we're not alone."

"What do you mean?"

"There are thousands like us who believe they're the reincarnation of souls murdered during the Holocaust. Often children, whose deaths were so premature ... There's a rabbi who has collected hundreds of these stories. He believes righteous families were chosen for these souls to be born into. My parents were certainly righteous—the finest people you could ever meet."

* * *

The other good friend I made that year was Giulia, an Italian writer who had moved from Milan to Paris with her young daughter to escape the broken Italian education system. We connected at once, sharing long lunches and excursions, including walks around Paris. She wore a white woolen cape that draped around her elegant frame, and seemed to do everything with aplomb—whipping up Italian meals, hosting soirées, generating endless pages of literary criticism—and became fluent in French with enviable speed. Her eyes always seemed to twinkle with irony, a half smile on her lips. Her English was perfect and literary, adorned with a gentle Italian accent. I see her still on her bicycle, as I wait for her at one café or another, careening around the street corner, long blonde hair flying behind her and her little dog, Ombra (shadow in Italian), sitting upright in the handlebar basket, his ears plastered back by the wind.

At the end of our year in Paris, my husband wanted to take our kids to Reykjavík, where he has family. Discovering we could not bring our dog without extended animal quarantine, I decided to stay in Paris with Sparky, pack up the apartment, and meet the family back home in New York. They left, and the days got gobbled up with sorting and packing, dealing with the endless things kids accumulate. Sparky skulked around in a cloud of anxiety. Boxes and suitcases always troubled him.

Two nights before my final departure, I met up with Giulia for dinner. She took me to a café, where we dined on cheese and cold meats served with crusty baguette and sparkling water that came in a bright-blue bottle. After dinner, we decided to take a long walk, a last hurrah for me. She adored Paris, and I was seeing it now through her eyes. We wound through streets in a residential neighborhood I didn't know. Finally, *finally*, my heart felt the fullness of beauty I'd longed for, a spectacular, unexpected parting gift from the city.

At the same moment, we both suddenly sagged with weariness, desperate for a rest. We were on a long residential street with not a café in sight. Rounding a corner, we found ourselves right in front of a hotel with a large café, its tables spilling onto the sidewalk. We looked at each other with delight and sank onto the wooden chairs. I noticed a postcard in a little stand beside the menu and idly reached for it. I was stunned to see a familiar face looking out at me with his distinctively troubled and yet gentle eyes: my beloved Joseph Roth as a young man, gazing ahead into his future. I turned over the postcard. *The Life and Work of Joseph Roth: An Exhibition.* I saw from the dates that the show ended the following day, my last day in Paris.

I looked up to find my friend scanning my face.

"What's up?" she asked.

I showed her the postcard and told her about my long-standing love affair with Joseph Roth. I relayed how some years earlier, my husband had come home to find me face down on the bed, racked with sobs. Alarmed, he asked what was wrong. I had just finished reading Roth's *Job.* I tried to explain that I wasn't weeping because the book was sad, though it is. My emotional outpouring was more complicated—existential, deeply personal, and connecting me to all of humanity. For me, Roth's book cut to the quick of the human condition, engaging my deepest yearnings and dilemmas. His powerful literary palm had pressed upon a bruise in my soul, at the same time taking hold of my aching writer's hand. In his retelling of the biblical story, Job was a Hasidic Jew in Roth's present-day Poland. The series of catastrophic events befalling this Job brought to life the realities such Jews faced. Roth also evoked Job's stoicism and refusal to relinquish hope, perhaps capturing something historically deep about oppressed peoples. Though trauma accrues, Job's resolve to survive and to celebrate life only deepens. In the end, he is rewarded with one of those everyday miracle coincidences, something astonishing and sublime that finds him, on the very last page, speechless with joy.

Lying on the bed that night, unable to stop crying, I felt catapulted by Roth's book to a vertiginous altitude, revealing a breathtaking view of humanity that left me terrified, joyous, hardly able to breathe—and keenly aware of the perils: the air dangerously thin, the beckoning of a catastrophic fall. The artist's strange double helix—misery and ecstasy. A vision that soars in hope and also seizes in despair.

The cauldron of feeling that overtook me seemed like a fundamental condition of *being*, the *everything of everything*. I was weeping because Joseph Roth had lived and been the person he was, who'd reached into his own vexed nature to create this book that from beyond the life-death boundary spoke to me so wholly. He felt like a long-lost soulmate in my own battle to make sense of it all, to move through the impossibly demanding business of just being alive.

How could I explain any of this to my husband? That I felt this to be at the same time the bleakest and happiest moment of my life?

And I couldn't explain this to Giulia now at the table, though her face had lifted with interest. Just as I was about to try, my eyes wandered, and I found myself looking up at a plaque affixed to the wall beside me. Distractedly, I scanned the words engraved on the plaque.

Joseph Roth, the Austrian writer, lived in this hotel until his death on May 27, 1939.

It took a moment to sink in. I was sitting at a café table in the very spot that Joseph Roth had certainly sat on occasion, looking at the same glass-paned doors through which he had walked to get to the bar. I craned to catch sight of the staircase beyond the café that led up to the hotel rooms, skirting the desk where the clerk had that evening, long ago, handed Roth the letter that would precipitate his final alcoholic binge.

I wonder now why I didn't think to enter the hotel that night to climb the stairs and walk the corridors. Try to intuit which room had been Roth's. Perhaps because those stairs, as Joseph Roth had climbed them, did not actually seem real to me, having existed until that moment only in my imagination, nothing to do with *this* reality of pointy corners and hard surfaces.

The next morning, I awoke early and worked frantically to get everything packed. I wanted to make it to the exhibition.

What I found when I got there was disorienting. Bits and pieces from Joseph Roth's life, all of it oddly sanitized, filled several rooms. There were handwritten manuscript pages framed in glass and hanging on the wall. One cache of letters detailed the terrible decline of Roth's wife, Friedl, along with details of the sanatorium he finally managed to find for her. Other letters displayed the bitter realities of Roth's many humiliations, and his repeated cries to his friend, Stefan Zweig, for help. The intent of the exhibition was undoubtedly to celebrate and memorialize Roth's life, but the result—a prurient sense of gawking—was mortifying. After half an hour, I fled.

I took the metro back to the house we'd lived in that past year on Rue Saint-Sauveur. I opened the massive wooden door in the high wall and crossed the courtyard, then took the seven long flights up to the little apartment, empty now of my family, and soon to be empty of me.

* * *

Some months after Paris, back in New York City, I dropped my daughter at a friend's house in Brooklyn Heights and took a detour down Montague Street, the main shopping drag. Passing the used bookstore, my eyes strayed to the table outside, which held cardboard boxes filled with bargain books, a dollar apiece. My husband and I were always lamenting that we had too many books and had made a pact to try to avoid buying more. I was about to turn my head away from the bargain piles when a book perched on the first box snagged my attention, its title flashing: *Beyond the Ashes: Cases of Reincarnation from the Holocaust.* The author was Rabbi Yonassan Gershom—surely the rabbi Margot recalled that evening in Montmartre, who had collected stories not unlike her own. I grabbed the book and went into the store, laying my dollar bill down on the counter.

I stopped in a café to read. Sure enough, dozens of stories, just like Margot's, recounted by people from all over the world. People who talked about being haunted from earliest childhood by memories and dreams that had led them to believe they had been murdered by the Nazis, their troubled souls finding their way back into living bodies.

I re-conjured the dreams that had visited me as a child, going back in my memory to before that day as a thirteen-year-old when the documentary film about the Nazis, *Night and Fog*, burned into my soul. Margot had embraced the history she felt certain was rightfully hers, converting to Judaism and adopting a Jewish way of life. I, on the other hand, had pulled away from the Jewish world I'd been born into, fleeing my own personal past but also the history of my people, which often felt like one and the same. Something new occurred to me. Perhaps all my racing around the globe was not just about running away. But also an attempt to find a new place to plant the roots for the next generations. Is it foolish to think one can undo centuries of dislocation? Silence a historical trajectory by attempting to start a new one from scratch? As if there were a logic to any of it—as if one were master not only of one's own fate but also of the fate of generations, of souls moving around in the outer reaches of the cosmos.

– 8 –

I Wish I'd Had You as a Mother

During the year I spent in Bogotá with my husband and teenage son, I got a call from my sister in Australia to say that our mother had taken a fall. She'd cut her head and lain in her own blood through the night, unable to move. The previous day, she'd angrily told my sister to stop constantly checking up on her and bringing food. "My fridge is overflowing! I'm fine, I can manage. Just leave me alone!" So, for twenty-four hours my sister had let her be. Of course, that was the day she fell, having left the panic button they'd bought for her hanging on the headboard of her bed. The incident felled the fury in my mother; she finally agreed to move into an assisted living facility.

"I'm coming," I said to my sister, who had borne the brunt of caring and planning for our mother. "You're going to need help emptying out her apartment."

I cleared a month and booked a flight, leaving my husband to hold down the fort with our son. Our daughter, midway through her freshman year of college, was living in the Boston area.

It was a long journey, from Bogotá to Lima to Santiago to Sydney then finally on to Melbourne. I didn't count the hours in the air, or the time spent in airports that all looked the same, sitting in one look-alike food court or another while FaceTime calling my daughter in Boston, my husband and son in Colombia, my sister in England, or mother, sister, and brother in Australia, my world a hopscotch grid sketched across the globe.

And then, there I was, on the other side of the world, alone in my mother's apartment, which was filled to the brim with her. I stood in the entryway, looking into the living room-dining room, with its picture windows holding breathtaking views of Melbourne. The city had transformed in the thirty years I'd been away, now a sprawling metropolis with a jagged skyscraper skyline off to the east, and urban districts nestled in greenery spreading in all directions. In the distance, the bay glimmered beneath an endless blue sky. The bright Melbourne light filled the apartment, touching everything with uncomplicated promise, a contrast to the heavy weather brewing within.

I walked the empty rooms. Everything carried my mother's eye and the anointing quality of her touch. Each fiercely adored item—furniture, pottery, blown-glass pieces—carried its moment of history in the epic of her life. I stood by the grand piano, aware of my mother's spirit hovering above the keys. A wall of cabinets held a musician's lifetime of sheet music, and hundreds of classical CDs, many still in their protective wrap. My mother preferred the radio—an effortless flick of a switch, and the surprise of the programming.

In the hallway outside the kitchen were cabinets designed for my mother's vast store of dishes: soup bowls with knob-edged handles; delicately glazed dishes from Japan; unusually shaped glass platters; goblets that caught the light, flashing rainbow fragments. I glanced into the dining room at the enormous table my mother had designed herself, inspired by a Chinese collectible. Set in the middle of a gold velvet runner was a brass bowl in the shape of a ritual dragon, baring its fangs.

I fancied I could smell my mother's creamed spinach soup with its peppery kick, and the intoxicating mixture of cherries and wine, the sauce that goes with her roast duck. I pictured the large round poppyseed cake slathered with melted dark chocolate, and strawberries, grapes, and tangerine slices gleaming with a brittle sugar shell.

I am there, a child (though I never lived in this apartment my mother moved to in her mid-sixties) as the room fills with my mother's guests. I pass around the hors d'oeuvres I helped make earlier that day that are laid on an enormous platter. I am especially careful with the platter, squelching my natural clumsiness with an urgent sense that my life depends on it.

I shook my head. There were no guests. There would never again be guests here. No soup simmering on the stove, no one, most likely, who would ever again make that poppyseed cake.

In her bedroom, I slid open the glass doors of the closets, revealing shoeboxes lined up on the top shelf, everything labeled. Immaculately folded sweaters and tops. Scarves and belts rolled in drawers. Everything in order, the world charming and arranged. Her meticulousness the opposite of my more blundering relationship to the material world.

My spirit felt crushed by the task facing me: the systematic undoing of my mother's carefully constructed world. It turned out that nobody would want most of her lifetime collections—that I would end up cramming so much of her life's ballast into the garbage bins at the back of the apartment building, incurring the wrath of residents who complained there was no room left for their trash. I would make endless phone calls to find someone to take the piano. No one wants pianos these days, it turns out, not even as a gift.

Every now and then, from her nursing-home bed, my mother would ask where something was—the mottled green vase, the Brahms serenades folio, her blue denim blazer. We'd thankfully found a home for her sheet music at a sheet-music library, tended by volunteers, and had sent bags of clothing to the Salvation Army. My sister and brother had taken some items to place in their own homes. We'd invited friends and acquaintances to help themselves to the crockery, furniture, and small appliances. As kindly as we could, we would tell my mother where the item was, avoiding mention of the Salvation Army. She'd glance around her nursing-home room, her eyes flitting about in hopes of landing on the item that was calling to her.

"It's all gone," she would say, her voice shaded with disbelief. "They've taken it all away."

* * *

That night, alone in my mother's apartment, I sat up in the guest-room bed looking out the window at the urban sprawl, the trees looming animate shapes—a kangaroo on its hind legs, a boar in rutting crouch, a panther with a glowing streetlight eye. The bay in the distance was a metal band stretched taut, sealing me into this shoreline, so far from my husband and son on one continent, my daughter on another, from homes I had forged in so many places.

My gaze grazed the city's eastern suburbs. Kew lay in that direction, where I spent most of my growing-up years, and then a little further east, North Balwyn, with the orange-brick house our father brought us to that long-ago day from the airport, when my baby eyes would have first taken in the distinctively white south-eastern Australian light.

I drifted into a half sleep.

I am all ages, and I am shelling peas. The pods come in a large brown paper bag. A bowl sits in front of me. Aged four or five, I am standing on a kitchen chair and as I grow, I shell them seated, and then later, as a teenager, I stand at the kitchen counter. I pinch the tip of each pod between forefinger and thumb, hear the satisfying snap, tear the pod open, and slide the peas out with my thumb. Every now and then I eat a few; they are crunchy and sweet.

The years tumble by and I am shelling peas, always aware of my mother, who is busy at the stove or countertop or sink. I am good in the kitchen, which means I am likely to get appreciative smiles, words of praise. She talks while we work—giving instructions and telling elaborate stories about her life. The details remain in place with each telling, as if my mother were reading from pages inked with mythic truth. In my child's mind, the stories tumbled together with the Bible stories I learned at the low-key Jewish Sunday school I attended for a year or two. Daniel in the lions' den; my mother growing up in Koppies, a tiny one-horse town in rural

South Africa. The Jews' expulsion from Egypt to wander in the desert for forty years; my mother's escape from South Africa, traveling to Australia by herself with three young children, since my father had already gone on ahead to find housing and work. Queen Esther in combat with evil Haman to protect the Jews; my mother doing battle with onerous obstacles from the day she was born, no one to help her, not her parents, not her brothers, not her husband. Mighty and fragile, heroic, embattled, alone.

But she was not alone in the kitchen, not while I kneeled or sat on the kitchen chair, or when I was older, standing at the counter beside her, my anxious, adoring presence enveloping her as I shelled or stirred or diced, listening, scrutinizing, memorizing, as her stories baked themselves into the substance of my own developing self.

"I was terminally bored, all the time," my mother would say. "All summer long, I did nothing but sit in a tree. Koppies was the end of the earth."

Known as a chatterbox from the time I started to speak, I went very quiet when my mother embarked on one of her stories.

"I wasn't meant to be born."

"What do you mean, Mummy?"

"My mother didn't want to have another baby. Tenth pregnancy. Can you imagine?"

I couldn't imagine. I see myself this time as six years old. I knew babies came from ladies' tummies and I knew that my own mother had been very sick every time, vomiting and vomiting and so exhausted that she could barely get through the day.

"I was about your age when she told me. She did everything she could. Ran up and down the stairs. Drank nasty things. Put things up there. She wanted to get rid of it, that's what she said."

"Get rid of what?"

"Me, you silly!"

My bafflement seemed to amuse my mother; she gave a sideways smile. "But I wouldn't be gotten rid of!" She ruffled my hair.

I bit my lip, stifling the tears. Her mother had tried to kill her, and she was smiling.

"I just hung on—for dear life. And here I am!"

I am twelve years old, and I am in charge of the hors d'oeuvres.

"We're *entertaining*," my mother would say. "Medicos and their wives." My father's medical colleagues. The women referred to themselves as *housewives*.

I had just finished buttering triangles of white bread and was wrapping them around asparagus tips I carefully removed from a jar.

"I hated my brother," my mother said. "He persecuted me, day in, day out." She had seven older brothers and ahead of all of them, a sister, who was eighteen years old when my mother, the unwanted last child, was born. One other sibling had died as a baby.

"My mother had a way of firing the older child when the next one was born. Harry was the youngest until I came along. The older one was supposed to disappear—they were a nuisance."

Don't be such a nuisance! This had always been my mother's way of telling us not to bother her.

She was melting sugar for the *friandises*—*free-un-daze* is how she said it. I recently discovered it is a general French term for sweetmeats.

"Harry made my life a misery. On the rare occasion I brought a friend home, he would taunt her, making sure she'd never want to come back. I'll never forget—"

I knew exactly what was coming.

"—when Mr. Kriege, the traveling salesman, gave me the most precious gift."

On cue, a beatific look on her face.

"We took in lodgers when we could. When Mr. Kriege came, it was so exciting! He had an enormous leather case that rolled on wheels—and always found something to give me."

This was my favorite part, imagining my mother's excitement as a nine-year-old, Mr. Kriege having magically reappeared in that terminally boring town in the Nazi-sympathizing Orange Free State. There, the Jews were the bottom rung on the social ladder before the drop into the abyss occupied by the Black population, who were on the receiving end of discriminatory degradation and abuse that infected all aspects of their lives.

"'Little Dee-Dee,' he said. 'I've brought you something special!'"

My mother held a strawberry in the silver confectionary tongs. The strawberries were never washed, since even a drop of moisture would ruin the glaze. I supposed that ingesting a bit of insecticide was the price one had to pay. She dipped the strawberry into the steaming liquid sugar.

"His leather case stood open like a giant book, filled with little shelves and drawers. Perfumes, shaving tools, ribbons, porcelain thimbles with gold edges. Dolls, toy soldiers, tiny farmyard animals."

I was forming small balls of cheese pastry dough, slipping a single stuffed olive into each.

"I longed to have the baby lamb with its little pink nose. I never mustered the courage to ask."

I heard *mustered* as *mustard*. Mustard stung the tongue—it took courage to tolerate, like the courage, I figured, to ask for something you wanted but didn't feel you had the right to.

"He pulled a box covered in blue silk from the bottom shelf. Inside was a miniature tea set, each piece in its own velvet compartment. Plates, saucers, teacups—the teapot and milk jug in the middle. I could not believe it was really mine. I went straight to my room and arranged the tea set on the floor. Then, I positioned my dolls, the dolls I made of mango pits. You know—"

"Yes," I said, jumping in. "You shaved the pit with a knife, left strands at the top for the hair. Painted the faces on. One had a purple bow in its hair."

My mother lowered the last glazed strawberry to complete the row.

"You can imagine how I felt when Harry appeared at my door."

I'd never met my Uncle Harry. He lived on the other side of the world. My mother had not seen him in decades. But he'd appeared in this story countless times throughout my childhood, filling me with terror.

"He was holding a hard ball in his hand," she said.

"The color of clay," I said.

"'Look what Mr. Kriege gave me,' he said. I knew that look in his face."

"He was quick," I said, judging the distance between the cheesy balls on the baking tray—a two-inch spacing was required.

"'It's a baseball,' Harry said, 'from the U-S of A.'"

I felt overcome with nausea. I left my station to get some cold water from the fridge. The glass jug was heavy. I had to use two hands. I poured slowly, not wanting to spill.

"I threw my body over the tea set to protect it, but at the last minute, my survival instinct kicked in—he'd said the ball was hard. What if it hit my head? I swerved my body and slid under the bed."

My throat tightened, closing off words. My mother would have to finish the story on her own. I stood there holding the glass of water, helpless before the story that was barreling toward me, unable to change the ending, unable to do anything but hear it through to the end.

"Harry was a perfect aim. One toss—he got every single piece. 'Stri-i-i-i-ke!' My tea set was smashed to bits. But—I realized I was holding a plate. I was so happy, to have saved one little plate!"

The worst was over. I managed a sip of water and went back to my task.

"That's when I got the idea for my trick!" A strange smile would take over my mother's face, along with the sinister twinkle that always made me nervous. My mother held up her pinky finger. "My weapon! I grew the nail, sharpened it to a point. Was he surprised when I tested it out!"

I looked at the baking tray with the cheesy balls perfectly spaced, room for just one more.

"That day, he came at me and threw me to the floor. I gave one quick swipe, down his cheek. I saw little beads of blood turn into a red line. I kept that nail pointy until he left home to go to the army."

That night, I waited up for the guests to go home so I could survey the leftovers. There were three blackberry *friandises* left—my favorites. Biting into the brittle glaze, I savored the burst of juice as it mixed with the sugary shards.

I was jolted awake early by jet lag, faced with the ongoing onerous task of sorting through the objects of my mother's life and figuring out what to do with it all. The sun was rising over the sliver of bay in the distance, dribbling honeyed blood. Image fragments scattered—one of them, a memory, skittered within, taking shape.

I am twenty and out shopping for my wedding dress. (The marriage, my first, will be short-lived, ending abruptly the week before my first date with the man I would one day tell my children was *my real husband, your father—I was only waiting to meet him.*) I had not been out shopping with my mother in years. She'd offered to come with me to buy the dress and told me to take her wherever I thought we might most quickly find one. I chose a fashionable store downtown: House of Merivale. I'd gone as a teenager, with friends who had vast clothing budgets. Such pricey, fashionable clothes had never been within my reach.

Once there I fretted, knowing how expensive everything would be. I took the first white dress I saw on the rack, scanning my mother's face while pretending to be lighthearted and happy.

"You go try it on," she said, pressing her hands into her eyes. "I need to sit."

In the dressing room, my attention fluttered anxiously toward my mother. Was she okay? How bad was her headache? Was she angry? Was I was taking too long? I looked at the tag. Two hundred dollars! I'd never bought anything so expensive. She'd never let me buy it. I didn't take a moment to wonder if I liked the dress—it seemed okay. I stepped back into my clothes then exited to where my mother was sitting.

"It's two hundred dollars," I said.

"That's fine," she said. "Do you like it? Will it do?"

"Yes," I said. "It is very nice."

She paid for the dress, already somewhere else. She was weary and needed a cup of tea. We found a tea shop with old-fashioned booths. I slunk in beside her, clotted with shame, the House of Merivale shopping bag hanging limply from my wrist. I was chattering desperately, unable to stop. My words clattered to the floor like rusty chains.

I am missing something. I look back, see my mother with her hands pressed into her throbbing eyes, her tea un-drunk. Beside her, the twenty-year-old me, feeling like a wooden block. Yes, this: only weeks earlier (or was it days?), my mother had heard the terrible news that one of her seven brothers—one she was close to and dearly loved—a husband and father of three children, had, on the first anniversary of their mother's death, kneeled by her freshly placed tombstone and shot himself in the head.

But my mother's distraction and self-absorption that day in the teahouse did not feel appreciably different or new. It was all too familiar, the way my throat closed with panic as I tried to find a way to reach her, tap-dancing with clever words, my stomach in knots, the false brightness chewing me up from the inside. The frantic attempt to bring her out of her misery—to help her, yes, but also in hope that I might cease to feel like a life-sized wood carving, if only I could get her to engage.

On our infrequent clothes shopping trips when I was a child, my mother was irritable, harried, and stingy, particularly when it came to her time, which she had a horror of wasting. (If I concentrate, I can superimpose over the memory of her angry youthful face an image of my shrunken aged mother, sitting up in bed at the nursing home, gazing at me warmly, the kind of expression I longed for as a child.)

In my mother's later years, she recalled those outings and expressed sorrow. She particularly regretted that she'd seldom allowed me to ride on those moving animals you'd find outside shops. *No, I don't have time, money doesn't grow on trees,* fury rising from her like smoke. I learned not to ask, but sometimes, I could not help myself, my voice fearful. On rare occasions, my mother acceded. I would feel the toxic rise of her impatience as the animal bobbed up and down. Perched on top, drenched in misery, I would monitor her for signs of eruption.

In my late twenties, some years after I'd moved to New York, my mother came to visit. Walking on Manhattan's Upper West Side, we passed an animal ride outside a children's store. She looked at me wistfully, suggested I climb up and have that ride—as many rides as I wanted. There I was, a grown woman, a psychologist working in a psychiatric hospital, reduced inside to a child quivering with panic.

I gave a little laugh, assuming she was joking, but then saw she was serious. Her eyes twinkled with fun, but behind that was mournful pleading.

"Please, darling," she said. "Do it for me. Back then, I was always so tired and overwhelmed …"

I looked into the face of the horse: flared nostrils, bright-blue mane, eyes stark with terror. I glanced around at the people walking by.

"It's okay, Mum," I said, praying she'd let it drop. Oddly, though, I also had a yen to get up on the horse, could feel a breath at my ear, some unknown kind of freedom. I heard my own voice, coming from far away, rehearsing the pat phrases that sprang to my lips of their own accord. *Mum, it's fine. You were a good mother, truly. You had such difficult circumstances*—. I was floating above, looking down on the scene, waiting to see my mother's face relax into a grateful expression.

The final area to tackle in undoing my mother's life was the walk-in closet in the foyer. Stacked on top of a filing cabinet was a tower of shoeboxes, filled with correspondence, each labeled in my mother's neat hand. I took out the box labeled *HEINZ*. Heinz was the man my mother lived with, after my father died. There were two other partners after Heinz, but no boxes of keepsakes bearing their names. I glanced through the contents: cards, notes, hand-drawn cartoons. Though Heinz was long dead, a quick glance through the contents of the box revealed a gleam of his being—his quirky wit, his adoration of my mother, his active, slightly pompous intelligence.

Who would want this excised chunk of my mother's life? A past incarnation of our mother, engaged with people and life, now also gone—not the elderly lady, gracious and sweet, who spent her days propped up in bed, who stifled expressions of excruciating pain and was a favorite among the nursing-home staff.

But no, not gone. The fiery woman in her mid-fifties to early sixties—she was here, with Heinz, in this box.

Coincidence had trotted at my mother's heels throughout her life, and when she recounted these tales, she was glorious. One involved a trip my mother took with Heinz to Phillip Island, which has a colony of over forty thousand fairy penguins, smallest of all penguin species. They spend long periods in the sea, but return to shore to rest, to mate and to nest. Tourists come to watch them emerge from the ocean.

My mother adored little creatures of all kinds, even ants. On a visit to us while we were living in Mexico, we were walking down the street with our young children when my mother noticed a column of ants making their way toward a tiny anthill in the middle of the dirt sidewalk. She stopped, drawing the children's attention to the otherworldly drama playing out at our feet, crouching down with them to watch the stoic little workers going about their business. They stayed that way for a half hour or more, the kids mesmerized by my mother's explanations and descriptions, their faces alight with wonder, lost in the exalted stretch of the moment.

I picture my mother filled with the same wonder as the penguins emerged from the sea. She is sitting with Heinz in bleachers cordoned off to give the penguins their space. The sky flares with color, and then, as dusk falls, the first dozen emerge, standing just twelve inches tall in their metallic gray-blue jackets, flapping their flippers. Now, hundreds spill tipsily forth until they number into the thousands. Their voices rise in crescendo, a chorus of bleats that amplify to almost deafening shrieks. They waddle with impressive speed, intent on reaching their burrows, which dot the landscape just beyond the sand, where the soil grips clumps of reedy grass. The park authority has created little wooden boxes with entryway holes to protect the burrow entrances; they sit like miniature cabins scattered in a tiny wilderness. Now and again, a pair of penguins stop to lean in for what looks like a kiss.

The next morning, my mother and Heinz have breakfast at a café by the beach. My mother becomes transfixed by the young server who crosses back and forth between the café and its patio, balancing her tray.

"She reminds me of someone," my mother says distractedly to Heinz. "Something about the way she walks. An unusual swivel of the hips ..."

"I was wondering," my mother says as the woman sets down her coffee. "It might seem like a funny question, but are your parents from Australia?"

"Actually, no," the girl says in a broad Australian accent. "I was born here, but my parents are from South Africa."

"Do you, by chance, have a grandmother named Dorothea?"

"Why, yes! She was from Benoni. I never knew her. She died when I was little."

My mother tells the girl she had known her grandmother forty-five years earlier when they'd both attended a Jewish summer camp for a few days in the countryside of South Africa's Orange Free State. "She was a lovely girl—so alive. We kept in touch for a few years. But then ... you know ..."

"I'm sorry. How could you have possibly known I was her granddaughter?"

"There was something about the way Dorothea walked. You walk exactly the same way."

The box labeled *HEINZ* felt heavy in my hand. I found myself out in the service area by the back stairwell of the building, gazing at the gray concrete walls and floors, avoiding looking at the metal panel of the closed garbage chute. I thought about calling my sister to ask her what I should do. She was at work. For so long her mind had been cluttered with everything having to do with my mother's illnesses and care—she'd had no peace for years. I was here to make these kinds of decisions, to shoulder some of the burden. I reached for the top of the metal panel and pulled, revealing the mouth that would swallow things down and expel them into huge metal bins in the basement.

The cellphone in my pocket buzzed. I put the box down to see it was a FaceTime video call coming in from my daughter, now in her freshman year of college, ten thousand miles away.

"Darling, hi!" I said, hoping the redness of my eyes would not be noticeable on the small screen.

"Hey, Mama! Where are you?"

She was walking outside—springtime in Massachusetts, glimpses of cherry blossoms floating by.

"In the back hallway, outside Grandma's apartment."

Her smile fell. "How is she?"

"Hanging in. What's happening?"

She told me about rehearsals for the play she was in. Of course, I would be missing it—remarkably, since we were living in Bogotá, it would be the only play of the year that I'd miss. I'd managed to make it to each one so far, planning my business trips around her performances. She chatted happily about her classes, her friends, her new life so far away from me.

Now, she squinted closely into the screen of her phone.

"Hey, you still in that depressing hallway?" she asked. I'd forgotten I was here; I'd been whisked away to sunny springtime, caught up in the goings on of my daughter's college life.

"There's a lot to do," I said.

"Well, whatever it is, why don't you finish up so you can get out of there. *Hey, David! David!*" She dropped from view as she raised the hand with the phone in it, likely to wave. The sky wafted about in the screen, swooshing back and forth, pale blue with white streaks, lit by the sun.

"Sorry, Ma, gotta go. *You going to the theater?* Bye, Mama, love you!" Before she hit the end button, I heard the ripple of her laugh.

I picked up the box I'd set down on the concrete floor, pulled out a handful of papers and cards and stuffed them into the mouth of the chute. I wondered if they still burned trash in Melbourne. I recalled the black smell of the smoke when I was a child; we'd smell the burning garbage when we passed by the council pit. Another handful into the chute and then a third. The box still seemed full, taunting me, as if it were planning to magically replenish with every handful I removed. I closed my eyes and saw the lives of my mother and Heinz going up in smoke: their happy years, their breakup, Heinz's grief at losing my mother, who—after his difficult marriage to another woman failed—had ended up being the love of his life. My mother, at the end, felt suffocated by Heinz's possessive jealousy, as she'd felt stifled by my father's stereotypical-of-the-times male behaviors, insecurities, and attitudes. There she is, in each handful I am disposing of; a woman fighting for her own self-determination, smothered by the controlling restrictions placed on her by the men she'd loved. All of it—the era, the times, the complications between men and women—and at the center of it all, my mother, going up in smoke. I could almost smell it, for a moment had the awful feeling that, were I to reach for a tissue, I would discover the inside of my nose was coated with ash.

When I returned to the walk-in closet, I found that the *HEINZ* box had been sitting on the final layer of shoeboxes, several of them making a little platform that had supported all the rest, each one labeled *HUSBAND*. My father.

Their long marriage started with two starry-eyed, well-meaning people, my mother just twenty-one, my father twenty-four, falling into betrothal after knowing each other a scant two weeks. Twenty years after my father's death, another of my mother's coincidences brought it back to her.

Aged seventy-four, still vigorous, my mother was standing in line at the supermarket in Melbourne, her home by then for forty-five years.

A much younger woman in front of her turned around.

"Excuse me, would you mind holding my place in line?" she said. "I forgot to get my biscuits."

My mother noted the woman's South African accent. *Maaah biskits.*

A minute or two later, the woman returned, biscuits in hand. "Thank you," she said.

"Where are you from in South Africa?" my mother asked, in her milder accent.

"Vereeniging. A small town in the Gauteng."

An hour and a half from where my mother grew up. She knew it well. "Not as small as where I'm from!" my mother said. "I'm from Koppies!"

"Why, I had cousins in Koppies. Second cousins. One of them got married in Johannesburg when I was—gosh, maybe three and a half years old. I was the flower girl."

"January 26, 1955?" my mother asked, searching the woman's face for signs of the sweet cherub who had strewn petals at her wedding.

Both stood there, dumbfounded.

"You were such a beautiful bride," the woman said. "It was a perfect wedding. I wanted to grow up and have a perfect wedding just like yours."

To the little flower girl, it had been perfect, that same wedding day my mother would always say she *hated*—her in-laws staging an enormous, splashy affair no one could afford, attended by hundreds of people, most of them strangers to my mother.

She had hardly known any of her many suitors. But it had been time to choose a husband, and she accepted my father's proposal the night he'd appeared in her doorway, two weeks after their first date. Within the constraining life-plan girdle imposed on her by her time and circumstances, this opportunity was shiny and bright: a proposal from a brilliant young doctor who was outgoing and charismatic, enchanted by her elegance and country-girl simplicity, who promised to cherish and take care of her, all their days.

The day after their wedding, the young couple boarded a ship for England, where my father was embarking on a four-year fellowship in surgery. Within eighteen months, my mother would find herself with an eight-month-old child and battling her first life-threatening cancer, which required a major, debilitating surgery. She begged her mother to come take care of the baby, but her mother refused, so instead she paid strangers to take her daughter—my sister—during her surgery and months of recovery. My father was working sixteen-hour days. It was 1956, and the idea of the man disrupting his career to take over childcare was simply not an option they even considered.

There is a photograph of my parents on the ship, dressed in costumes my mother fashioned for the Fancy Dress Ball, for which they won first prize: my mother in a cylinder made of cardboard, with the word *HONEY* written on it, a giant lid on her head, and my father sporting a large cutout of a moon. She once told me that the first night of their honeymoon had been *disappointing*. When her words were spare, I would always read in her face what she wasn't saying. In this case, *disappointing* meant something catastrophic— that the consummation of their marriage had been a disaster, that all her young girl's fantasies had sheared away, that the reality of marriage, of *this* marriage, had slammed into her with terrifying force. Perhaps on that first night, my mother glimpsed the truth:

that an unbridgeable gulf lay between them, two people of glaringly different sensibilities, with little in common. That marriage would not turn out to be the ecstatic, perfect togetherness she'd dreamed of. I believe there were some good periods, and that they were connected in a soulful and meaningful way, which included shared parenthood. But the connection sputtered and accrued a bitterness that was marked by loneliness and isolation. Perhaps on her honeymoon my mother had a trembling intuition about how awry the whole configuration was, not just between her and this husband she barely knew but in the very scheme of things—everything that marriage might end up being for a woman like her in that corrosively repressive, exploitative era.

With the force of her tremendous will, the young woman on the boat—told all her life she was stupid, a foolish girl incapable of determining her own fate—decided she would find a way to bring the life she'd long dreamed of into existence. She would work fiercely to be the perfect wife, to be supportive to her husband, to bury her own needs even further underground, if that was what was required. To be always elegant, beautiful, svelte. To cook the gourmet meals that as a little girl she imagined her doll family of mango pits had made for their cultured friends. To create and maintain an exquisite home, raising the four children she'd planned on having, who would always be beautifully presented and given *every opportunity*, all the opportunities she'd been denied. And she wouldn't stop there. There was also her own artistic development as a singer and pianist, and who knew, maybe one day she would even earn the university degree her brothers had deemed her unequal to. She would love this husband she had chosen from the posse of suitors, this man who had no idea who she was, whose acute scientific intelligence, surgeon's talent, and unflagging work ethic would grant him a gleaming career but who did not have access to the realms of experience that animated her being, as perhaps she had little access to his.

* * *

A filing cabinet held the mementos from my mother's life in music. One drawer contained programs from every concert she'd sung in, over many decades, with the Melbourne Chorale. The choir was made up of mostly young singers, my mother the oldest, by many years. Auditions were required every year. For twenty years the undimmed beauty of my mother's voice secured her place. I found the flashy program for Barbra Streisand's *Timeless* concert in Melbourne, the one my mother performed in as an additional backup singer, aged sixty-six, not long after she'd been diagnosed with breast cancer.

Of the singers sent to audition for Barbra Streisand, my mother was one of four chosen. Never mind that she spent three days a week in aggressive six-hour chemotherapy sessions, during which patients would typically be reduced to a condition of collapse— hours of vomiting, crippling nausea, headache, inability to eat. Both concerts fell on chemotherapy days. After the treatment, my mother drove home, showered, and changed, donned her stylish gray wig, and then headed to the stadium where she sang backup before 31,000 enthusiastic fans who'd paid from $140 to $1530 to hear Barbra Streisand perform.

"It was exhilarating!" my mother later said. "I wish you could have been there."

I remember the day my mother called to tell me about her cancer diagnosis. I was in the kitchen making dinner, recently home from the hospital where I'd spent a month battling hyperemesis gravidarum while pregnant with my son, still unnaturally thin, though my belly was beginning to bulge.

"Stage four," she'd said quietly, almost hoping, I think, that I wouldn't hear what she was saying.

"Does that mean it's spread?" I asked, watching the spatula I was holding drip oil onto the kitchen counter, my stir-fry forgotten on the stove.

"It was in seventeen lymph nodes—they took those out. Otherwise, not as far as they can tell."

I always felt as if I could hear the vast ocean in the background whenever I talked on the phone to my mother. I felt its weight sometimes as I imagined the phone cables set down on the ocean floor, climbing submerged mountains that can rise to twelve thousand feet and then dip into underwater valleys never touched by sunlight. I'd imagine the ships dragging tens of thousands of miles of cable across the earth, cables that were now conducting my mother to me and me to her.

"How long have you known?" I asked.

"Darling, you need to focus on regaining your strength."

She told me she was about to have a mastectomy. Radiation and chemotherapy would follow. I was still on medication for the intense nausea, which had tampered with my emotions.

"You can't die, Mum, I mean it! I'm about to have a baby ... I'm not ready to lose you!"

Going through my mother's filing cabinet, it came back to me—our long telephone exchanges, traversing oceans and decades. How could I have misplaced this ethereal Atlantis, stifled it in the experience and memory of my mother's long years of suffering and decline? That connection had opened up for us once I moved to the United States. In those long hours of talking by phone, we got to know each other in new ways. When we talked, I was typically busy doing something—putting away groceries or preparing food, mending or hand-washing clothes. The distance seemed to clear our relationship of its barbs. She was generous, then: attentive, invested, engaged. We talked about people, career developments, and, once I had children, my kids. We talked about music and writing; she was keenly interested in hearing me talk about my plot lines or characters.

"You always had a vivid imagination," she'd sometimes say.

Now I remember how much it meant to me when she said things like that. I was speaking and my mother was listening. My mother had heard what I'd said.

Two weeks into the work of going through my mother's things, I dreamed about my own birth.

Johannesburg, South Africa, 1960. A vile, racist society, as distant to me now as Mesopotamia. My mother held me in her arms. I was the third child, another daughter, much to the dismay of my father's parents, who wished for her to produce a son. But to my young mother, a country girl with flashing dark eyes and a song in her soul as big as her coloratura voice, who had once again pushed out a baby with no pain relief, the new life in her arms was perfect. In the dream, she stared into my face, her heart swollen with love, finding within my eyes a shiny soul to mirror her own.

You will help to make things right, she whispered, her capacious dreams flooding my being, along with her yearnings, in which deprivation and generations of persecution were lodged.

Song, you are my little song, she thought, losing herself in the newness of my tiny being. *I have the perfect name for you*, and she mouthed the Hebrew word that captured the meanings of both *poetry* and *song*.

In the dream, I see my own newborn self from above, a creature bursting with eagerness for miraculous life, peering up at its creator over the edge of its otherworldly wisdom and responding to the call: *I will be your mirror and your salve, a daughter, but also the loving mother you never had, I will fill you to the brim with the life that is in me*—tripping upon an echo of a prayer from the Jewish people she had just joined—*and I will strive all my life, and with all my being, to grant you peace.*

* * *

At the nursing home, there were different kinds of normal. Mrs. Hannity, in a hospital gown, howled all day long from her reclining contraption. Mr. and Mrs. Berger walked by, elegant and fashionable, Mrs. Berger's hair dyed black, her lips bright red, Mr. Berger dapper in corduroys and a cashmere sweater.

Sitting in my mother's room with her, I glanced up at the portrait of her mother, given pride of place on the wall across from her bed. In my mother's stories, my grandmother was a looming, dangerous figure who controlled her sprawling, tumbledown home with cold disregard for most of her nine children's feelings (bar her declared favorite, the son who eventually shot himself at her grave). Hardship shrouded my mother's childhood—the family's financial struggles, bullying at the hands of that one brother in particular, vindictiveness from teachers and classmates at her Nazi-sympathizing Afrikaner school, the wider exposure to a malicious racist society.

My mother followed my gaze, her eyes settling on the portrait of her mother as a woman of about seventy, matronly, stocky, with purple-tinged hair and impenetrable eyes, showing none of the elegance and charm that had always flashed from my mother's being, and was still evident now.

"Why did you put her there?" I asked.

"And why not? She's my mother."

"She was just so awful," I said, readying to join with my mother's long-expressed view of her own mother's monstrous cruelty and neglect.

"I'm surprised you'd be so negative," my mother said. She was sitting up in her hospital bed, recently coiffed by the in-house hairdresser, her cheeks touched with rouge. "She wasn't a bad woman. She didn't have an easy life. She did the best she could. And what a raconteur! No one told a story like she did …"

Shocking to hear—at complete odds with what I'd carried around, on behalf of my mother, for a lifetime. And yet there it was, pouring from my now elderly mother: empathy, kindness, forgiveness.

"Darling, could you get me my manicure scissors?" She pointed to the drawer of her bedside table. The scissors she'd had for sixty years, one of those childhood objects that carried for me a visceral, earth-anchoring familiarity. (I have those scissors now; I keep them in my desk drawer.)

The drawer was neatly crammed with little treasures, organized in small boxes my mother had collected over the years, each with a memory attached. Feeling around at the very back, I touched something smooth and cold, then drew it out. A small porcelain saucer. I'd never seen it before, though I'd heard the story of the tea set the whole of my life.

"Is this from the set Mr. Kriege gave you?" I asked.

"Yes. Have I never shown it to you?"

I shook my head, no.

"I want you to have it," she said, taking my hand. There was longing in her face.

I looked at the saucer, a remnant of that singular gift that had embodied the inventive longings of a child, a lifetime ago on the other side of the world. It felt hidden and yet familiar, like the dark side of some inner moon.

Such warmth in my mother's face as she lay there, shrunken from cancer, the radiance in her eyes undiminished by years of physical suffering, endless surgeries, and rounds of treatment in her relentless quest to hold tight to life. My mother may not have ended up singing in the world's great concert halls, as she'd dreamed in her youth she might, but in many ways—in all the important ways—the outlandish dreams of that forlorn, neglected, bullied child had come true. Yes, there had been disappointment, and anguish, but there had also been achievement and satisfaction, artistic fulfillment beyond what the child could have imagined: many and varied singing performances, creative growth, artistic and intellectual experiences of all kinds. Pride taken in children and grandchildren, a vast network of close, like-minded friends. Volunteer activities, endless social engagements, and concerts, opera, ballet. Gourmet meals cooked, travel to all the places the child had dreamed of. For more than forty years, she taught hundreds of students, including the children of former students, and then some of their children. Years of hosting a radio show on the classical station, and after the death of my father, a period of dating that would rival a debutante's, settling into first one long-term relationship, then a second, and in her late years, a third. Life fully fought for, embraced, lived.

I looked down at the porcelain saucer. "I'll treasure it."

In that moment, I saw something that I hadn't as a child, when my mother's stories thundered toward me as I stood, panic-stricken on the tracks, staring down the eye of the train. These treasures my mother held so closely told a story of survival and flourishing. Despite a bitter slamming down throughout her life, including the societal constrictions she bore as a woman (which infected everything, including her marriage), my mother prevailed. I saw now the ferocity with which she resisted being crushed. I'd witnessed that fury, had been in some ways at its mercy, a casualty of her refusal to be destroyed.

A year and a half later, I made the final trip to see my mother.

"This time," the doctor said, "she really is at the end. A week, ten days at most."

My mother of course defied this prediction, as she'd defied all the ones that had come before; it was to be six weeks, not ten days, until her death.

My sister, who was the coordinator of an annual psychiatry conference, had booked a place for me at that year's event, which was being held on Australia's Gold Coast. Our mother, who was holding steady, insisted that we go.

"You need a break," she said to my sister. She was keenly aware of how her ongoing medical crises had turned my sister's life upside down for seven long years. My sister certainly did need a break, and even though the conference work was demanding, the trip would be a much-deserved respite.

"The Gold Coast is so glorious," my mother said, delighted to see my sister lit up with the energy of her professional self, and happy to think of her two daughters having the adventure together.

In fact, we had a marvelous time. The conference was a big success. It was a treat to see my sister shining in her milieu, smart and vivacious, handling everything with aplomb. The Australian Gold Coast was as beach perfect as the travel pictures promised. The three days passed in a whirl of activity—lectures, meetings, meals, everything overseen by my sister, who was electric with purpose. The resort had a faded, old-world feel, with wooden overhead fans that circulated the hot air, and sliding glass doors overlooking the rippling ocean.

My sister and I spent a lot of time with a couple she knew, a psychiatrist colleague of decades and her husband, Aarav, a builder who had recently retired. On the final evening, we sat with a group of attendees on the beach to watch the sunset. The sky swirled with color, pink that deepened to magenta, blue to violet, yellow that burned to orange. All was transformed when the sky dipped to dusk, discreet as a gray fedora, quietly hinting at noir. I looked around, noticing that the five of us represented four different countries of origin.

"I'm curious to know how you each ended up here?" I asked.

One young psychiatrist told us how he'd arrived in Australia with his parents as a refugee from Vietnam. "They called us boat people," he said. "I think those were the first two English words I ever heard. *Boat people.* I had no idea what they meant."

Aarav was the son of an Indian man and a white woman from Britain. "I knew English, of course. And because I look almost white, I found it easy to adjust."

In the racist milieu of Australian society in the 1950s and 1960s, this meant that a way of existing, denied to his darker-complexioned father, was open to him.

"There was always a distance between my father and me," Aarav said. "I'm ashamed to say—I was embarrassed by his accent, by the way he talked, by the way he dressed. Terrible, that a son would feel that way ... and by the time I tried to do something about it, it was too late."

It was only toward the end of his life that his father talked about his experiences during the Partition. His generation seldom talked about the horrors, too traumatized to revisit the memories. In 1947, the British colonial rulers hastily drew up borders to separate Muslims from Hindus and Sikhs, creating Pakistan as a Muslim homeland. The British were eager to make a speedy exit, not wanting to preside over the civil war they saw looming. What ensued was mass murder on both sides and widespread kidnapping and rape. In one short year, between five hundred thousand and two million people were murdered, and fifteen million driven from their homes, the largest mass migration of the already grim twentieth century.

Aarav learned his father had spent months driving what came to be called *ghost trains*, back and forth between the newly birthed Pakistan and the newly defined India.

"The corpses were loaded into trains," his father told him. Aarav supposed that his father had decided, sensing his own death was near, to finally speak of his experiences. "The bodies were ferried to whichever side they now 'belonged.' There were also trains carrying refugees from one side to the other. These were the trains I drove. They were frequently attacked. When that happened, everyone on board was killed. So much silence ... when we arrived, there would be blood seeping out from under the doors."

We sat on the northern Australian beach watching the sky's colors morph as a massive flock of sulphur-crested cockatoos appeared from nowhere, fanning out in disarray, their yellow plumes flattened to discreet tubes. I recalled Margaret Bourke-White's photographs of the mass cross-migration between East and West Punjab. Two years earlier, she'd photographed Buchenwald on the day of liberation; she had photographs of local townspeople, brought by the liberators to see the reality that had for years been in their own backyards, wandering among piles of corpses and past emaciated survivors. "We didn't know!" they all said. Margaret Bourke-White, snapping roll after roll of film, had her response: "You *did* know, you *did*!" Her urge to record, to show, was greater than the value she placed on her own safety. Time and again, she endangered her life to take on the mantle of witnessing.

Two years later, walking the streets of Kolkata (then Calcutta, until its name changed in 2001) as the Partition was under way, she would remark that Kolkata's streets "looked like Buchenwald." In his essay published in the *New Yorker* in 2015, "The Great Divide," historian William Dalrymple noted that the Partition "is central to modern identity in the Indian subcontinent, as the Holocaust is to identity among Jews, branded painfully onto the regional consciousness by memories of unimaginable violence."

And there we all were sitting on the Australian beach, close in our fellow feeling, each of us hugging our origins and yet also free in ways that our immediate forebears would have wept to know.

* * *

Back in Melbourne, our mother was changed. She seemed to have relaxed her fierce grip on life, as if finally, wearily accepting the approach of death. I sat by her bedside, aware of the grimaces of pain on her face, as she faded in and out of consciousness. Dying from pancreatic cancer is not an easy death. Even on morphine, she endured extreme pain.

Time thickened, glugging noiselessly, the world an airless tunnel.

Her eyes snapped open. "Darling, why do you look so anguished?"

"Because I can see you're in pain, Mum. I'm worrying about you."

It was not an entirely truthful statement, though at the time, I couldn't tease apart what was wholly true and what was not. I could feel that old disingenuousness (which all my life had marked my relationship with my mother) frothing around the edges of my soul.

Though as I write this, I question the story I am telling myself. Are not the masks we make for ourselves also a form of truth? The strategies we develop allow other parts of us to flourish. The byways to the self are full of secreted twists and turns. Full-bodied relationships are like works of art, defined by hiddenness and shadow, by the bits of emptiness and silence, by the unsayable. Was it *not* disingenuousness but perhaps a deeper wisdom that prevented me from saying what I now wish I had been able to fully know in that moment, and to say?

Had I screamed *that* version of truth, it would have come out as something like this: "Don't die!"

And now, I hear the echoing sound of my nine-year-old daughter's voice—*Don't leave me!*—as I left the Pátzcuaro schoolyard those many years ago, when she was fearful in her new school in the woods.

One truth was that I hated my mother for dying. For being about to leave me forever. For being in such pain. I grieved for the suffering she'd endured in her lifetime, for the vastness of her unfulfilled artistic yearnings, for the betrayals she'd had to endure. For her loneliness, for the many ways she'd been abandoned—including by me, the daughter she did, after all, love, who left more than three decades earlier, yes, for adventure and education but perhaps also to put some distance between us.

I grieved that she did not love me as wholly as my infant-child-teenager-adult and now middle-aged-woman self might have felt adequate. Perhaps this was my failing as a daughter. To not walk away from that gape-mouthed infant self within. And here's the thing—I hated myself as well. For being unable to become myself without fleeing, for causing—well, this very moment, which had arrived because I had deprived us both of the opportunity of growing together into the kind of realized, differentiated womanhood a mother and daughter can perhaps achieve if given the chance to evolve side by side. In depriving my mother of that, I'd also deprived myself of becoming something I had not become, perhaps would never become.

This was my reason for the emotional opacity, this was the reason we—who had at times been so close, two souls who *did* know each other, who *did* see into each other with recognition, connection, and love—could not fully reach each other during those final visits. We both made intense and honorable efforts, though. Finding no words, I simply sat by her bedside, watching the life leak from her. Instinctively I knew that here, at the end, there was no space for the shameful rage I felt—there was space only for gentleness, for the love I prayed would flood my soul and give me the courage and strength to help my mother die.

But then … something happened. My mother closed her eyes and a peaceful smile floated to her lips.

"Don't worry about me, darling," she said, her voice whispery and gentle, the gentlest voice of the most loving mother. "I'm a very, very happy woman."

I sat on the edge of her bed, dripping with sadness for this brave woman now reduced to suffering and incapacity, who castigated herself for her decline (*Stupid old woman!* she would scold when she thought no one could hear).

She opened her eyes. She was looking at me with pure longing—and what was that? I fought it, tried to push it away, so practiced had I become in steeling myself against the Big Disappointment. Yes, love was coming at me in waves from this suffering creature who was my mother. She took my hand and was looking right into my soul, wordlessly telling me so many things, telling me, I think most of all, that she saw my pain and was sorry.

"You're a wonderful mother," she said. "Your children are so lucky." Her voice was a shadow, dancing in the light. "I wish I'd had you as a mother."

I wanted to reach out to this sad, diminishing woman who'd been so unloved—more unloved than I'd been. I wanted her to know how much she was loved by me. I also wanted to reach back in time and tell the little girl–me that her mother had loved her after all: that we were, both of us, beloved.

− 9 −

A Mahogany Door, Leading Down

I'd been longing for a break from the city, with all its grime, and jangle, and my idea for this book found kindness in the form of a writing fellowship, a month in New Hampshire at a place whose motto is "Freedom to create." My cabin was nestled in a wild, wooded landscape. It was January, and the snow was thick on the ground.

I was two weeks into my stay when, one night, I found myself unable to sleep. I kicked off the heavy gray comforter. The fire I'd made earlier had long since sputtered to ash. The cold air on my limbs felt soothing. I rose and dressed in my fleece-lined pants and the nubby sweater I'd had since I was fifteen—a miracle it was sturdy as ever, since most every other piece of clothing I'd ever owned had been stretched, worn thin, or lost. I put on my down coat and then, I was outside, standing under the stark sky.

I stumbled, tripping on a jutting stone. My eyes acclimatized to the near darkness; shapes sprouted all around and I slipped easily among them. Something went very still inside, even as I increased my speed until I was almost running. Deep in the woods, drinking in the cold air, I was unperturbed by my loss of directional sense. I closed my fist around nothing, imagining a demagnetized compass with a wildly spinning needle. The image filled me with a sense of freedom. I felt victorious: alone and intensely alive.

The sky spat out icy specks that landed tartly on my face. A wind rose and the trees around me gave a shivery applause. Since arriving, I'd seen white-tailed deer, an owl, several beavers, and two

enormous raccoons up on their hind legs, nosing around in the gut-
ted hole of an ancient oak. The birds were silent as ghosts, though
I felt their presence and pictured them as feathered buds lined up
on branches, heads tucked tight. Creatures huddled in burrows,
waiting out what was brewing to be a storm. My mother's singing voice—a coloratura, which is a light and agile soprano with an
expansive range— bloomed in my head, music I'd not thought of in
decades. Schubert's "The Shepherd on the Rock." Now, within me,
my mother's voice rose:

> *Der Frühling will kommen,*
> *Der Frühling, meine Freud',*
> *Nun mach' ich mich fertig*
> *Zum Wandern bereit*

> The springtime will come,
> The springtime, my happiness,
> Now must I get ready
> To wander forth

The moon was high overhead. My hands were cold, even in my
insulated gloves, telling me I'd been walking for some time. The
path opened to a clearing. I felt a pang of longing for shelter and
rest. I leaned on an enormous birch presiding over the clearing.
Even through my glove I could feel the bulge of scar tissue on the
tree. I turned to see what looked like a thick diagonal slash, about a
foot long, and trunk growth, years thick, bulging around the wound.

It was then I noticed the peculiar house, set in the middle of
the clearing, bulky in its four-story height, giving the impression
of being both ramshackle and well maintained. The house seemed
uninhabited; it lacked the aura of human presence. The cloud
drifted away from the moon, upending white light down onto the
scene. The house, its wooden shingles painted steel blue, jutted out
in unexpected places; clearly, bits had been added to the original
Queen Anne architectural form. A generous porch wrapped around

the main body of the house, with filigreed metal railings and over-hang draping down from the eaves. I counted four triangular gables. The oddest addition was a slender tower rising from the back of the building, topped with a bright-red pergola that looked like it belonged in a Japanese garden.

I walked up the stone path and climbed the wide stairs to the porch. I waited for a moment on the broad unpainted planks, as if for a sign, but when nothing happened, I approached the front door and turned the cut-glass handle.

I'd expected the door to be open. It was.

My mother's singing rose again in my mind's ear. The door clicked shut behind me. I heard a beautiful melody, my mother's exquisite voice as I had heard it throughout my childhood, saw again her young-mother face: hair pulled up into a perfect chignon, delicate features arranged in artistic concentration as she worked the muscles of her mouth, jaw, and throat to coax the sound from her diminutive frame. In her eyes, the look of an artist who has lost themselves in service to the gods as they connect to their own deepmost core.

I reached for the switch on the foyer wall. A chandelier over-head filled the space with light and my mother's voice vanished. Elegant rooms opened out from the foyer, appointed with furniture from several periods—Victorian, but also touches of the mod-ern, and items from distant lands—a Japanese screen, an African beadwork doll, an Australian Aboriginal painting, two Indonesian masks mounted on the wall. In the formal living room to the right, I made out the contours of a Danish coffee table, early 1960s, and in the dining room to the left, a Ming dynasty–style carved table with matching chairs. I glimpsed cork wallpaper in the room beyond the living room, and beyond that, a solarium with a glass wall, the panes set into blue-green metal struts. The house echoed with a feeling of unlived-in splendor, vibrating with people who were no longer here, as if the stories of their lives hung in the cur-tains and fluttered in the air as invisible golden dust. Everywhere, shadows and silence.

I walked from room to room, my footsteps oddly noiseless. I found myself in what was likely once a porch, glassed in and made cozy by a brick fireplace. The needles of a massive hemlock spruce scraped against one window. I sat in a leather armchair by the corner window, taking stock of the feeling that this house had been waiting for me, had drawn me to it and was pleased, even relieved, that I was finally here. A feeling of calm spread through my limbs. I wanted to stay in this chair forever. I looked down to where my arms lay on the armrests, saw the way the maroon leather, softened by the years, gleamed in the light of the brass floor lamp.

The formal rooms of the ground floor were conventionally laid out—living room, dining room, sitting room, library, and the winterized porch. Beyond these were a series of spaces that made little sense: a large supply closet in the middle of everything—brooms, buckets, cleaning supplies in extreme quantities; I counted twelve mops, for example, and in the corner was a hamper filled with clean rags, torn from old pillowcases and threadbare towels. A door in the back of the closet opened onto a children's playroom with bins of toys—wooden things, dolls and puppets, board games, and a croquet set. There were two kitchens, one leading onto the next, the first large and commercial, such as you'd find in a restaurant, the second compact and sleek, stylish according to today's standards, with shiny appliances and a quartz counter the color of pearl.

Beyond the opaque glass door at the far end of the modern kitchen, the treads of a narrow staircase twisted upward, looking like what they used to call "servants' stairs." It likely led to the bedrooms, and now I imagined these rooms with beautiful paned windows looking onto a lawn bordered by a formal garden, the wild woods kept out by tall wooden fencing.

Back in the library, with its floor-to-ceiling bookshelves and smell of leather bindings, I found a door in the corner, tucked behind a sliding ladder set on metal rails. I slid the ladder aside. The door was mahogany, the top half dominated by a piece of frosted glass etched with flowers and leaves. The metal door handle was rusted where its black paint had peeled. The mechanism turned easily. I peered in. The pale light filtering in from behind me revealed a wide steep staircase leading down. I felt overcome by vertigo and feared I might tumble but steadied myself, holding on to the doorframe and taking a deep breath. The air was cold and smelled of stone. I stepped over the wooden saddle to find my feet were now on concrete; I could feel its solidity pushing up through the soles of my shoes.

The stairs below came into view one at a time. I stepped down, down, farther down, the air becoming cold and damp as I descended, as if I were burrowing below ground. Finally, I reached a dimly lit corridor with a hardwood floor and walls covered with paper in a dainty floral design. I heard sound that seemed to be coming from far away. I paused beside a door to my right, from which I could hear strains of music—piano, a Chopin prelude I knew in my bones. I leaned against the door. The cut-glass handle was warm to the touch.

I opened the door a crack, startled by a full throttle of light and sound, the familiar, lilting melody of the prelude lifting from the keys, and drenching sunlight from a picture window on the far wall.

At the piano, my mother in the full burst of young womanhood I have seen only in photographs. On the floor beside her sits a bassinet, not far from the foot pedals of the baby grand, its raised lid turning the instrument to an enormous one-winged bird. A soft, amoeboid motion alerts me to the presence of an infant tucked beneath the folds of a white blanket—and there, a little hand, pulling out from the fold. The room wavers oddly—with the realization that the infant in the bassinet, new to the world, reacting to the light and sound, and of course oblivious to the fact that I am standing here taking in this scene, is me.

The doubling feels unbearable. I close the door.

I turn the handle of the next door, opening it a sliver.

I hear them before I see them, my parents—both young, my father's hair already streaked with silver. They are fighting, angry, withdrawn from each other. Dread pours through me, everything aches. And then, a sudden splash of light from somewhere. They both spin around—they have seen me—and their faces change, sparking with warmth. My father smiles generously, my mother flashes her radiance, eyes alight. The scenery in the room swivels around to reveal the kitchen of my childhood home, with its white wooden cabinets and windows looking onto the street. My mother is wearing an apron over her evening dress. She leans over the electric frying pan I used to pride myself on scrubbing clean of its tarred grime. (How I would glow, hearing my mother's praise, "Darling, thank you! That's just perfect!") The pan simmers. The smell of tongue in wine sauce wafts over to where I am standing as I peer in through the sliver-opening. The scent is pungent with leeks, carrots, celery, and I know the meat will be flavorful. But now my mother has turned again, this time at my father's approach. My father reaches out his hand, his index finger pointed, and my mother puts down the runcible spoon, also reaches out a forefinger so that the tips of their fingers touch. I close the door, carefully, the sound of the latch a heavy thud, like the hefty stone lid of a sarcophagus.

I peer down the length of the corridor, try to count the number of doors, but they recede into shadow. I skip several doors then stop before one that is much larger than the rest—double width, reaching to the ceiling. I can barely take hold of the elaborate handle, the kind one might find on the door of a museum or church. I grasp it in both hands and turn, this time opening the door wide enough so that I might enter. Beyond is the deep scent of nature's greenery.

I have entered a maze of wall-high bushes, trimmed flat. I reach up to steady myself. The cut ends of the shrubbery prick my palm. My feet guide me and soon I am lost in the twists and turns, filled with panic, a sooty dread hanging in the air. A halo of illumination accompanies me. I round a corner to find my little brother—he must be eight years old—standing in a corner made by the maze and bouncing a ball, delight in his face. Beside him, our new Labrador puppy; she's doing a happy-puppy leap and wag, trying to catch hold of the ball. My brother laughs, turns his sparkling brown eyes my way. My heart leaps, but he looks right through me. I keep walking. My brother is gone, and there is darkness again, but then another sheen of light rises around the next bend, and there, in a corner, I see a child curled up on the ground, whimpering. I see it is one of my sisters, and I know she is in pain. I lurch around this corner and the next, and another circle of dim light, and now I catch sight of my other sister, her face turned toward the hedge. I see only her back but of course recognize the shape of her, every curve and line, and I see her shoulders are heaving, her head pressed against the hedge. I cannot bear the pain coursing through me. I tear around the next corner and come to an abrupt halt, faced with something that socks the breath from me. It is me, my own face, a child, staring wildly, in terror—. I slam my eyes shut. I want only to leave this place, but I am tangled in the maze. A sob rises in my chest. I sidle up to the hedge and inch forward, hoping I might find a way out without having to open my eyes. I shuffle along for some time, the sharp twigs spiky on my palms. My skin is pierced in places, and I picture blood, black in the darkness, leaving sticky traces on the leaves of the hedge. I wonder if it glistens.

And then, of a sudden, the air brightens and clears. I can feel it in my lungs. I open my eyes. I am back in the hallway. I have somehow leapt the length of it and find myself at the end, standing by a window that opens out onto the night sky. The window is wide open. Fresh, cold air is pouring in.

Beside me is the final door. Of regular size, another cut-glass doorknob. I reach for the handle and turn.

This room is silent and in shadow, lit only by a small floor lamp in the corner. My mother is here—I see her profile. She has a vicious look in her eye, dragging a child—I know the child is two years old, though I don't know why I know this. I suspect it's a girl, but I cannot be sure. I wonder if the child is me. The image terrifies me, recalls a dream image that haunted me for years that somewhere along the line I'd shut away and buried: a woman, holding a young child in an awkward and unwieldy way, its arms and legs hanging down, a blank and horrifying look on its face. I know the child is injured. Vigorous shaking springs to mind, the kind that can injure a small child's innards and brain.

I slam the door shut before I can think. I race along the corridor, then blindly leap up those steep and treacherous stairs, the air thin in my lungs. Up and up and farther up, and then through the glass-paned door, along the elegant hallways, on through this room and that, the furnishings a blur in my peripheral vision. I know this house as intimately as if it were a house I'd once lived in. I reach the foyer, and without pausing to flick off the light-splintering chandelier, I am out the front door, down the stoop steps, and tearing through the woods.

I come to a halt in a silencing thickness of fresh snow and hear from my gasps that I am having trouble breathing. I crouch on my heels for a moment to regain my breath. I brush my hands through the snow. I rise and then, at a steady walking pace, continue through the woods.

Mum, how you would have loved these woods. How you'd have flourished, if you'd been given the chance to walk them, to walk them here, with me. To have had the chance to open your voice, unencumbered—.

I come to an abrupt halt.

I turn around, not racing, this time, but moving steadily back to the house. Back through the foyer, the light no longer splintering but luminous and soft, on through each room until I come to the library with the door that leads to the basement. I turn the doorknob and make my way back down.

I know exactly which door to open to find my mother with the crazed look in her eyes and this time, I do not feel terror. My mother—how young she is, how weepingly beautiful, despite the cruel look in her eyes. Her mouth gives it all away. I see, when she turns to me, that her lips are trembling with desperation. Seeing me there, tears spring to her eyes as mortification floods the whole of her. It flows down her arms, drips onto the floor.

"Darling, I'm so sorry." Her voice comes from that volcanic source deep within the earth.

I shake my head, as if to say there's no need for that, really.

"Mum, come with me," I say, reaching out my hand. I only register later, back in my cabin, where I will watch the sun rise over the

tips of the snow-crusted hemlocks and blue pines, that the child
who had been there earlier had vanished. My mother, upon seeing
me, had let go of the child, who dropped in an ungainly way to the
ground and then, it was as if she just dissolved into the floor.

My mother's eyes stream with tears as I lead her up the concrete
stairs. She glances around the house as we walk. Several times, she
opens her mouth as if to speak, but each time, she closes it without
making a sound. Neither of us says anything, not a word, though I
can feel an otherworldly communication flowing through our fingers,
where I clasp her hand, which feels small and childlike in my own.

And then, outside in the cold New Hampshire night, I peel off
my coat and put it around her shoulders.

"Come," I say. Something like love fills her features, and in
that moment, her face is the most beautiful face—*mother*—I have
ever seen. My own eyes fill with tears and then I lead her off the
roadway and onto a path that opens in the thick bank of trees. It
is an overgrown hiking path with little signposts placed every now
and then. Fallen branches litter the way, and here and there we
climb over a felled trunk, me first and then behind me, still holding
my hand—how delicate her touch, how trusting and thankful—
my mother. At one point, she stops and withdraws her hand from
mine to zipper the coat I have given her all the way to her chin.
She pulls the hood up over her hair, which has come undone from
its chignon in places so that strands hang around her cheeks, fram-
ing her face. She gives me back her hand, and we continue. I know
exactly where I am going and know what I will find. After a time,
we come to a halt. I scan about for a clearing I know is somewhere
right about here, trying to locate the spot. Sure enough, up ahead
perhaps three hundred yards, I make out an opening in among the
thicket of trees.

"Come," I say again, and a few minutes later, we find ourselves in a sizable clearing soaked in moonlight. In the open space
stands a sturdy cabin with no windows and a lofty roof. The roof
glints, suggesting it is made of glass. My mother lets go of my
hand and side by side, we approach the cabin and enter through
the front door.

Moonlight rains down, the light ricochets off the wood paneling of the walls. In the center of the room stands a magnificent grand piano.

"Go ahead," I say, gesturing toward the piano. I see the yearning in her face. "It's okay, it's there for *you*. Play for as long as you like—and when you're ready, sing."

She looks around nervously, then turns back to me with a querying look.

"Really, there's no one here. Not even me." An odd thing for me to say, but it feels right, and something dips in her eyes, a recognition.

"I know, it feels impossible, but it isn't," I say.

In that moment, I know that had my mother had these snowy pathways, this chance to walk and listen to the silence of the world, this unencumbered freedom to create, she'd never have done any dragging, nor slapping of small children's faces, nor cracking of a sharp knuckle against a child's skull. Yes, I will say this time that it was a little girl, a sad little girl so stunned and confused that the marvelous creature she worshipped, whom she'd have unthinkingly laid down her life for, whose smile and loving gaze she coveted with the full hotness of her little soul, that this marvelous creature could become a monster, could inspire such fear that the little girl would wet her pants in the face of the wrath, even in anticipation of the wrath that sometimes, mercifully, did not come.

"Go on," I say. "Open your throat and sing."

I leave her there and race back to the house, running the way a child runs, with abandon, the air rushing into my lungs, my legs strong, the movement filled with freedom and grace.

Joy leaps within me as I go back into the house and through the already familiar rooms. Through the library, beyond the elaborate door, down the concrete stairs. I come to a stop before the door I know will be the final door that I open.

This handle doesn't turn easily—it sticks a little, as if it needs oiling. The hinge, too, is tight—the door creaks slowly open. My mother is sitting all the way on the other side of a pleasing room at a small desk, concentrating on something, one hand propping up

her head, the other holding a pen. At the sound of the door opening, she turns to me, her face relaxing into a generous smile.

"Darling, how lovely of you to come!" she says, jumping up and
crossing the room. She leans in for a hug. My own body stiffens,
though I try to shake it off. Her hug is relaxed and warm, though
she pulls away first. A familiar yearning pours through my veins.

"Come in! I'll make some tea."

I take in the room—modern, lit by three elegant lamps. The
gold curtains are drawn.

We sit over tea, my mother's smile electric as she tells me about
the art history course she's taking at the university, having decided
in her early fifties to go back to serious study. Her eyes dance, her
voice dances, *everything is so fascinating*, she says. I gaze at her lovely
face, gaze and gaze, an infant, again, taking it all in.

* * *

The house I have just described—with its impossible stairs leading
hundreds of feet down into the earth, where, in its subterranean
reaches, empty windows sear light into cavernous rooms, where one
door leads to an outdoor maze of perfectly trimmed hedges ten feet
tall—is as real to me as anything. It is a savior of sorts, allowing me
to open my eyes just enough to snatch glimpses of the things that
have puzzled me for so long. Why do we need to do this, we suffering humans—to stare down the silent, hidden things that take
root in our souls, spreading barbed tendrils that coil dangerously
through the seasons of our being? It has something, I suspect, to
do with reclaiming, though I do not know why we feel this might
make a difference, hands in front of our faces, fingers slightly spread
before our eyes. We dare in our fright, I suppose, to discover.

* * *

Toward the end of my stay at the artists' retreat, we were warned
that a major storm was approaching. I decided to drive into town
for supplies.

The snow came down in thick clouds, stirred by the wind to sideways gusts of white. The country highway was still drivable, so I settled in for the half-hour drive into town. The traffic was heavier than I'd expected with the encroaching storm, but then locals were used to this kind of thing. They hardly batted an eye.

There was a line at the general store. I bought firewood and milk, eggs, butter, carrots, broccoli, and a blueberry pie. By the time I turned back to the country highway, the snow was coming down heavily. I could see nothing ahead of me. The beam of the head-lights showed only dense, swirling snow. I drove at a crawl. Every now and then, faint red taillights would appear a few inches in front of me. Oddly, I felt safe. We all seemed to be in this together, taking extreme caution, hoping to inch our way home without incident. Time thickened and became one with the swirling whiteness. I kept my foot very lightly on the pedal and lost myself in the atmo-spheric daze.

The white suddenly lifted. For a moment, the headlights cut through and I could see the road ahead. Not a single car. I accel-erated, hoping to take advantage of the respite in the storm. The road unfurled softly beneath the car, a silky white ribbon. The trees beside the road were laden with snow. Everything was utterly quiet and oddly static. My eyes wandered for a second to the speedom-eter—the needle was hovering at around eighty. I couldn't possibly be going at such a speed. But then I realized my foot was almost all the way down on the pedal, and a foreboding, metallic with danger, overcame me. I pulled my foot up off the pedal and heard a sudden screeching, and then, I was spinning. I tried to right the car, but the wheel didn't respond. The car was now just moving on its own, out of the spin into a slide. Branches smacked the windshield. A crunching, cracking sound reached my ears. The car slammed to a halt, and I felt myself thrown forward in the seat. Then, there was only stillness, and silence.

My neck hurt but not terribly. I reached for my phone on the dashboard. No signal. Reception at the cabin had been patchy at best, and here it was altogether nonexistent. I'd been driving for some time. It occurred to me that perhaps I was not far from the cabin I'd visited in the night. I sat for a while, my mind strangely blank. The headlights opened a wide swath before me, into the woods. Layer upon layer of birches. The two beams converged in the distance, an arrow pointing me to where I was supposed to go. I grabbed my gloves, hat, and scarf and opened the door.

I picked my way through the trees, my feet falling into the powdery snow. My feet knew where to go, as if I were being reeled in. Relief poured through me. There was nothing for me to do but go where I was going. In my ears, the sound of my breath; in my veins, a vital pulsing, my legs strong, my feet canny. Time evaporated in a way that felt right, as if finally, I could settle in—well, just here, in this moment, walking through the woods, my car having veered off the road. No one knew where I was. No one was expecting me. There was no one I needed to take care of, and no one who needed to take care of me. I was alone in the cold, swirling white of the world, my breath turning to little specks of ice.

A trail opened in the tangled underbrush, marked by a wooden post with a red square. It looked familiar—yes, I had seen it before. A large chunk at the top of the post was gone, as if it had been damaged in a storm, leaving a jagged edge. I was able to make out the path—the snow was smoother underfoot, and I followed it as it wound through the trees. There, another post and, a few hundred yards deeper into the woods, another. I now knew where I was—I was on the path that led to the clearing and the remarkable, familiar house. I walked with a growing sense of excitement. There was something so unlikely about this—about the fact that I would veer off the road into the woods and then chance upon the very path I had walked when I tripped upon the house. It had to be purposeful—I could feel, in my bones, that it was. Feel that I was being drawn to—what? My fate? Yes. I was being drawn to my fate. On the page, the word looks portentous, dramatic—the thought a teenager might have, at the center of her own epic drama—but that is not how it felt as it pressed itself softly into my mind. No, it was more like this: the feeling that as far away as I was from, well, from everywhere, as far-flung as I was in this life I had made for myself, I was where I was supposed to be. I was here, simply here, and this was right.

Now, I couldn't wait until I would see the house again! The house, with its cobbled-together feel and elegant rooms and unexpected storeroom, and magical, frightening basement world, all of it was about to appear again and invite me in. A warm place to ride out the storm. It was just around this next curve, I felt sure of it, and my heart skipped a beat. The wind picked up. I could feel the snow whipping against my face, icy needles stinging my cheeks. I blinked once, twice, could feel the ice on my eyelashes. I pressed forward, determined, undaunted. Soon, I would be coming upon the house.

Yes! There was the enormous birch, taller than the rest; I had stopped to admire it that black night when I'd stumbled upon the house, thinking it was some kind of watchman or guard. I trudged close to the tree and, sure enough, there was the diagonal gash, shoulder high, carved into its trunk. I wondered who would have done such a thing, sliced at the tree in that way. I took off my glove and rested my hand in the groove of scar tissue. My hand froze immediately upon contact with the frigid air. I slid my fingers back into my heavy ski glove and turned, aware of the gleam of happiness that seemed to rest over everything. The path curved and I knew that in a moment, I would come upon the clearing that held the house, and wondered if I'd see, through the glass transom above the front door, that the chandelier was alight. I wondered if the house would be expecting me once again.

I took the curve. Sure enough, here was the clearing. The broad swath of land, the open sky, just as I remembered it from that night.

But no house. No structure of any kind, just a wide patch of fresh snow, startling and untouched. There was only the clearing and the steadily falling snow.

- 10 -

The Moving Forward

I suffer a peculiar affliction. I'll give you an example of what it is like.

We are spending the summer in Oviedo, a small, bustling city in Asturias, in north-central Spain. My husband is working at the university here. They've provided an old apartment on the main square, beside the Gothic cathedral. Four times each hour, the cathedral erupts in a lengthy clanging of bells in the tune of the Asturian anthem. Ninety-six times a day. The hourly version is twice the length of the half-hourly and three times the length of the quarter-hourly.

The chiming has become a family joke. Both our kids, aged six and eleven, break into grins if I catch their eye when it starts up. When the bells are mercifully silent, one of us might begin to hum the melody, sending the others into smirks.

We've been here for a month, and this is the thing. As of yesterday, when the bells sound, I find myself no longer there with my family in the moment, but in my private elsewhere, ahead in the future: in the hospital bed, unable to move, attached as I am to the machines that invade me with plastic tentacles.

Here I lie, staring up through weak eyes at the crackles and peelings of the ceiling, in hope that today, though I cannot remember the day or the date or the year, one of my two children, now the bearers of what life remains for me, may come to visit.

There she is, above me. My daughter, the clear eyes of her youth shining, though her skin shows signs of age. How old could she be? Forty? Fifty? More? I have no way of knowing but to ask, and I would never shame her or myself by doing this. She smiles her generous, inclusive, life-affirming smile, and I pull the oxygen mask from my face. Her face shades with concern. I hear the ugly, slap-sucking mechanical gasp of the machine. She reaches for the mask, is trying to replace it, but I wave her arm away and nod to indicate that I'll be fine for a minute or two without it. You see, I want to reclaim our ancient joke.

Da da dah—la la-la lah, la-la lah—la la-la lah, la-la lah.

When I smile, I feel how dry my lips are. They are sore and the smile gives birth to a new little tear in the skin. I touch the fresh wound with my tongue and taste a fleck of blood.

My daughter smiles too, though not the smile I remember—no, not remember, I can also see her smooth eleven-year-old face right now, right this second, and behind her, the gleeful pixie-grin of my little imp boy, who throws back his head to release a ripple of laughter. The air is warm, within it a fresh touch of cool. I watch the dappled light filter through the trees of the park as we watch a woman throw a tatty rag-toy to her dog.

But no, my daughter's face has those strange signs of aging, and her smile now is not one of freedom. It is filled with pain and loss. Gone her childhood. Gone her energetic mother with her firm protective arms, the mother full of plans for her children's lives, the mother who would—and did—move mountains so that her children might evolve in the light of goodness, adventure, hope.

Tears leak from my eyes, down my cheeks, pooling atop the oxygen mask, which appears to be back over my face. My broken body has no trouble extruding tears; they are vigorous in their flow.

Sweet child, I want to say. Sweet child who is no longer—and yet sits beside me, woman-child.

I don't say this. I only stretch my mostly toothless mouth in an attempt at a smile.

It is a cruel trick of time—for here I am, back in the park, our summer in Spain not yet over, though soon it will be, and then it will be home to New York to face the new school year with all the anxieties and expectations of entering sixth grade (my daughter) and first grade (my son).

The infernal chimes, there they are again.

Each of my competing *presents* feels like the real, the solid, the only one. I don't know which one to hold on to or trust.

I have, however, figured something out.

The present up ahead—what I've come to think of as the Final Place—is static. It waits up there, drawing me toward it, like Tolstoy's last station.

The other present moves forward. Once, in that present, I was young. Now, here, in the Plaza San Francisco of Oviedo, I am in early middle age. At some point I came to think of this realm as the Moving Forward.

I have come to realize that the two realms awkwardly coexist, unequal and full of tension, the Moving Forward unseeing as it hurtles toward the Final Place that is knowing and smug—by definition, the other realm's ultimate instant.

One feeling has plagued me throughout the Moving Forward. Now, in my bed, alone with the tubes that are the medium of my subsistence, I recall that odd pulsing instinct that was with me once I had my children, subterranean and imperative, like the steady beat in the wrist the physician touches to see if the patient still lives. When they were born, I frantically wished that nothing bad happen to them, that I would reach my own death only when they were firmly established in their adult lives with families of their own, so that my passing would not unbalance the foundation of their being.

I suppose one can get used to anything. And this peculiar, doubled condition I am describing—this temporal telescope—is not, in the end, so very demanding.

I wonder if tomorrow will be a day on which my son, still an imp, though a grown one, graying at the temples, will come to visit?

The tube that enters my chest beneath the cup of my throat is hurting again. I must bear it for some hours until a nurse appears who might inquire how I am and attempt to adjust it.

There is a good deal of shame that goes along with this condition. It has to do with realizing one is not fully in this life because of it—and yet also more fully in it than others might be, because at every moment, all experience is passing through the lens of imminent death. Who knows if others share the condition; it is not something I could bring myself to discuss in the hard-edged brightly lit world of quotidian life—at dinner parties, by the workplace water cooler, or on walks with friends.

Although, as I write this, I realize I do have clues that perhaps I am not, after all, alone, that a great many *do* share my condition. The clues are in books and films set in the future or past that bear the stamp of a *present-day* consciousness coupled with an *other* consciousness that oversees everything: Toni Morrison's *Beloved*, Terrence Malick's *Tree of Life*, David Malouf's *Fly Away Peter*, Elizabeth Rosner's *Gravity*, Tatyana Tolstaya's *Aetherial Worlds*. While engaged with such work, I feel joined and understood.

When the time comes, my passing will feel like a double loss. A loss of the Moving Forward—of the journey—as well as a loss of the backward-looking state of the Final Place, the eye that has watched it all unfold, whose presence has made the passage more piquant, achy, and precious. Most of all, I have trouble imagining the subsiding of the ache ...

Though perhaps this is what lives on, in disembodied form. Perhaps this is what constitutes the soul, that essence-of-living that some believe endures. Perhaps there is, after all, an afterlife: a great and ever-expanding collective yearning.

This lying-in-the-bed-with-the-tubes, then, is what I yearned for all these years: this, the fulfilling of my dreams. To have watched both my children thrive and strive and labor and love, as Simon and I had the luxury of doing.

When they strain to make eye contact with me over the mask and the tubes, I try to communicate that this is *not* one of those awful situations one silently prays against in the course of the Moving Forward. No, this is victory, the win.

What can it mean to have had the chance to live fully, and without significant suffering, and for a robust number of years, when in any event death will come and wipe it all away? Of course, it *does* matter, in the same way that birdsong matters, or the scent of jasmine. For an instant the air is alive with melody or sweet with perfume. Someone smells it or hears it—or not. But it is there.

I look at my son's face—yes, he has come.

That's all there is for me now. No antidote or cure for the terrible things in this world.

They will remove all these tubes when there is no more that these tubes can do.

I see him again, he is almost three, his hair, flaxen curls, giving off that sweet little-child scent, we are lying together in his new big-boy bed as I read him a story. I am aware of the beam of his concentration and the relaxed press of his little body up against mine. Slowly, absently, he strokes my forearm with his fingers.

And now, we are in Paris, where we spent a year. My son is eight, I am reading to him up on the attic platform that serves as his room in our small seven-story walk-up apartment on Rue Saint-Sauveur.

"Mama," he says. "I'm dreaming of a clubhouse. So big." He gestures upward with his slender arms, making a wide V, his gaze boring through the ceiling, beyond the pitched roof and into the planet-speckled sky. "There's a big room to play in, and then on top of that, a science lab. And then, and then ..." He is leaning up against me in the bed, and I can feel his little heart pounding in his thin chest. "On the top, the very top, a glass ceiling, like a circle ..."

"A dome?"

"Yes, a dome. How you look up at the stars. With a huge telescope," he says.

"An observatory."

He nods, lets his arms drop, his heart still pounding as he stares into his creation.

"It sounds amazing."

"Can we build it? In our backyard? When we get back to Brooklyn? Can we?"

"We could build a clubhouse," I say. "I'm not sure we could build one quite that big. Maybe a cabin?"

When we return to Brooklyn, we go to Home Depot and buy supplies. A friend who works in construction supervises us and, together, we build a one-room structure with four little double-glazed windows in the concrete patch that is our backyard. We cover it with cedar shingles, using four nails for each. We tile the pitched roof with simple tar squares. It takes a couple of months of weekends to complete, down to sheet-rocking and painting the interior, though we never quite finish the caulking.

The night the cabin is complete, I come in to say goodnight. By now, we are reading the Narnia books aloud. He has the book closed on his chest, not yet ready to begin.

"I can't believe it," he says. "We actually did it."

"Yes, we did."

"I can hardly believe that I dreamed about building a clubhouse and then our family actually did it."

My daughter? Will she be here soon?

And now, another of the moments I stroke again and again in the limpid space of memory. My daughter, not yet two years, several years before the birth of my son.

We have driven to a lake. I peel her from my arms, the place she most likes to be. She was a fretful baby who startled easily and clung to me in the way of a marsupial, as if she needed more time in a quasi-womb. I pass my daughter to my husband so that I might take a short swim. Her brow furrows with anxiety, but I dive in nevertheless. I swim out to the center of the small lake—four minutes or five—then turn to head back to the shore. A languid breast-stroke: with each bob of my head above the water, visual gulps of the fuzzy image of my toddler in her bright-blue floral bathing suit, trying to suppress her distress, straining at the water's edge to reach for me, her Mama, whom she can't bear to have beyond her grasp.

And then, I am at the shore, breaking through the water, shedding sunlit droplets, and I take hold of her as she throws herself into my arms with relief.

At the time, I knew I would carry these moments with me forever.

I remember precisely when my condition made itself known for the first time. I was ten years old, sitting in my classroom at Deepdene Primary School, doodling surreptitiously on the desk.

In the space of an instant, I was not only myself, listening with quickening heart to the words of my favorite teacher, Mr. Savage, but a different me, too. I was lying somewhere—yes, in a bed.

It is difficult for me to move my head, but with some effort, I move my eyes. I see I am in a bed with shiny metal bars around me. The feeling of tiredness strikes me. Not the usual tiredness I feel after hours of running around playing British Bulldog and cricket with my neighbors in the cul-de-sac where I live, but something else: a weakness, a feeling that I am fading away.

Everyone in the classroom just sat there, as if nothing had happened. Mr. Savage continued his discussion of the book and children raised their hands.

Me, an old woman. The tubes, the oxygen mask, the feel of my own wasted muscles, and wrinkled skin that hangs in folds.

The classroom faded in the way that a photograph would become undone if one could reverse the developing process, and I was left only with the me-in-the-bed—a hospital bed—and surrounded by people I didn't know, and yet toward whom I felt strange and compelling feelings.

Funny, the idea of giving birth to my Death Self—to the self that is closest to passing. My *dying self* coming to life to accompany my *living-evolving self* throughout the passage.

So perhaps, then, not two selves, two lives, happening simultaneously. Perhaps the older, wiser, finished self spawned as a guide to accompany my naïve self on the journey.

It was only after my children were born in the Moving Forward realm that I finally realized who these middle-aged adults were—these people who'd sat with the me in the Final Place for so many hours, who looked at me so tenderly.

When I first held my newborn daughter, I recognized the look in her eyes. This baby was the same person as the woman who had, all these years, come to see me as I lay in the hospital bed, who'd hovered around me with love and concern and grief.

So even though my son had not yet been born, I understood that my two main visitors in the Final Place were my own children. At that stage, when the Final Place first came clear, they were of course much older than I was in the Moving Forward realm. Old enough, in fact, to be my own parents.

In this condition, one gets used to a great many things, paradox chief among them. One's children being older than oneself, for example, and for such a long stretch of time.

I've tallied my calculations so many times; it has become a habit, like cracking your knuckles or chewing your nails.

I've had to rely on estimations, though these have become more fine-grained as the years pass. At first, I guessed my Final Place age to be about seventy-five. I've come to realize that it's more like eighty-five or eighty-six. A good long life.

Because this second self has always been there, for almost as long as I can remember, I believed it would miraculously exist for all eternity. It somehow followed from this that my Moving Forward self would also therefore endure for eternity. The living equivalent of an asymptote, a line that goes on forever, perhaps coming very close to the horizontal baseline but never meeting it.

It is only recently—within the last few minutes, in fact—that I realize this has been an illusion, another of the cruel tricks played on me by my condition.

What is that wonderful feeling at my feet? I cannot inch myself up to see what it is. Oh, wait, now I know. My daughter has come.

She is here again, rubbing my feet. She has removed the fluffy bed socks and is rubbing the papery skin, deepening the massage slowly and carefully. The soothing energy of her hands pours into my body.

Time, I've discovered, is intent on deceiving: drawing you in, allowing you to believe again and again that you have been granted one last reprieve.

There I was in Spain, the suitcases packed, waiting to leave the rented apartment—it was so old, filled with disquieting odors no amount of scrubbing would dislodge. I was excited at the thought of returning to our more modern, clean place in Brooklyn.

The front door is open, the luggage is stacked in the hallway, I hear the children running one last time through the vast apartment. I am waiting for my husband to take down the bags. How long have I been waiting?

Wait—why did we not go back to New York? What has happened to what was supposed to happen next? The new school year, and then the next summer, another big family adventure abroad—were we not talking about Colombia? Concerned to keep up our children's Spanish, which we'd labored hard to give them (the year in Mexico, for instance). What happened to all those years that were owed me? Why am I still standing at the door of the apartment, waiting for my husband?

Now, only this: me on the bed, me with the tubes going in and coming out.

My throat heaves. I feel cheated beyond all reckoning.

What happened to the last forty years? The period I was waiting to *experience*? I was so eager, so expectant, I could hardly breathe, choked with anticipatory joy.

I clench my aching head: flashes, glimmers, faded snapshots seen through a cloud—perhaps some kind of proof that these years were not entirely snatched? But these flickering glimmers are not rich and full and unfolding in the liquid narrative of time-happening as the rest of the Moving Forward was. They are stilted and dry.

Another flicker, in among the rest: a smattering of words. My daughter, my son, the two of them attempting to explain something to me, to do with my health. My memory, my brain.

I am not in this bed. There is no oxygen mask, there are no tubes. I am sitting up in a chair. I recognize that painting hanging on the wall opposite me. Painted by someone connected with my husband's Icelandic family, is that it? A lunar-like landscape, rendered in metallic colors.

"You will continue to remember the distant past," my daughter is saying.

She is distressed, but I am not. I am only happy to be looking into her face. When the other teenagers broke out in great blotchy pimples, bringing misery into their lives, my daughter's skin stayed smooth and golden, her lips unnaturally rosy, as they'd been since she was an infant. People used to think I put lipstick on her.

"The rest will be patchy," she says. She is trying to stifle her distress.

"It's okay, darling," I say. "I don't mind things being patchy."

I smile.

Tears slide down her beautiful cheeks.

"Don't worry, darling," I say. "I'll be fine."

I feel as if I've been telling her that—*don't worry, darling*—since the day she was born.

My son is calmer. His soulfulness, like my daughter's, goes all the way down. He can be anxious, but I can see that he has accepted something, yes, that's it, not resignation but acceptance, wise and knowing, a gentle glow in his eyes, an adult gaze now, that intense beam of concentration fully harnessed. *Stay steady*, I would tell my son. *Your wondrous mind that whizzes around to grab on to everything all at once—grab on to it, let it buzz and whizz, and also, hold tight.* The pixie glitter-sparkle still flashes at times. He takes my hand, says nothing, only gently smiles.

A flicker of anxiety passes through me.

Has the Moving Forward caught up so now it is one and the same with the Final Place?

Have I, in fact, finally arrived?

If the Moving Forward *is* now the Final Place, who will remind my daughter not to worry when I am gone? Who will remind my son to stay stay steady, to hold tight?

But oh—perhaps they no longer need reminding? Perhaps everything is already in place?

I am tumbling again through old happenings that bolt up within and grab hold of me, snatching away the tubes, and throwing me into confusion. I seem to have lost that clarity that in the past helped me keep the alternating time frames in order. I've had this condition a very long time, but I knew how to navigate its unlikely byways, the way denizens of Venice conduct orderly lives in a city of baffling narrow waterways.

I think, though, that I must accept what seems to be the truth. Without properly clocking it (the fault of dementia? Yes, that was the word they used, that is a word that comes through the fog). Yes, indeed I must have lived through all the years remaining between the happenings of the Moving Forward realm and the Final Place.

I always thought I would have time to prepare.

I must do more tidying up before I leave. Clear out the closets, clear off the shelves.

How can I do it, though, chained as I am to these tubes, to this mask?

I gesture to my daughter—there she is by the bed. She seems to be reading a book. Perhaps she does not realize I am awake; perhaps she thinks I am sleeping.

She does not see my gesture and I realize why. I am only squeezing together my forefinger and thumb, squeezing them so tightly that a sharp little pain flashes across my wrist and up my arm.

It is all I can manage, so I do it again. I keep doing it until the nerve pain in my arm is red hot.

What does it matter, the pain? It is bearable, I almost welcome it.

What does it matter now, my getting her attention? I've always had her attention, and she's always had mine. And my son, he will be here soon, I know it. He's always had my attention. I've always had his.

The infant, frantic at the breast, little fists balled against my skin, pounding and pressing so the milk might flow more quickly. I marveled at how they both knew to do this—knew that pressing urgently with their tiny little fists would mean they might gulp more milk.

I stare at her face, I cannot get enough of her face. My son—he is also here! He is sitting beside my daughter. He, too, is reading. I stare at his face—manly! He is a man!

When as babies they slept, my heart ached with missing them.

Look at me, dear daughter, dear son. Know how I feel.

But she doesn't. He doesn't. They keep to their books.

I shall miss watching my daughter and son in their becoming.

I am sorry I have come to the end.

I close my eyes.

Not a now-happening, but a memory.

I am with my son in the hospital. He is a little boy of six.

It is hot—the worst heat wave ever recorded in northern Spain—and my son is in excruciating pain. We are in the hospital, and the medical residents and interns take turns vigorously palpating the site of my son's agony. He maintains his dignity and grace through it all, even pausing to notice the Picasso print in the hallway.

"Mama, that painter messed up. He drew the face all wrong." He listens intently as I tell him a little about Picasso and what he was trying to do.

My son has fallen into an exhausted sleep. The surgeon finally appears and says he must operate immediately. He almost runs down the corridor, removing his outer clothing in preparation for donning operating garb.

They wheel my son away. I hurry beside the gurney, my hand on my six-year-old's feverish brow. His hands are flung up over his head in the way of a sleeping infant—both of my children slept this way well into middle childhood. Thin at the best of times, at this moment my son is gaunt, a tiny narrow form on the gurney, his arms two smooth sticks ending in the exquisite curl of his hands.

"Not beyond here," the attendant says when we get to the double doors.

I stand at the door and watch him disappear down the corridor, relieved that my son is asleep and therefore unaware of the parting, though this feeling of relief is quickly gobbled up by the thought that minutes from now, the surgeon will be slicing open my child's belly. There is no air-conditioning in this hospital, as far as I can tell; I only hope that the operating room is the exception.

It is over, and we are leaving the hospital. We stop in the cafeteria on our way out for a drink.

"Mama," my son says. "One day Papa is going to die, right?"

"That's right, darling, he will, but that won't be for a very long time."

"Then you'll die, and then sister, and then me."

"Well, that will be a very long time, too, maybe longer than you can imagine."

And then, serious and calm. "Mama, I don't want to die."

"I don't either," I say steadily, but with lightness in my voice. "Why don't you?"

"Because I'm having too much fun being alive."

I open my eyes again to see that my daughter and son are no longer here.

My things, all the things in my house. The things that I know. The things that know me.

What does it matter?

I close my eyes. Perhaps, when I open them again, I'll find that my children are back.

Perhaps they're keeping vigil.

In fact, I've noticed the appearance, now and again, of faces that are familiar but that I can't place. A niece? An old friend?

A man as old as I am. Could it be I have a brother?

I smile, when I can, to let them know I recognize them, even if I can't exactly put my finger on who it is that they are.

Recently, I found myself smiling and sending warm eyes at a face hovering over me. The person tried to return my warmth, but I could see that she seemed perplexed. When I realized that she was taking my blood, I knew she was a nurse, and not some intimate relative or friend, after all. I felt a little foolish, but I suppose that's how things go.

I haven't mentioned my husband. This is not because I do not think about him—I think about him constantly. I loved my husband wholly and without cease for many decades. I do not mention him because he died some years ago and I have spent all the years since grieving for him. It has been an agony I learned to live with.

And because, in going, I am not leaving him.

It is the children I am leaving. It is my adult children who must go on living with me no longer in the world.

How can this be?

I want to smell them, I want to smell their hair.

And now another conversation comes swimming back. My son, ten years old?

"I feel sad for myself. For when I'm older," he says.

"And why is that?" I ask.

"One day, you'll be gone. I don't know how that will be." His eyes are not twinkling now, they are cloudy with anxiety.

We're a family of seers, I think.

And then—are they living doubled lives too? Are they both *here* and in *their* Final Place? I can only hope it is restful and safe, as mine is, and that they arrive at a ripe old age.

It is my time.

What will happen to it all?

The mask is off. I can breathe.

The discomfort of the tubes—finally gone. How long has it been? My body, unhampered, free.

I am free now to go.

The faces of my adult children, their dear faces, are stained with tears. They are trying to smile, I see them straining to leave me with a look, in their faces, of peace.

There's something I've forgotten—

There's something I want to say—

I don't know when I last managed to speak. I know only that for some time now I've not had the use of my voice.

The world is no less full of language, though. If anything, it seems fuller of words; they streak across the horizon, which is to say the far wall of the room—it is painted beige—

There's something I've forgotten—

There's something I wanted to say—

No matter, I have said my fair share. I have, in this life, used a surfeit of words.

So much of the world—oneself so little—how could there not be a lot left to say?

The little boy singing jingle bells. Running the words together—*inaonehorseopensleigh*—he cannot know their meaning.

And still, in the face of my grown son, that crinkling of the nose, the joy muted, though not so much—is he thirty or thirty-five, maybe already forty? And my daughter, forty-five?

He is showing me a toy. His face lit up, an inner sun that pours out light.

It is a little red car. He puts it back into his pocket.

"Do you like it, Mama? Do you like my red car?"

"I love it."

He is happy, more than happy. He is satisfied and proud.

Now, my daughter: "You found it! My Kelly doll!" She is shaking with joy. "Thank you, Mama! Thank you!"

We are together. We are walking through a park. My son on one side of me, much taller than I am. He holds my arm. My daughter on the other side, her arm around my shoulder. Diminutive, even she is now taller than I am. My children hold me steady as we walk.

It is a beautiful day. I don't know where we are. I know that the great leafy trees spread their branches above us, stroking the sky with their felt tops. I know I am withered; I can feel it all over, the way my skin hangs on my bones.

But that's not what they see as we walk. They see *me*. They see their mother.

I can no longer protect them.

Tears slide down my cheeks. I can feel the trace they make on the wrinkled surface that soon will no longer be me, that soon will be nothing and no one.

I gasp—

Anguish floods both their faces—

No! I want to shriek. Not pain—*it is a gasp of joy!* This struggle for air, for one final breath, one final gulp of glorious life, one final vision of you, dear children, *vida*, as they say in Spanish—

They are there still, at my bedside. They have been there for all the decades of the Moving Forward, so many years frozen in their respective ages—the ages they will always have been when I was on my deathbed. Suddenly, I know. My daughter forty-eight, my son forty-three, and me having just reached eighty-three, which is to say safely at the finish line.

I turn my gaze for an instant from my children—the briefest moment, less than a breath—toward the window. It is open. The bleached light of early evening slants into the room, settling onto the linoleum floor. A ripple of air passes across my face. Blissfully free, at last, of the oxygen mask, I breathe in the fluttering remnant of breeze, faintly aware of all it contains: the places it has traveled, the people it has passed over, all the world that I sense but will never know.

Is it possible that I'll never again need to frantically rush around the house, trying to find our son's beloved cuddly bedtime toy, Robert, gone missing again? Or my daughter's Softy, a little stuffed dog I took once to the doll hospital to have his nose replaced when our friend's living canine chewed it off? Or rush to grab the soccer ball so that on the way back from wherever we're going, my husband can kick the ball in a park with my now eight-year-old son? Where is it? my husband asks. Where have you left the ball? The toy closet, I say, and if not there, try the hallway, under the bench.

But my husband is not rushing to fetch the ball. He is many years gone and buried, and my son is at work where he is a senior engineer. He has no time for kicking the soccer ball endlessly around a park and besides, his Papa is gone.

Who, then, is in the park?

And where is our ball? The blue-and-white one that my son slept with sometimes, his long, skinny arms wrapped around it, his sweet sleeping face tucked into its curve.

No one sees this face anymore but me. Or my daughter's baby face. I am the only one who thinks about my beautiful son-child's and daughter-child's sleeping faces, which sometimes I still glimpse beneath their aging skin.

It's a headlong rush. I feel it—I'm a young woman, full of vigor, I've just done two loads of laundry, cooked dinner, read books to my son and helped my daughter with her homework, greeted my husband with a loving kiss, tidied the closet, written three letters, settled down happily to read in bed, the prospect of lovemaking ahead, and then a languid tilt into sleep—but no, behind all of that, all that steadiness and dailiness and planning and pleasure and hope, the truth. A plunge into whitewater rapids toward a treacherous, thunderous fall, exhilarating but doomed, nothing left after the plunge but a violent froth of spray, dispersing rapidly into the air.

All of it, all that living. All the striving, my heart swelling and leaping and sometimes just gliding quietly, or still with the sheer and ludicrous wonder of it all. It has all come to this, to my small, personal, universal end.

Not bursting with joy, this old heart, but straining to squeeze just one more beat, and another, not wanting the next to be the last, and yet knowing the last is near.

No, not joy.

Just longing and ache and disbelief.

I do not believe all memory of my children's sleeping faces will cease. How could that be possible? Was that not for eternity? Was that not the promise?

When my husband died quietly in his sleep, having survived with good health into his ninetieth year, I knew I had become the last keeper of those precious images, of all our mutual recollections. I had not, though, anticipated this.

One more breath, one more, please another—

One last encounter with the world—

My daughter, my son, how kindly, how gently they helped me free myself from these tubes. The tears are flowing down their faces.

Don't cry, my loves, both of you my sweetness, my life.

No children were ever more loved.

I can no longer speak. I am clawing at the air. They hear my thoughts. I am certain of it.

With my eyes I say—I am not afraid. Only sad to be leaving you, after all—the leaving I could never imagine, that I've been tricked all my life, until now, into believing would never, could never, come.

I can see that you hear me, both of you. I can see that you know what I am thinking.

You nod, daughter, I see that. You are wiping your tears. And you, son, you nod too.

Both of you give me your angel smiles.

A sudden splinter of light—I know something, suddenly, and now, yes, a surge of the old joy, beautiful and vivid and white. Yes, it does endure, somehow, my images of you, my memories and happiness and love.

My daughter, my son, your faces are near, you are pressing my cheeks with kisses, my withered skin leaps to the soft warm feel of your lips, of baby lips I endlessly kissed so long ago, so recently—

Can I go, dear children? Can I?

You are nodding again? That little smile clamped on your face, daughter. And son, the touch of glee you've always had in your eyes. Both of you soulful, as you've been from the day each of you was born, from the first time I held your new beings, fresh in this world, close to my own ecstatic heart—

I grasp your hands, one in each of mine—

I feel the warm imprint of two hands I have known so intimately, whose shapes I feel in the entirety of my being—

And I tell you, instead, with my eyes, what it is I have to say, look deeply from one to the other, into the panic I see growing in your faces, my own eyes not panicked at all but calm, truly calm, and filled with a great pool of love—

Don't grieve—
Only live—

Epilogue

It is ten years since that moment in Arturo's taxicab in Bogotá when things changed for me, not long after I'd dropped my daughter off at college. I realize that the story I've been trying to tell has come to a natural close. As I put the final touches on this memoir, I am still in my late middle age, not old yet. As I suspected would be the case, coming to the end of the writing, I am left feeling the gaps, aware that the wish for some ultimate wholeness is, at least for me, misplaced. As illusion comes clear and disappointment sags, truth presses itself against me, no longer deflected by the armor that is youth. I have learned to live with certain confounding contradictions, though they can tar my spirit.

The condition of *mother* lies deeply at the heart of it all for me—the mother I was born to, and the mother I became once I'd found my own *bashert* in love and living. I've learned that the Jewish concept of *bashert* applies not only to a romantic soulmate but also to the broader fact of our lives—that we must choose every day how we live, and therefore who we become.

I began this reckoning by describing the end of my active years of mothering, which I experienced as a fracturing of my being. Toward the end of this memoir, I grappled with the foundational fracture within of my own daughterhood, born to a mother whose daughterhood had also involved a shattering, as was likely true for her mother too, a legacy tied to the sociocultural and religious persecution and geographical dislocation that courses back through generations.

I feared my mother; I loved my mother with all my heart. History boiled out of her like magma, and into me. Her personal history with its traumas, misery, longing, and rage along with the history of my people, their traumas—all of it blended within me, one blistering torrent, no getting out of its way.

My mother was gracious, charismatic, wickedly talented; that's what I wanted to see, what I wanted others to see. I didn't want people to know that my mother could turn into a different person, her face strangely twisted. I didn't want people to know about the tension and misery of our household. I burned with the ferocity of a child's wish to protect her parent—from the eyes of the world, from the pain of the truth, both for the child herself and for the parent. That truth: well, that was to be a secret, I knew that before I knew much of anything else.

But I remember the sudden sharp hand reaching out, leaving five red finger marks on my cheek, and where the palm was, a misshapen heart-print, my blood raised to the surface of me as if in search of her, desperate to have the hand that had made its mark take hold of me in kindness. Well into adulthood, I would cry when I saw parents being kind to their children.

Those tears were replaced with joy when the time came for me to hold my own children, to turn those stinging fingers into a clasp that cradled. My own children, that was where I could find what I had yearned for the whole of my life. In my own arms.

I believe my mother bitterly regretted the rages she flew into when we were young. Only now do I recall her saying this, that day, in my apartment, as she balanced on the edge of the bathtub, looking into her own reflection as she worked those tiny little brushes between her teeth. "I knew what I was doing. I did. But I couldn't stop it." That's when she said those unexpected and baffling words, an apology, I now see. "I feel I failed you as a mother." Who was she talking to? She was looking in the mirror at her own reflection. I could see her, but could she see me, or was she seeing only herself?

But now, I think I glimpse something else—a kind of wisdom in her face. An acceptance of the reality that people betray each other—that a mother who loves her children can betray them, as perhaps a child can also grow up to betray their parent. As her husband betrayed her, as she, in her way, also betrayed my father. Do we all disappoint each other? Are these disappointments always betrayals? And where, in all of this, is love?

At the end, propped up in her nursing-home bed, did my mother forgive me for not having found a way to fully open my heart to her as she lay dying? To set aside my own anguish and disappointment and accept her as the flawed human being she was? To let *her* take charge of her own suffering and pain—to free myself of the burden—which might have freed her of feeling she had, in her own words, *failed* me?

Wait—. Perhaps I am misguided in the way I have been using concepts like betrayal, disappointment, failing each other, failing ourselves—positing them as impediments to love.

I have often wondered why it is that love needs to feel perfect to feel like love. It insists on hyperbolic qualifiers. *Endless, undying, boundless. Absolute, consummate, ideal.* And when the flaws become apparent, it can cease to feel like love. But having come to the end of writing this book, I have finally shed the fallacy that for love to be love, it needs to be perfect. I've come to understand where love *is* in all of this. It is in the messiness, in the gaps and lapses and illusions. It is simply there, at the core of everything.

The last few nights, I've been waking at 2:35 in the morning—tugged from a deep sleep, suddenly alert. I sit up in bed. My husband is sleeping quietly beside me. Always a slender man, he is entering the stage of seeming physically smaller. He takes up less room in the bed than he used to. He likes to sleep under a great pile of blankets. Suddenly awake, I reach out to pat the pile of blankets, just to make sure he is there, and there he is, so slender, like our children, whose bodies are shaped like his. Buried under the blanket, the long mound barely visible in the dark, he's quietly breathing. He is peaceful at night; he slips easily into sleep. He seldom remembers dreams. He is older than I am by eleven years. Healthy, fit, he rides his bike to work, runs and walks and plays tennis. I fear the day when I will pat the bed and find that he's not there. There's no knowing who will slip away first, but because he is older, there is reason to think it will be him. All our complicated everything—what, then, will happen to that? To the endless conversation, to the fraught reaching for things we expect of each other but sometimes do not find, to the world-dissolving, world-embracing lovemaking, and periods of disconnection that leave me sad. What will happen to the oneness we have become, the joined memories, the unique pleasures and idiosyncratic irritations, the tender appreciations, the shared past and regrets, the everything we are? Where will it all go if he is gone before me? What shoreline will be lost to me then? Will I still be me?

It is 2:35 a.m. Again.

I get up and go downstairs, open my computer, and locate the digital copy I have of my mother's death certificate—it is in a file labeled *MUM*. There, the date: December 14, 2015. But no actual time of death noted. I write to my sister in Australia, the family chronicler (due to the time difference, it is late afternoon there), to ask what time our mother died. She writes back that she recalled leaving the hospital at 5:45 p.m. to run home to make dinner. By that point, the death watch had been going on for more than two weeks. Once again, my mother was defying the odds. No sustenance already for nine days, no water for three. And still, she lingered. At around six-thirty p.m., perhaps 6:35 or 6:40, my sister received a call to say our mother had died. I did the math—the time difference between New York and Melbourne in December. Melbourne: sixteen hours hours ahead. Melbourne's 6:35 p.m. would have been 2:35 a.m. in New York.

I hold on to certain moments (the way I held on, all that summer before my daughter left for college, to the hallucinatory memory of her birth): my mother in the nursing home propped up in bed, right at the end, her arm flung up, crooked behind her head, her face alight with love.

"I'm going to miss you, darling," she said.

She knew I was leaving in the morning. *She has a week, at most,* the doctor had said when I'd arrived six weeks earlier. My son had final exams, my husband had to travel for work. I did not want to leave, but I felt I had to.

"And I'm going to miss you too, Mum," I said, my heart breaking into little pieces.

A week later, I was asleep in bed, so far away, the phone beside me. My eyes snapped open, I stared at the phone and knew that in a few seconds, it would ring. My husband was in Italy, my son was asleep, my daughter away at college. There—the ringtone.

"She's gone," my sister said across the airwaves, across the oceans, from that distant squiggle of a shoreline that was the shape of the country I grew up in but that was no longer mine. The voice of my childhood self echoed within—*Where did she go? When is she coming back?*

I wept. I should have been there. I should have been there to hold her hand as she took her final breath, as she was there to hold mine when I took my first.

Still, today, I don't know what to do. I reach for my mother—all the turmoil of who she was, who she is to me. The pain, the longing, the love. The misery. The child in me still smarting from the sharp hand so hurtful on my cheek, still bewildered that the mother I adored would do those things she did, and me reaching out to her for comfort, though her face had turned vile. *Please, Mummy, love me, care for me, be nice. Let me know that I am a good girl, that I don't deserve—this.* I am now the mother of two grown children and have navigated the world, yet still I am that little girl, and also all the ages of me, right up until now, a woman in late middle age, tipping into the final phase of life. She is always there, my mother, and always missing, always longed for, always loved and now, so finally and forever, gone.

Have you been coming to me at night? Are you coming to me at the time of your death to tell me something? To tell me to let you go? To tell me to live my life—without all the complications of you? All that curdling agitation, the tendency to find fault and to blame, the way I can turn other people into you and then bristle with distress. Are you here, as I come to the end of writing this book, to tell me what I imagined I would one day, through the slight movements of my eyes, tell my own children, as I myself lie dying? *Don't grieve—only live—?*

In reading over this epilogue one last time, I see something new. That these words, which I imagined speaking to the middle-aged versions of my children (they are, in fact, still in their twenties), may be a final bastion of illusion. The brutal truth is that there is no way not to grieve. To live is to grieve. Shorelines never only offer welcome; they're ever hearkening departure. An old prayer, God Be in My Head, comes to mind. In its contrapuntally sung version, a hundred voices tenderly harmonize its beauty. Its final line is "God be at my end, and at my departing."

Of course, the end is a departing. Each of us inevitably leaves those we love, just as our own beloveds have left or will finally leave us. If there are no answers, there is perhaps solace in the appeal to be accompanied by the Divine, whatever form in our soul the Divine takes, in the moment of our final departing. And I would extend this appeal to include our beloveds. I pray that God also be with them, at my departing, as they take their turn, as we all must, in being left behind.

Does such divine accompaniment, I wonder, transform the condition of being stranded—not only as one is left behind but also more pervasively regarding the condition of being alive? Is this what is meant by *faith*?

* * *

Finally, last night, dear mother, you came to me in a dream.

You are there, in the nursing home, propped up in bed. *Oh, darling*, you say. My heart swells, and for a moment, our two souls touch.

Six long decades ago, you created me. So long ago you held me, newly wrenched from you, as I blinked my eyes at yours. Mother, earth, heaven, sun and sky, all the world I could see and know. In the dream, I can feel the fullness of the love you must have given when the monster was at rest, and I look into your eyes and I love you back wholly, and I cry that I am lost without you. And then, I hear you. *You are not lost. Daughter, in all your wanderings, you have found yourself. You made a family that is tethered. It's not about the shoreline. I learned that in my own exile. It is about the commitment to tethering … to making the life that is our own …*

She reaches out a hand—so soft, so beautiful, so gentle—and takes my hand in hers. She is holding my hand, she is clasping me to her, and for all time.

* * *

It's an unseasonably warm November day—almost eighty degrees, perfect and strange. The leaves are in full autumn glory, beautiful, dying, ablaze. The sky is spring blue and bright with floating summer clouds, all of nature bemused and glorious. This day of sun hearkens back to my happiest days in childhood, to youth's ecstatic callings and love's first exotic blooming, and to the simple passions of new parenthood, reliving the wide gushing joys of a child's thousand firsts. And yet all this heat not belonging here, not in November. It recalls for me the terrifying beauty of scenes in that most uncanny movie, Lars von Trier's *Melancholia*, an homage to humanity—to life, to the earth—that is both celebration and dirge, that plunges the viewer into a free fall that is at once desperate apocalypse and the discovery of God. Its characters become like Icarus, giving over to the engulfing heat, embracing the final combustion for having found and experienced *the all*—the meaning, the light.

This is what I think as I drive through the quiet suburban streets of the New Jersey town we moved to some years ago so that our son could attend the town's small, welcoming high school. I find myself thinking about the term *postmemory*, coined by literature professor

Marianne Hirsch, in talking about the intergenerational transmission of trauma. It refers to the holding of the traumatic past of others as if it is one's own, experiences transmitted, usually to offspring, "so deeply and affectively as to seem to constitute memories in their own right." Hirsch talks about the way in which historical trauma can crowd out the inner life of a young person, an occlusion that is itself traumatic, effacing the young person's self before it has a chance to develop. A sad birthright for too many peoples to count, the young bearing the psychological burden of forebears extending back through generations.

I have found myself stranded on many shorelines. At the same time, I have also built for myself a home, a jumbled-up home comprising people, and written pages that became books, and long hours in the air above oceans. Always packing and unpacking and then packing up again. Anxiously searching—for things that were secret or hidden or pulsing mysteriously behind the everyday, or that were stolen or buried or destroyed in a distant past, calling me to come looking.

I'm struck to realize that now, having struggled in the pages above to lay my hands on the inchoate wholeness of my own life, I have arrived back at the place I began decades ago, when I first set out to write. And I suddenly understand the first sentence that came to me, of the first novel I wrote—a line that ended up being the last sentence of the book. I would discover that the sentence, which burst into my mind fully formed, contained within it the entire novel. I devoted myself to unearthing the story, to finding the novel that lurked, opaque and unreachable in some dim space, and that I yearned to grasp and make sense of.

What I saw, in that book-birthing moment, was an elegant man, weary and spent, standing before a fireplace in a beautifully appointed Victorian room—in England, I supposed, in the kind of apartment they used to call a bedsitter, the kind of room a gentleman who had fallen on difficult times might have rented. An apartment almost respectable for a man of his standing, whispering, as such arrangements did in that era, of a mysterious past, of events that churned in shadow, which settled on the individual a transgressive allure. Standing apart, free of suffocating convention—a man to be pitied, but also, perhaps, to be envied. A history of pain hovers about him, and though he is stoic, anguish and loss ripple out from his being like an aura. Handsome and refined, he is also relatively young—certainly not over forty-five—and yet he wears life with the air of an old man contemplating his end with wisdom, acceptance, and grace. He is considering a covered vase that sits on the mantelpiece. The vessel is painted with a bucolic scene of a man walking through fields, balancing a yoke of water pots.

I saw him as if he were standing before me—he *was* standing before me, and also within me. Since writing that sentence, I have wondered, on occasion, if the man was some kind of *me*; he came into giddy focus in a way that was personal, that had everything to do with who I most mysteriously was to myself at that moment in my life, but also with who I was destined to be. As if in conjuring him from the depths, I was confronting something essential about the life I'd been born to live, imagining myself into a fullness of being that would otherwise have gone missed.

So, the man, who earned the name Oscar, is wondering if the vessel is a funeral urn—wonders if it holds the remains of some stranger, though he's not had the courage to open the lid. He finds himself drawn to the piece, spending long moments before the marble mantelpiece lost in thought. Here is that line, the last line of my first novel, *A Mind of Winter*:

At times, gazing at the lovely, distant, peaceful scene—another world entirely, a forgotten era—I feel that I am somehow like that funereal porcelain, a vessel for the ashes of the dead.

Driving on this recent November day—this day of high spring in what should be late fall, everyone commenting on the weather with astonishment, knowing that to beam about "such a lovely day" would be to belie the knowledge that the climate we grew up with is no longer the climate we have—it comes to me. Beauty has always been this way; it is in its nature. Of course, I am not the first to think this, to have that intuitive flash that destruction may lie coiled within all beauty. (I hear you, Wallace Stevens—"Death is the mother of beauty; hence from her, / Alone shall come fulfillment to our dreams / And our desires.")

Yet, perhaps there is now something new—not just leaves dying in this unusual heat but the earth itself offering its more comprehensive death-knell blaze. Not a small something of course, but then maybe the certainty of some fatal ending was ever thus, the earth itself no less mortal than any of its inhabitants. The ground beneath our feet, its torn acres, the breath of soil released by the plow's wound in the end much like our own breath, beauty's hidden truth being implosion, destruction, *the end*. This is what I sensed to be true of my character, Oscar, standing before the funereal porcelain. He, in his complex, disturbing allure, was like this beautiful, perturbingly unseasonable day: everything and nothing like what he appeared—*are any of us?*—a riddle of identity and history, layers of secrecy and torment, of morally dubious deeds, and yet many deeds that were saintly. Suffering, innocence, culpability, guilt, all of it swirling around the room. And me, the consciousness holding it all, the vessel for *all these stories*—like Oscar, and perhaps like all artists, a mere mortal breaking under the weight of my duty. A calling I did not ask for yet had to heed, strapped to the mast by my own longings, tormented and delighted by sirens who urge me to break free—to reach for illuminating ecstasy that carries with it the risk of being dashed to pieces on the rocks. A glimmer of understanding peeks though, regarding the privilege and burden of being, along with everything else, a vessel for the ashes of the dead.

I pull over to the side of the road and get out of the car. I strain to see the horizon in the distance, shimmering faintly beyond the trees. I stand there, the warm air soft on my cheeks, then crane back my neck to look up into this violet afternoon. I turn my attention inward, focusing intently, and listen, awaiting an image or sentence that might emerge from the hiddenness for me to grab on to.

Texts

Margaret Bourke-White, *Witness to Life and Freedom: Margaret Bourke-White in India and Pakistan*

Rachel Carson, *The Edge of the Sea*

Joan Didion, *The Year of Magical Thinking*

George Eliot, *The Mill on the Floss*

Rabbi Yonassan Gershom, *Beyond the Ashes: Cases of Reincarnation from the Holocaust*

Heinrich Heine, *The Prose Writings of Heinrich Heine* (ed. Havelock Ellis)

Katrin Himmler, *The Himmler Brothers: A German Family History*

Marianne Hirsch, *The Generation of Postmemory: Writing and Visual Culture After the Holocaust*

Henry James, *The Golden Bowl*

Immanuel Kant, *The Critique of Pure Reason*

David Malouf, *Fly Away Peter*

Toni Morrison, *Beloved*

Jay Parini, *The Last Station*

Peter Read, *The Stolen Generations: The Removal of Aboriginal Children in New South Wales 1883–1969*

Elizabeth Rosner, *Gravity*

Joseph Roth, *Job*

   The Radetzky March

William Shakespeare, *Cymbeline*

   Julius Caesar

   Macbeth

   A Midsummer Night's Dream

   Richard III

   The Tragedy of Antony and Cleopatra

Wallace Stevens, *The Collected Poems*

Tatyana Tolstaya, *Aetherial Worlds: Stories*

Virginia Woolf, *To the Lighthouse*

Film and Television

Irwin Allen, *Lost in Space* (1965)

Marvin J. Chomsky, *Holocaust* (1978)

Bob Fosse, *Cabaret* (1972)

Joe Glauberg, Garry Marshall, Dale McRaven, *Mork & Mindy* (1978)

John L. Greene, *My Favorite Martian* (1963)

Yves-André Hubert, *Les Parents Terribles* (1980)

David Lean, *Brief Encounter* (1945)

Terrence Malick, *Tree of Life* (2011)

Alain Resnais, *Night and Fog* (1956)

Sherwood Schwartz, *Gilligan's Island* (1964)

Lars von Trier, *Melancholia* (2011)

Peter Weir, *The Truman Show* (1998)

Chanoch Ze'evi, *Hitler's Children* (2011)

Acknowledgements

I REALIZED, through the writing of this book, that the real shoreline for me is constituted by my family and friends, some of whom are no longer living, though they remain alive within me. This book is dedicated to them all.

For generous involvement, which included offering from their own store of memories, I thank my siblings Michele, Ilana, and Marc, and my friend Yitzhak (Ian) Ajzner. Michele was my first literary role model, and has provided crucial editorial input and encouragement on this and other books over many years. Ilana has been deeply involved in the writing of this book, and bountifully supportive of my work over decades.

I acknowledge with gratitude and love my parents, Jack Nayman (obm) and Doreen Nayman (obm), who lie at the heart of this book—especially my mother, who lived almost thirty years beyond my father.

I thank dear friends who read parts or all of this manuscript and gave valuable feedback: Yitzhak (Ian) Ajzner, Diane Fischer, John Bussey, Lynne Sachs, Lydia Dean Pilcher, Elizabeth Cuthrell, Odette Vaughan, Michele Rockoff, Merritt Janson, and Judith Cox. I am also grateful for the love and support of dear friends Gina Rosenberg, Sharon Seyd, Tammi Litke, Michele Diamond (obm), Andrea Masters (obm), Lisa Gornick, Ben Moore, Brian Zeger, Omar Lotayef (obm), Livia Manera Sambuy, and Kevin Knight.

Thanks also to Michael Hofmann and David Mikics for expert input and corrections on the Joseph Roth chapter.

Two excerpts from this book were published in *Tablet Magazine*, and one in *Tikkun* magazine. And I was fortunate to receive a MacDowell fellowship in support of this work.

I am indebted to two editors of unsurpassed talent and generosity. Alexis Gargagliano gave invaluable editorial guidance and encouragement through several stages of the book. Margo LaPierre was involved from an early stage, has read more drafts than is fair to her, and has been meticulous in preparing the manuscript for publication. I continue to be astounded by Margo's talents and am thankful for her friendship. And I am grateful to Guernica for once again giving my work a home.

And how profoundly blessed I am for the shoreline that is my husband, Louis, and my children, Juliana and Lucas. Ultimate grounding, ultimate home.

About the Author

SHIRA NAYMAN is a clinical psychologist and writer who lives in Brooklyn with her husband. The author of five books, she has also published in *The Atlantic, Tikkun, Tablet Magazine, New England Review, Psychoanalysis and Contemporary Thought, Georgia Review,* and elsewhere. She is the recipient of three Australia Council for the Arts Literature Board grants, a Hadassah-Brandeis literature grant, a Cape Branch Award for Women Writers, and a MacDowell Fellowship. Her work has been broadcast on NPR and staged in New York in collaboration with composer Ben Moore.

Also by Shira Nayman

Awake in the Dark
A Mind of Winter
The Listener
River

MIX
Paper
FSC® C100212

Printed by Imprimerie Gauvin
Gatineau, Québec